Black Colleges in America

Challenge, Development, Survival

Charles V. Willie
and
Ronald R. Edmonds

EDITORS

Teachers College Press,
Teachers College, Columbia University
New York, London

This project on Racism and the Sociology of Knowledge–Black Education was
supported by a grant from the Center for Minority Group Mental Health Programs of
the National Institute of Mental Health, Grant No. MH 27322-02.

Library of Congress Cataloging in Publication Data
Main entry under title:

Black colleges in America.

   1.   Afro-American universities and colleges–United
States–Adresses, essays, lectures.   I.   Willie, Charles
Vert, 1927-   II.   Edmonds, Ronald R., 1935-
LC2781.B44   378.73   78-17147
ISBN 0-8077-2528-5

Manufactured in the U.S.A.

This book is dedicated
with joy and thanksgiving
to our
preacher, teacher,
president, and politician

Benjamin Elijah Mays

President Emeritus of
Morehouse College
Atlanta, Georga

Contents

Preface

In the past, information about the adjustment and adaptation of blacks tended to be written by whites affiliated with prestigious institutions. Because of the settings out of which the pronouncements came, these studies were published and acquired the status of standard references on the black experience. The counterinformation usually was slow in surfacing because of the heavy teaching loads of black scholars. As a rule, when black academics did write they had difficulty getting their material published.

At Harvard we have tried to take a step to eradicate racism in education through holding the Black College Conference from which this book developed. The Black College Conference and this volume are a way of challenging the practice of having the majority speak for the minority. The conference was held in separate two-day sessions in March and in April 1976, at the Harvard Graduate School of Education under the auspices of the Harvard Black College Conference Project, with the support of a grant from the National Institute of Mental Health.

A small number of minority scholars are now members of the faculty and staff of some of the elite colleges and universities. They therefore have an opportunity to contribute to the accumulation of knowledge about black education as well as to public understanding of it by conducting research, disseminating findings, and challenging distorted information—sometimes from the same institutions from which misinformation has emanated. In view of Harvard's unfortunate record on this score, it was an excellent setting from which to launch a major investigation into black education and the education of blacks under the direction of black scholars.

The Black College Conference tried to avoid errors of the past by insuring that more than one version of the truth would be presented. Participants were deliberately chosen from diversified backgrounds. They were black and white, male and female, born in the North and the South, young and old, with both extensive and limited experience as faculty and administrators of black schools. Some had attended black colleges as students; others had given financial support to black colleges. Of the approximately 120 predominantly black colleges and universities in this country, they represented private, independent, and church-related schools as well as state-related and public institutions, in the North as well as the South.

The story they told of black colleges as well as the way that they told it was impressive. Such enthusiasm and joy as that which greeted Benjamin Elijah Mays (who led Morehouse College for twenty-seven years) when he was introduced to the conference was an unusual demonstration for a Harvard audience. A three-hour session led by Mays and Samuel DuBois Cook, his former student and a classmate of Martin Luther King, Jr., who is now president of Dillard University in New Orleans, Louisiana, prompted a staff member of the Harvard News Bureau to say she had not heard such superb speaking ever—any time, any place. As the speaking got good, someone chimed in, "Yes, Lord," and an "Amen" was heard here and there from time to time. Such responses reflected not only the religious background and the oratorical splendor of some of the conference speakers but also the excitement and inspiration generated in the audience.

The Black College Conference at Harvard enabled the educators connected with black institutions to set the record straight, exposed the Harvard community to black college presidents and faculty from several states (Alabama, Florida, Georgia, Louisiana, North Carolina, Pennsylvania), caught the attention of the national press, and presented an opportunity for sociologist David Riesman (who together with Christopher Jencks had fired a broadside at all black colleges a decade earlier) to publicly state that his characterization of these schools would not be the same now as in the past. The fourteen papers presented at the conference have been revised and, together with an introductory and concluding chapter, are now issued as a coordinated volume so that this important information can be shared with a wider audience and thereby contribute to a new definition of black education, the education of blacks, and higher education in America.

The book is a serious effort to lay before the public an analysis of what black colleges and universities do for themselves and for the nation. It presents a comprehensive analysis of what is, has been, and can be. The point of view of the authors is an interesting mixture of the pragmatic and prophetic. Material is presented in descriptive and analytical styles. The different themes discussed and the contrasting modes of presentation reflect the rich heritage and varied structure of the system of higher education in America as it has developed among blacks. Some of the most serious educational problems of the nation are confronted in the book, including those associated with racism, sexism, and elitism.

The book is not a defense of black education and the education of blacks. Rather than dealing with charges based on ignorance and misperceptions, the authors proceed to answer the question which should have been asked before, but was not: How have black colleges and universities done so much, so well, with so little? The answers are of value to any school struggling with issues of racial desegregation and integration, limited financial resources, and students of varying backgrounds and academic preparation. The methods and techniques that black colleges and universities have used to transcend their difficulties and to transform their students are a mystery and a miracle story, which is presented in the pages of this book for the edification of our nation, the community of scholars, and educational administrators everywhere.

The editors were assisted greatly by the wisdom and administrative acumen of Blenda Wilson, senior associate dean for administration of the Harvard Graduate School of Education, who was a member of the leadership staff of the Black College Conference Project at Harvard and served as its codirector. Ronald R. Edmonds, acting director of the Center for Urban Studies, which provided space for the project at the Harvard Graduate School of Education, was the other codirector, who worked with the senior editor of this book, the conference director. They served with a loyal staff, including Ann Craig, administrative assistant, Marlene MacLeish, research assistant, and Benjamin Walker and Nanette Reynolds, who coordinated student volunteers for the conference. After the conference, Chester Hedgepeth, Jr., Gregory Kannerstein, and John Williams joined the project staff as research assistants and participated in editing the manuscripts for publication. The contributions of these persons were of inestimable value as was that of Jane Keddy of Parameter Press, Wakefield, Massachusetts, who with professional skill and loving concern functioned admirably as editorial consultant.

Other assistance that facilitated planning for the conference and preparation of this book was rendered by Gillian Charters, Anne Hebald Mandelbaum, Richard Stafford, David Bailey, Marion Crowley, Curtis Harris, Rita Albertelli, Walter Leonard, Paul Ylvisaker, Mary Sue Willie, and Preston Williams. Acknowledged with appreciation is grant number 5R01MH27322-02 that supported this project. It was provided by the Center for Minority Group Mental Health Programs of the National Institute for Mental Health. James Ralph and Richard Shapiro of NIMH exercised helpful administrative supervision.

Charles V. Willie
Cambridge, Massachusetts

Black Colleges in America

Chapter 1

Racism, Black Education, and the Sociology of Knowledge

Charles V. Willie

Minorities make many kinds of contributions to a society like the
United States. Often they go unrecognized. This has been
particularly true of the predominantly black institutions of higher
education in this country, which have long labored under the handicap
of a negative stereotype bred of ignorance and bias. The goal of this
book is to present an accurate picture of the predominantly black
colleges to a nation in need of educational reform. The facts about what
these institutions have accomplished and how they have done it—in the
face of tremendous odds—could benefit all colleges and universities at
this time.

Underlying the achievements of black colleges is a distinctive aspect
of the social role of minorities, which sociologist Robert Merton
articulated in a profound observation made several years ago. "It is not
infrequently the case," he wrote, "that the nonconforming minority in a
society represents the interests and ultimate values of the group more
effectively than the conforming majority" (1949, p. 367). Merton
gathered up the wisdom of the ages when he pointed out that the
morally committed minority may be responsible for the preservation of
a society's values. William Coleman, former U.S. Cabinet-member,
must have had a similar idea in mind when he stated that American
whites owe a debt of gratitude to American blacks for making the
Constitution work. The same conviction provides the point of depar-
ture for the analysis of black education and the education of blacks
offered in this volume.

3

How do you explain the misconceptions about black colleges that seem entrenched in the public mind, and in the minds of policy-makers as well? In preparing the Black College Conference at Harvard, we identified the problem as one of racism, first of all. Beyond that, we identified the sociology of knowledge as a useful theoretical tool for unraveling the processes at work.

This field of inquiry deals with ideas, ideologies, concepts, beliefs, and other forms of knowledge that are socially generated. Basically, it is concerned with understanding the relationship between knowledge and "other existential factors in the society or culture" (Merton 1949, p. 217). Because of the kinds of issues with which the sociology of knowledge deals, it is particularly appropriate for analyzing the contributions of black colleges to higher education in the United States as well as the assessments of and reactions to these contributions.

The sociology of knowledge offers a theoretical perspective that alerts us to the importance of determining who defines public problems, a matter of crucial significance because the public definition of a problem anticipates a probable solution. Specifically, with respect to black higher education, the sociology of knowledge provides a framework for analyzing (1) definitions of the purpose and appropriate content of higher education for blacks; (2) variations in definitions and their relationship to the social locations of individuals and groups in society; and (3) the conditions under which information about In-groups and Outgroups (Merton 1972), including races and social classes, is believed or accepted. With reference to social scientists, Merton has stated that their values, implicit and openly acknowledged . . . may help fix choice of problems for investigation, formulation of these problems and, consequently, the utility of findings for certain purposes and not others" (Merton 1949, p. 367).

We know what is accepted as truth is related to the historical society in which it emerges. That which is true of educational and other activities among blacks, for example, cannot be understood apart from the time and place in which it occurs, according to the sociology of knowledge. Yet Merton informs us that too often social scientists and others assume that "the aspect of psychosocial reality which [their] concepts help us to understand *are the only ones worth trying to understand*" (Merton 1972, p. 39). The same could be said of racial, ethnic, and social-class groupings.

The discussion takes us back to the definition of the situation and indicates its significance in this field of inquiry. With reference to black education and the education of blacks, who determines what is problematical? Who determines what is relevant? Who determines what is believable and acceptable?

Defining the Black Situation

Blacks and black colleges have been victimized by inaccurate definitions of their situation and inappropriate proposals for remedy. For example, the political scientist Daniel Moynihan—now a U.S. senator—in an influential report issued by the Department of Labor (Moynihan 1965) tried to define the economic insecurity of blacks as primarily a function of family instability rather than of discrimination. Accordingly, the solution he proposed was a national program that would obliterate any distinctive characteristics of black families that differed from the norm of the majority. He wrote, "It is clearly a disadvantage for a minority group to be operating on one principle, while the great majority of the population, and the one with the most advantages to begin with, is operating on another" (1965, p. 29).

Moynihan almost got away with it until other social scientists entered the debate and attempted to set the record straight (Herzog 1966). The following account of the White House Conference on Civil Rights in 1966 indicates how close the Moynihan definition of the situation came to being the basis of public policy:

> In a Howard University speech . . . the President promised to convene a White House Conference which would have as a major objective ways to help the American Negro people to move beyond opportunity to achievement. The words of the President in that speech sounded similar to the phrases in the Moynihan Report which suggested that poverty might be perpetuated among black people in the United States largely because of their unstable family structures. Moynihan, of course, did not rule out increasing the economic resources of the Negro family as a way of contributing to its viability; but it is clear that the social integration of family members should receive priority attention, according to his analysis. . . .
>
> Leaders in the black community and particularly leaders of religious organizations warned that if conclusions about the Negro family in the Moynihan Report were used as a basis for a national policy, the Freedom Movement would suffer a major setback. As preparation for the White House Conference on Civil Rights (actually named the White House Conference "To Fulfill These Rights") continued, many black leaders believed that the Conference was an effort by the Administration to refocus the Freedom Movement from court cases, street demonstrations, legislative

lobbying and concern with *changing institutions and systems* which deny opportunities to concern with *changing individuals and families* of limited achievement. The White House Conference was held in June of 1966. Because of the intense controversy which was sparked by the Moynihan Report, published a year earlier, the participants were divided on the goals which they wished to achieve. The gathering, which was billed as the conference of the century to hammer out a blueprint for action, became nothing more than a fading ritual low in vitality and confused in purpose. (Willie 1970, pp.1–2)

Even though the Moynihan proposal to stabilize the black family was never adopted as official governmental policy, it did influence public opinion as the report quickly became a bestseller of the Government Printing Office. The public visibility of the author of the report and the power and authority of the United States Department of Labor made a major impact upon race relations programs in our national life, with ripple effects in other institutions.

This episode presents clear and present evidence that the people who define the situation have the upper hand in proposing a solution. Those who offer a definition or explanation for the existence of a problem and orchestrate public acceptance of their definition do not always have their way, but their proposals tend to get a public hearing while others are ignored or shunted aside. In effect, those who define the problem have the home-court advantage of a basketball team or the inside-lane benefit in a track event. The members of the opposition are on the defensive and therefore at a disadvantage. They must establish the demerits of a premise they did not choose and may not understand.

In an approach similar to Moynihan's, Christopher Jencks defined educational attainment among black children as a problem of intellectual capacity or individual luck rather than one of a deficient school system. Said Jencks, "Unsuccessful parents will inevitably pass along some of their disadvantages" (Jencks et al. 1972, p. 4). Thus "variations in what children learn in school depend largely on variations in what they bring to school, not on variations in what schools offer them" (Jencks et al. 1972, p. 53). Further he said, "Neither school resources nor segregation has an appreciable effect on . . . educational attainment" (Jencks et al. 1972, p. 8). Finally Jencks stated that the line of reasoning is wrong which asserts that "equalizing educational opportunity would be an important step toward equalizing blacks and whites, rich and poor, and people in general" (Jencks et al. 1972, p. 52). Jencks, in assigning family circumstances a more influential role than schooling in educational achievement, is attempting to identify reasons for poor academic performance by blacks. His study was supported primarily by a prestigious and powerful philanthropic foundation, the Carnegie Corporation of New York. This undoubtedly enhanced the visibility of the book, *Inequality, a Reassessment of the Effect of Family and Schooling in America,* in which findings of the study were presented. It was published by Basic Books, received a prize from the American Sociological Association, and was widely discussed in the daily press.

Jencks's definition of the situation was readily embraced by a public that was experiencing economic troubles and competition between educational and other programs for dwindling public funds. The answer seemed clear: If schooling did not make a difference, why spend more money on schools when money for all programs was scarce? Jencks had offered indirectly a definition of the problem of how to deal with competing demands for scarce public resources. Harold Howe II, for one, has concluded that "the initial result of Jencks' work . . . hurt children" (Howe 1976). The rebuttal of Jencks's work by knowledgeable critics, according to Howe, "did not appear in time or get the public notice to undo the harm" (Howe 1976).

Who Is Believable?

Saunders Redding, a black intellectual, a gifted writer, and a former professor at a black college, produced a revealing book, a powerful personal document, entitled *On Being Negro in America;* it first appeared in 1951. It was a book, said the publisher,

> which takes you inside the Negro world as no other book ever has before! Here, in the words of a Negro writer is a stark, penetrating portrait of what it actually means to be a Negro child, parent, man, woman, human being in white America. Here is a deeply personal account of how the Negro actually views himself, his future, and the white world which has humiliated and oppressed him. (Redding 1964)

These observations were echoed by writer William L. Shirer, who stated that the work was "eloquent" and "passionately written" and provided "great insight" on what life is like for a Negro in the United States (Redding 1964). While it dealt with Redding's own experience, the book had a message for all. His goal was "to externalize the struggle and set it in the unconfined context of the universal struggle for human dignity and wholeness and unity" (Redding 1964, p. 114).

Notwithstanding this broad thrust and the glowing comments, *On Being a Negro in America* never received the attention it deserved.

John Howard Griffin's book *Black Like Me* also tells what it is like to be black in America. It won an award from *The Saturday Review* and an Anisfeld-Wolf Award in Race Relations, was widely acclaimed, and has gone through more than forty printings. According to the publisher, Griffin used first-hand experience as a basis for sharing with the reader what it is "really like" to be a Negro in the Deep South. Griffin, a white humanist with a deep interest in justice, experimented with a number of chemicals and eventually was able to darken his skin temporarily without any permanent side effects. Then he traveled throughout the Southland for six weeks as if he were black.

Note the publisher's emphasis: What it is *really* like to be black. Presumably this account, written after the publication of Redding's book, was more authentic than earlier personal statements by people who were actually black. Indeed, the *Atlanta Journal Constitution* seemed to hold this view; it described Griffin's story as one of the most "penetrating documents yet set down on the racial question" (Griffin, 1961). Could it be that *On Being Negro in America* was ignored or forgotten by whites because of the author's minority racial status? Was Griffin's account of being black more believable as "really real" because of his majority white status? Griffin gives some indication that this may have been so in the question that he raises at the beginning of his book: "How else except by becoming a Negro could a white man hope to learn the truth?" (Griffin 1961, p. 7). His six-week experience as a temporary black person presumably answered that question for him personally and for hundreds of thousands of whites vicariously. Would the simpler approach of asking a minority person to tell what it is like to be black in America reveal less of the truth?

Griffin's truth should not be denied any more than Redding's. Indeed, the statement by Griffin toward the close of his book that "the Negro does not understand the white any more than the white understands the Negro" (1961, p. 156) is an insight that could be achieved only by a white person who has thoroughly immersed himself or herself in the black way of life, and the same situation holds in reverse. This, then, is an understanding that can emerge only from the experience of diligently trying to know another. It is entirely valid but different from the other equally valid truth that is the product of diligently seeking to understand oneself. Both kinds are needed if, as Bogdan and Taylor propose, truth is seen "not as one objective view but rather as the composite picture of how people think about . . . each other" (1975, p. 11)—and, we would add, about themselves.

Truth, Believability, and Racism

The issues of truth and believability force us to confront the fact of racism when black education and the education of blacks are viewed from the perspective of the sociology of knowledge. Stated simply, people are more inclined to believe what is reported by someone like themselves, even when the experience concerns people who are different from themselves. Thus whites are more inclined to believe what it is like to be black in America and what it is like to be educated in black schools if the report is made by a member of their own race. They tend to find it more truthful than a report on the black experience in America offered by a person who is black.

For this reason, black scholars are likely to be treated as invisible persons. Their research reports, interpretative articles, and book-length analyses are seldom cited in the scientific literature. Their version of truth may indeed be different from the version of truth reported by white social scientists, not, however, because black scholars are more or less scientific in their methods of investigation than white scholars but because they may have asked different questions of the same data and therefore obtained different answers. The sociology of knowledge helps us to remember that "what is taken as 'data' and what as 'problematical' " are significant in scientific analysis (Merton 1949, p. 221).

With reference to the black family, for example, most white social scientists ask questions about its weaknesses, and most black social scientists ask questions about its strengths. An adequate sociology of black family life requires truths about both its strengths and weaknesses. Thus the various versions of truth provided by social scientists who represent different locations in society may complement each other in providing the whole truth. Any other approach represents a truth that is partial. The fact of the matter is that all of us—black and white—are stuck with a truth that is partial when we rely completely upon our own version.

Michael Polanyi observed that "each person can know directly very little truth and must trust others for the rest" (quoted in Merton 1972, p. 10). This is where the issue of racism comes in. In America, as we have stressed, whites tend to be more trusting of other whites than of blacks to advance their knowledge of the black experience in this nation. For

example, several years ago the Carnegie Corporation looked around
for a scholar to do a thoroughgoing study of the Negro in the United
States. Gunnar Myrdal, a Swedish economist, was selected for the job.
Myrdal is white. His study of the Negro in the United States was
published in *An American Dilemma* which first appeared in 1944 and
was widely read. It was evaluated as "the most penetrating and important book on our contemporary American civilization" by
sociologist Robert S. Lynd (Myrdal 1975). The scholarly works of E.
Franklin Frazier on *The Negro Family* (1939) and *The Negro in the
United States* (1957) never attracted the widespread readership
achieved by Myrdal's book, even though Frazier, a black man, was an
outstanding sociologist and past president of the American Sociological
Association.

Merton (1972) has claimed that Myrdal was retained to study the
Negro in the United States because he was an Outsider. Using the
nation-state as a frame of reference, Myrdal was an Outsider but, using
the majority race in this nation as a frame of reference, he was an
Insider. We claim that he was retained to do a study of blacks in the
United States because he, like John Griffin, was an Insider, whose
findings would be believed by whites. Also he was a good scholar.
Scholarship alone, however, hardly could have been the determining
factor. There were several knowledgeable black scholars, some of them
hired by Myrdal, who were capable of studying the adaptations of
blacks in American society. In addition to Frazier and Charles S.
Johnson in sociology, there were, among others, Kenneth Clark in
psychology, Ralph Bunche in political science, John Hope Franklin in
history, St. Clair Drake in anthropology, Abram Harris in economics,
and James Nabritt in law. Myrdal's Swedish origin tended to mask the
racist Ingroup–Outgroup syndrome that is related to how black ways of
life in the United States are understood.

David Riesman and Christopher Jencks published as a chapter in
The Academic Revolution (1968) their article on "The American Negro
College," which had appeared in the *Harvard Educational Review*
(Jencks and Riesman 1967). This chapter, like the article, displayed a
gross misunderstanding of the complex and unique culture of blacks.
Probably the best example is the statement that "Southern Negroes
never had a revolutionary tradition" (Riesman and Jencks 1968, p.
406). It is almost inconceivable that such a statement could have been
written in a book published during the age of Martin Luther King, Jr.,
and the explosive action of the civil rights movement. In 1970, the black

sociologist Harry Edwards stated that the black student revolt that began in 1960 in Greensboro, North Carolina "continues to rage" (1970, p. 202). Apparently, Jencks and Riesman discounted this rage and revolution. A lack of knowledge about black schools was revealed in their assertion that ambitious blacks would probably bypass predominantly white schools as providing "better preparation" because they are unhampered and unhandicapped by "the seemingly predominantly white schools as providing "better preparation" because they are unhampered and unhandicapped by "the seemingly inescapable burden of Southern history" (Riesman and Jencks 1968, p. 417). Such a statement reflects a misunderstanding of blacks as well as of the South.

As the author pointed out in a conference sponsored by the Educational Testing Service, "The poor and disadvantaged have some ideas of their own about what they would like to get out of formal education. . . . Learning how to endure, and how to develop a positive concept of the self, and how to gain a measure of control over one's environment probably are as important to the poor as gains in I.Q." (Willie 1973a, p. 82). Thus blacks' definition of "better preparation" and that of Jencks and Riesman may not be the same.

In the proceedings of a conference on the benefits of higher education, I further pointed out, "The black college is an example of an institution that has experimented with different ways of involving students in relevant community experience" (Willie 1973b, p. 235). Edwards, who has studied black students in southern, northern, and western settings, has indicated the kind of education or preparation that blacks want and need. He found that they "continue to push for education which teaches Black people to solve the problems facing Black communities" (Edwards 1970, p. 202). John A. Williams illustrates this point in his chronicle of the sit-ins:

> The decade began with a rush. The activities seemed to be in command of youth. It was the time of the sit-ins. Each escalation of the civil rights movement has a date and a place. The sit-ins commenced on February 1, 1960. The place was North Carolina A & T College in Greensboro. The students were directly influenced by the Montgomery bus boycott with its nonviolent philosophy. Its effectiveness persuaded black youth that they, too, could successfully employ it. (Williams 1970, p. 37)

Following the sit-ins came the freedom rides. They, too, were led by black students. These efforts to desegregate the public eating and traveling facilities in the South led to beatings and humiliation. But they were effective. As I have pointed out before, "These black students [in predominantly black colleges] were getting educated all right. And the education they were receiving was relevant. They were helped and supported by their teachers in their effort to change the world, in their efforts to make it just" (Willie 1973b, p. 236).

The role of black college students and college-educated blacks such as Martin Luther King, Jr., in the civil rights movement demonstrates the revolutionary stance of southern blacks that was overlooked by Jencks and Riesman as well as pointing up one of the most reliable and distinctive functions of the black colleges. I tried to sum up this function in a Founders' Day address at Morehouse College: "Morehouse College has sons who can debate. Morehouse College has sons who can demonstrate. This is the breadth of its involvement in the community" (Willie 1966, p. 9).

Jencks and Riesman came to the conclusion that "by almost any standard these 110 colleges are academic disaster areas" (Riesman and Jencks 1968, p. 433). This judgment ignores one set of data illustrated by the following for Morehouse, my alma mater: It leads all Georgia four-year colleges in the percentage of alumni who have earned doctorates; one out of every ten Morehouse alumni has an academic or a professional doctorate. Moreover, Morehouse has produced alumni who are administrators and professors in several predominantly black and predominantly white colleges and universities, including Harvard, Yale, and Columbia, and it is one of four Georgia colleges with chapters of Phi Beta Kappa (*Morehouse College Bulletin* 1973). One of the past presidents of the United Chapters of Phi Beta Kappa, incidentally, is John Hope Franklin, a graduate of Fisk University—a predominantly black school.

These successes probably should not be generalized as characteristic of all black colleges. Neither should all black colleges be lumped together and dismissed as "disaster areas." Such a generalization is bad social science as well as poor citizenship. Yet this is the current practice, which stems from ignorance as well as institutional racism.

To overcome the misconceptions and to correct the mistaken information about black education, the chapters that follow define the purposes and goals of education from the perspective of a black minority that is preparing young people for survival in a society dominated by a white majority. Because of the social location of blacks in American society and their disadvantaged circumstances, black educators such as Benjamin Mays, to whom this book is dedicated, knew that their students had to be astute in communicating and calculating skills; but they had to have more.

In 1945, when Martin Luther King, Jr., was completing his freshman year at Morehouse, Mays said in a radio address: "It will not be sufficient for Morehouse College . . . to produce clever graduates, men fluent in speech and able to argue their way through; but rather honest men, men who can be trusted in public and private—men who are sensitive to the wrongs, the sufferings, and the injustices of society and who are willing to accept responsibility for correcting the ills" (quoted in Bennett 1977, p. 78). In this passage, spoken more than three decades ago, a black college administrator established a set of priorities in which honesty, a cultivated characteristic, is more valued than verbal facility. Ten years later in the Montgomery Bus Boycott of 1955, Martin Luther King, Jr., acted out the words he had heard from his college president.

Probably it is inappropriate to identify Mays as representative of all black college presidents. He does qualify, however, as their "ideal type." As such, his set of priorities for black education is that to which others aspire. In summary, Mays defines education as a moral experience that motivates one to be concerned about others, especially those who are oppressed and treated unjustly. Apparently, Mays's social location in American society as a member of a disadvantaged racial minority group has affected his definition of the situation.

The priorities set forth by Mays and the ideas, ideologies, and concepts of others that are presented in this book will be understood better if readers recognize that their tendency to accept or reject them is based, in part, on their own social location in society and their deliberate attempt to transcend a necessarily limited perspective.

Part I   History and Purpose

Overview

Chester M. Hedgepeth, Jr.,
Ronald R. Edmonds,
Ann Craig

Expressing a firm belief in the equality of all people, Benjamin Mays emphasizes the religious roots and the democratic spirit of black colleges when he states that the black youth of America "must develop whatever gifts God has given them and share the fruits of their minds and souls with humanity." The history of the black college in America has embraced both the notion of service and the goal of training for leadership in a complex technological society. Founded by the American Missionary Association and other benevolent societies, private black colleges trained their students for educational and religious leadership as well as for agricultural and industrial pursuits. Disputes between blacks and missionaries over the nature and scope of education made difficult the establishment of a clear objective for the teaching of blacks, as pointed out by Jane Browning and John Williams.

Some southern whites and missionaries advocated industrial education (or manual training) for blacks, which reflected their belief that black talent lay only in labor with their hands. The passage of legislation establishing trade schools with the aim of training blacks in mechanical and agricultural skills was the fulfillment of this belief. In the early decades of the 20th century, the debate on the efficacy of vocational education versus liberal arts education surfaced in the now famous Washington–DuBois papers. These "warring ideologies," Gregory Kannerstein notes, have subsequently come together so that at present black colleges intertwine social, vocational, and academic programs in their overall mission to educate for "leadership in democracy."

Samuel DuBois Cook, in his essay on the social and ethical role of black colleges not only advocates strong academic programs in these colleges but also efforts directed at social change. The final objective of a sound educational enterprise is the achievement of social justice,

17

which is the "key to a good society," writes Cook. "In the search for a better world," he continues, "there must be a blending of rational humanism, sober idealism, and existential personalism."

The idea of reform, of social change for a just society, is recurrent in the literature on the history and purposes of black colleges. The goal of the black college, therefore, is not education for its own sake but for a continual challenge of the status quo in oppressive race relations and social behavior. The historical preeminence of this mission is attested to both in the number and quality of black political, educational, and religious leaders who have graduated from predominantly black colleges and in the recent activist role of black college students in the integration of racially separate facilities in the South. Thus the role of the black colleges in American society is multifaceted.

The social role of black colleges is defined not only in terms of reforming an oppressive social order but also of providing services to their immediate communities. Kannerstein, in his study of the image of black colleges, finds a strong emphasis on service as part of the institutional mission. "Some colleges," he explains, "see the community as an extension of the university." He further indicates that open admissions and minimum costs are among the ways colleges respond to community needs.

The heterogeneous student body of the black colleges gives them unique status among institutions of higher education. The policy of open admissions goes beyond the acceptance of students with varying preparation for college work. It includes the acceptance of African, Asian, Caribbean, Mexican, European, Latin American, and white American students. Black colleges agonize over a potential loss of identity, however, should the composition of the student body or faculty become too diverse.

Mays reminds us that the black image in America has been kept alive by black colleges. The strength of the leaders of these colleges, the diversity of the students and faculties, the dual academic role (the inclusion of both black and white heritage in the curriculum), and, above all, the resourcefulness of the administrators assure these institutions a continuing role in American higher education. To assess the history and purpose of the black college is to focus on its ability to educate blacks for service with minimal financial resources but with an unparalleled belief in the worthiness of each individual in society and in the value of his or her potential.

Chapter 2

The Black College in Higher Education

Benjamin E. Mays

I have never been deceived as to who I was and who I am. I knew at the age of six who I was. I knew the value of black teachers and black schools. I was not brainwashed into believing that my people were inferior and that God had sent them into the world to serve the white man, to hew wood, scatter guano, draw water, pick cotton, pull fodder, and plow with a mule. I never believed what my ears heard and what my eyes saw. The environment, with its crippling circumscriptions, told me that God made me inferior. The way Negroes behaved in the presence of white people, cringing and kowtowing, tipping their hats to white folks, saying, "Yes sir, Boss," told me that I was never meant for great things, never meant to dream dreams, to chase ideas, to reach for the stars, and to grasp after the moon.

I did not believe it because I was selective in the passages of the Bible I read at evening and morning prayers when my mother requested me to read the Bible. The minister told us, and the Scripture supported him, that God is no respecter of persons, that he created of one blood all races of men to dwell on the face of the earth. He preached to us that in Christ there is neither Jew nor Greek, neither bond nor free, neither male nor female, for we are all one in Christ Jesus. I knew the source of my existence, that my status comes from God, not from the white man, not from the state, and not from the federal government, but from God.

This fact was further drilled into me, ingrained in my mind, muscles, and sinews, when I went to the four-month school at the age of six. A fourth-grade sister had taught me to read a bit and to write and spell.

19

My teacher marveled that I could do these things; no other entering student could. The second Sunday in November—church services were held only once a month—the teacher told my parents—before me and an assembled audience—that Bennie was smart and that he would do great things someday.

Again at eight, I got my first feel of the public. For Children's Day, the second Sunday in June, I had committed the fifth chapter of Matthew for my piece. To my surprise and amazement, when I finished, the congregation went wild. Young people applauded loud and long. Women waved their handkerchiefs, and, as in a dream, I saw the whole house standing. From that day on, I was a marked boy. I shall never forget this experience. The minister said that I would preach. The minister and the people had put their mouth on me. They expected me to be different, not to do the things that other boys did. I felt and I feel now that I cannot let these people down.

Who did this to me? Negroes did it to me. The people at my church in rural South Carolina were untutored but intelligent people. They helped me to believe in myself and said to me, "You are valuable, a person of intrinsic worth and value." And I realized that God had called me to do something worthwhile in the world. So, at a tender age, I was completely aware of my obligation to Negroes.

My heroes were and are black. I adore George Washington, but I dearly love Frederick Douglass. Douglass is mine. I think Douglass was a greater man than George Washington, though I recognize Washington's high place in history as Father of His Country, first president of our nation, a great general; but Washington was a rich Virginia farmer and white. Douglass was a slave and black. Yet Douglass became a free man and became a greater abolitionist than Garrison. I admire Harriet Beecher Stowe, credited with precipitating the Civil War with her authorship of *Uncle Tom's Cabin.* But give me Harriet Tubman, who by way of the underground railway carried 300 Negroes to freedom into Canada. Tubman is mine. We had only a few books in our house: Webster's *Blueback Speller,* books on the lives of Douglass, Booker T. Washington, and Dunbar. They were my heroes. Their pictures hung on our walls.

Competing in a White Man's World

The role of the Negro in the education of blacks and the need for it were dramatized in a college circle at South Carolina State where I did my high school work and at Virginia Union in Richmond where I spent my freshman college year. What did I find? I found black teachers who were competent and had a special interest in the black student. I graduated in 1916 from South Carolina State as valedictorian of my class and earned a prize in oratory, despite the fact that I was twenty-two years old when I finished high school. As you see, I was a bit retarded because of having only four months of schooling per year in South Carolina. I graduated from college at the age of twenty-six. The teachers at South Carolina State encouraged me and helped me to plan for further study.

I went on to Bates College in Maine, graduated with honors, won the declamation prize in my sophomore year, was one of ten to compete in the junior and senior prize speaking contests, was selected by my class to be their Class Day speaker, served three years on the debating team, and was captain of the team that defeated Tufts College in 1919. Later I was selected for Phi Beta Kappa by Bates. From Bates, to the University of Chicago. I entered Bates with $90. I entered the University of Chicago with $47.

I had gone south to see my newly wed wife, who was teaching at Morris College in Sumter, South Carolina. I had married Ellen in August 1920 in Newport News, Virginia, arriving there with time enough to marry Ellen at the end of the summer school at Hampton Institute.

I tried to work my way from Columbia, South Carolina, to Chicago, but no luck. As a railroad employee, riding a deadhead Pullman car, I found myself on a train headed for Richmond, which was where I ended up. A friendly conductor let me ride on my Pullman keys from Richmond to Washington. I knew I could get from Washington to Chicago. I had about made it. The sign-out man in Washington gave me a sign-out to Chicago, but then he looked at his list and discovered I was wanted in Boston. As soon as I reported in Boston, the Boston man told me I was fired.

A friendly porter was in Boston, though. I had helped him when he took sick one summer day on the job and had to rush to the hospital. He had never forgotten what I did at that time. I had taken charge of his passengers, collected $6 in tips, and then boarded the street car and carried porter Bryant his $6.

In Boston when Bryant learned that I had been fired, he wanted to help. First, he was going to give me his sign-out slip to Cleveland. But, on second thought, he knew he would be fired if he did that. Then he offered to take me as far as Cleveland in his car with the understanding that I would hide from the conductor after the passengers had been checked. I did this. When the conductor had checked his passengers and gone to his room, Bryant put me behind the linen in a linen closet and tied a knotted loop on the door to keep me from smothering. In Buffalo, Bryant put me in an upper berth to Cleveland; the conductor did not check that upper berth. In Cleveland the Pullman man in charge was short of porters. Bryant said to me, "Get up! Cleveland needs a porter to go to Toledo, Ohio." I went to the office and argued the man into letting me go to Chicago as a swing man, a porter who is allowed to work his way without paying the fare. He agreed, if I would make down the beds for the Toledo porter, who was doubling out— foregoing his layover time to help in a shortage; the porter could go to bed and sleep while I guarded the sleeping car. I agreed. I told him I had to be at the University of Chicago the next morning for registration. Luck was with me. I got to Chicago, matriculated, found a place to lodge for the school quarter, and got a job washing dishes in the university commons.

Professor N. C. Nix, my high school mathematics teacher at State, was responsible for my choosing the University of Chicago. He had attended the university one or two summers and had loved it. He talked about the University of Chicago frequently in his class, indicating the quality of the work he did there and the respect that the teachers, who were white, had for his ability. Then there were Levister, Butler, Watson, all from Lincoln University in Pennsylvania, from whom I got encouragement. Also from Julia Mae William from Fisk. All these were able, competent teachers, and they were black. At Virginia Union, where I spent my freshman year before going to Bates, the faculty was able. Among the best were black professors who had studied at Union, Colgate, and Chicago.

All these contacts led me to know that all this talk about white superiority was a myth designed to make Negroes accept meekly their role as inferior persons. I had learned through my own experience that I could compete successfully in a white man's world. Thus the role of the black colleges and their continuing existence has never been a problem to me. I have never been deceived into believing that black colleges were interim institutions, that would go out of existence when white colleges became liberal enough to accept Negroes without discriminating against them. I have argued for as long as I can remember that the image of the black man and woman in education and their contribution to American life must be equated with the black colleges.

What Desegregation Should Mean

On May 17, 1954, the United States Supreme Court handed down the decision outlawing segregation in the public schools, a decision which paved the way for the uprooting of segregation in all facets of American life. Shortly after that decision, I gave a speech at Livingston College. In that speech I make clear my position on what the Supreme Court decision meant. I quote from that speech:

> Since 1935, when the Appellate Court of the State of Maryland ruled that the University of Maryland had to accept Murray, the NAACP Legal Defense and Educational Fund, the NAACP, the Southern Christian Leadership Conference, the Congress of Racial Equality, and the Student Nonviolent Coordinating Committee have spent millions upon millions of dollars to get America desegregated. Desegregate and integrate to what end? This is the question.
>
> I hope to develop the thesis that desegregation and integration are not ends in themselves but mere means to ends.
>
> Certainly, the end of desegregation in church and school, in train and plane, on land and sea, in hotel and motel, in employment and recreation, is not for blacks to be with white Americans. It is not to give one a false notion of his worth, to make him believe that he has arrived, that he has risen higher in the world, that he, automatically, is more important as a person because he can eat in the finest restaurant, sleep in the swankiest hotel and work side by side with any American and socialize freely. These are not the ends of a desegregated and eventually an integrated society. If these were the ends, they aren't worth the sacrifice. Americans disguised as communists, intent on overthrowing the United States government, Nazis, spreading the poison of hate, the members of the Ku Klux Klan, the wealthy who make their millions in the underworld of prostitution, alcoholism, and dope can and do enjoy these luxuries unsegregated and without embarrassment.
>
> Desegregation is not and certainly should not be designed to perpetuate or create an inferiority complex in Negroes or a superiority complex in whites to the end that we feel that desegregation can come about only one way—only if we abolish all banks and insurance companies, all churches and educational institutions, all newspapers and magazines, all businesses and professions built and established with Negro brain and sweat. Rather, the aim should be to incorporate everything that is good and everything that is needed into the mainstream of American life.
>
> To state the case more positively, the end of desegregation, and eventually the establishment of integration, should be to unshackle the minds of Negro youth, loose the chain from the Negro's soul, free his heart from fear and intimidation so that he will be able to develop whatever gifts God has given him and share the fruits of his mind and soul with humanity around the globe in the arts and sciences, in the professions and sports, in business

and industry, in medicine and law, in music and dance, and in painting and sculpture.

To be unshackled, to improve the mind, to mold the character, to dream dreams, to develop the body, to aspire for greatness or to strive for excellence is the birthright of every child born into the world. And this birthright is given not by Christianity nor by democracy but by God and by virtue of the fact that the child is born. No society has the right to smother ambition, to destroy incentive, to stifle growth, to curb motivation, and to circumscribe the mind.

We strive to desegregate and integrate America to the end that this great nation of ours, born in revolution and blood, conceived in liberty and dedicated to the proposition that all men are created free and equal will truly become the lighthouse of freedom where none will be denied because his skin is black and none favored because his eyes are blue; where the nation is militarily strong but at peace; economically secure but just; learned but wise; where the poorest will have a job and bread enough and to spare, and where the richest will understand the meaning of empathy. For if democracy cannot function interracially as well as intraracially in the United States, I fear for its survival in the world. The battle for democracy is being fought out at this very moment in the streets of America and in the Congress of the United States.

What am I trying to say? I am trying to say that Negroes, with low incomes, poor academic backgrounds before college, unfortunate home conditions, and ancestors handicapped for three and a half centuries, are now required to compete in the open market with those who have been more favorably circumstanced for several centuries. Our inadequacies have been printed in the press, flashed over the radio, on TV. Nobody explains the reasons for our shortcomings.

What can we do? We can blame it on the past, but that will do no good. We can accuse the environment, but this will not change our conditions. We can curse and rave, only to develop ulcers. We can wring our hands and cry, only to find that nobody is moved by our tears.

The Contribution of Black Colleges

At this point let us note the contribution that Negro colleges have made to this country and what they have done to enhance the image of blacks in education. Let me give a few examples. Morehouse College, which is a men's college, has graduated more students with the A.B. degree who have gone on to earn doctorates in the many disciplines of higher education than any other college of comparable size in the United States, irrespective of race.

Morehouse men, though few in number, have done exceptionally well. If a college is to maintain a high level of academic excellence, it must have not only a competent faculty and a good plant but also a large number of able students. In the final analysis, a college or university must be judged by the achievements of its alumni. On this score, Morehouse college has a proud record.

By 1967, Morehouse had 118 alumni who had earned Ph.D. degrees; in 1967 alone, one of every eighteen Negroes earning doctorates had received the A.B. or the B.S. degree from Morehouse. This figure is impressive on two counts: Not more than 4,000 men had graduated from Morehouse since its founding over a hundred years ago. In addition, Negroes have been graduating from white colleges since the first black received a degree from Bowdoin College in 1826. Since 1967, there have been 25 or 30 Morehouse graduates who have earned Ph.D. degrees, making a total of 148 Morehouse graduates with doctorates. These degrees have been earned in the last thirty years, for it was in 1932 that Samuel Milton Nabrit (Morehouse '25) became the first when he received the Ph.D. from Brown University. Since 1932, Morehouse has averaged three and one-half Ph.D.s a year.

Morehouse men have received doctorates from forty-five different universities since 1932. Such a record is hardly an accident. It is a tradition at Morehouse that an A.B. or a B.S. is not a terminal degree; every outstanding student is encouraged to continue his studies. It should also be noted that many of the Morehouse men who have earned doctorates were early-admissions students, before the Ford Foundation initiated their plan for college entrance before graduation from high school. With Morehouse it was a method of survival. World War II had so diminished our enrollment that the chairman of the board suggested closing the college for the duration of the war. Actually nobody took the chairman seriously; but we did get busy recruiting bright young students who had not finished high school. Among those so recruited was Martin Luther King, Jr., class of '48.

Morehouse stands among the first four Negro institutions in the production of graduates who go on to medical and dental colleges. By 1967, more than 300 Morehouse men had earned M.D. and D.D.S. degrees, and 40 of the 300 had achieved distinction as medical specialists — diplomates in medicine. A high percentage of Negro physicians are graduates of Morehouse. Combining the degrees in medicine and the Ph.D.s in other diciplines, 1 out of every 9 Morehouse graduates has earned an academic or professional doctorate.

It took from 1953 to 1966 to persuade representatives of Phi Beta

Kappa to visit Morehouse to determine whether it qualified for membership. In August 1967, the United Chapters of Phi Beta Kappa, meeting at Duke University, voted to admit Morehouse College to membership. Only seven other institutions in the nation were selected that year. On January 6, 1968, Delta of Georgia was established at Morehouse College, thus rewarding fourteen years of effort.

On Friday, May 17, 1968, Delta of Georgia was proud to initiate into Phi Beta Kappa the first Morehouse students to qualify for membership: Benjamin Ward, Michael Lomax, Frederic Ransom, and Willie Vann. The installation and the initiation of the first Morehouse students into Phi Beta Kappa were historic events, which culminated a journey that really began in the basement of a church in Augusta, Georgia, where Morehouse was founded. Each triennium during my administration, we had sent credentials, and after each no we worked harder for the academic excellence that would qualify us. Now the dream had come true.

Adding to the Morehouse contribution, let us note what has been done at such colleges as Howard, Fisk, Talladega, Atlanta University, Spelman, Clark, Morris Brown, Shaw, and Bennett. The vast majority of black leadership has come from these and other black institutions.

Howard University is the most integrated educational institution in the United States. Every state in the Union is represented in the student body, as well as Africa, Europe, and South America. A representative number of white American students are enrolled. The faculty is also thoroughly integrated—all under the leadership of a black president. Most of the black physicians and dentists have come out of Meharry and Howard. Our black lawyers, judges, and high-ranking government officials are mostly from Howard.

Unity in Diversity

This is no time for black colleges to apologize for their existence, to become weak-kneed, to stop striving for excellence, and to stop trying to raise money for their support. All foundations that are tax exempt—Negroes have helped them make their money. Negroes drink their share of Coca Cola. The Rockefeller Foundation became wealthy initially through a monopoly on the gasoline market; Negroes use their share of gas. Negroes also buy their share of Ford cars, including Lincolns. God knows Negroes buy their share of liquor and beer; the liquor and beer people have their foundations. Negroes buy and smoke tobacco produced by Reynolds and Duke. Blacks and their colleges ought to receive support from these and other foundations.

On the basis of these facts, if America allows black colleges to die, it will be the worst kind of discrimination and denigration known in history. To decree that colleges born to serve Negroes are not worthy of surviving now that white colleges accept Negroes would be a damnable act.

No one has ever said that Catholic colleges should be abolished because they are Catholic. Nobody says that Brandeis and Albert Einstein must die because they are Jewish. Nobody says that Lutheran and Espiscopalian schools should go because they are Lutheran or Episcopalian. Why should Howard University be abolished because it is known as a black university? Why pick out Negro colleges and say they must die? Blot out these colleges: You blot out the image of black men and women in education.

Clinging to an image is inherent in national, ethnic, and racial groups; national, racial, and ethnic identity is inherent in life itself. We are born into a specific group. We are born English, French, German, or American. We are born Jew, Negro, African, or Greek. Almost at birth, we are proud of our country, our ethnic heritage, or our race. We are proud of our city. As a rule we tend to gravitate toward our kind. The English are proud to be English, and we are proud to be American. In traveling abroad, we are elated to run into someone from the United States. In an international contest we cheer for the home team and want them to win. I love to see anybody perform well, but I thrill more when a black person reaches the top, when Joe Lewis knocks out the German heavyweight, when Hank Aaron becomes the home-run king of the world, when Muhammad Ali is the world's boxing champion, when Marian Anderson has the soprano voice of the century, when Charles Drew is founder of the blood bank, when Martin Luther King, Jr., is one of the most famous men in the world.

Greeks boast of Plato, Aristotle, Socrates, Homer, and Demosthenes. The English boast of Shakespeare, Tennyson, and Kipling, and their great generals and statesmen. France idolizes Napoleon, Joan of Arc, and Foch. So, I for one will fight to maintain the black image in education and fight for the survival of black colleges. Integration must never mean the liquidation of black colleges. Every good college and every college that is needed has a right to live. I believe in unity in diversity. This is what America is all about.

The black colleges have a role to play that is unlikely to be carried out

if they do not do it. The white colleges are designed primarily to meet
the needs of white America; their curricula are so designed. The black
colleges have a double role. They must be as much concerned with
Shakespeare, Tennyson, and Marlowe as the white colleges. But the
Negro institutions must give equal emphasis to the writings of Paul
Dunbar, Countee Cullen, and Langston Hughes. As much emphasis as
white colleges to white sociologists, but equal attention to black
sociologists like E. Franklin Frazier and Charles S. Johnson. The black
colleges must include works of great white historians like Schlesinger
and Toynbee, but they must also include the works of John Hope
Franklin, Carter G. Woodson, and Charles Wesley. It is not enough for
black colleges to teach their students the economics of capitalism. The
graduate of a black college must also understand the problems of the
small black capitalist and be able to help him and must know something about cooperatives. These examples are what I mean by the double
role of Negro colleges.

   Let me say one final word. Black people, working hand in hand with
a few white people (the holy remnant of whites) can commit their souls
to this task. A decent world, a world of justice and equality can be
accomplished if God has called you and me to build America to what it
ought to be.

Chapter 3

Black Colleges: Self-Concept

Gregory Kannerstein *

Black colleges provide valuable perspectives on American education
and society. This chapter is an attempt to define those perspectives
through an analysis of how black colleges see themselves. The research
materials are the statements of self-concept, purpose, aims, and objectives provided in the catalogs, bulletins, newsletters, and alumni publications of a substantial sampling of black colleges.[†] I have also
attempted an informal comparison with similar statements of certain
predominantly white colleges, roughly matched with the black colleges
on size, location, sponsorship, and general academic status.

This is a study of the ideals that black colleges proclaim for themselves: it is not an examination of their achievements. That subject is
dealt with by other writers in this collection. It will become evident,
however, that the statements of purpose by these colleges and their
self-definitions demonstrate their dedication to the twin goals of
academic excellence and community service.

In *The Souls of Black Folk,* W. E. B. DuBois spoke of the eternal
"double-consciousness" of black people in America, "two unrecon-

*I wish to express my gratitude to Professor Charles V. Willie of the Harvard Graduate
School of Education, whose inspiration and guidance made this chapter possible; also to
Ann Craig and Marlene MacLeish of the Center for Urban Studies of the Harvard
Graduate School of Education for their encouragement and advice.

†The collection of college publications in the Center for Urban Studies at Harvard's
Graduate School of Education has been the source of most of the statements cited.

ciled strivings" and "two warring ideals in one dark body, whose dogged strength alone keeps it from being torn asunder" (DuBois 1961; pp 16–17). Almost all Afro-American institutions incorporate this duality, none more clearly than black colleges and universities (Jones 1971). Nevertheless, an examination of their official publications reveals that these colleges are moving from antithesis to synthesis, from contradiction to cohesion. Today, more than seven decades after *The Souls of Black Folk,* black colleges still incorporate DuBois's double-consciousness and are successfully dealing with it, reconciling seemingly opposing strivings, harmonizing ostensibly warring ideals, uniting apparently divergent educational philosophies and experiences, merging, in the words of DuBois "their double self into a better and truer self" (1961, pp. 16–17).

The self-concepts and the purposes of black colleges are the products of many historical currents, some of which flowed together quietly and easily, others of which erupted in agonizing public controversy. The most well-known controversy was, of course, the debate between DuBois and Booker T. Washington over the nature of black education, which has had ramifications beyond the issue of industrial education for the masses versus liberal arts education for the "talented tenth." Even this violent rupture "knitted together" somewhat, as DuBois hoped it would (1973, p. 5). Today we see career education and liberal arts comfortably coexisting on black college campuses, while educators elsewhere around the nation struggle with the relative importance of these approaches.

The historian Michael R. Winston has said that the black college "has occupied a more strategic intermediary position in race relations and has been therefore more of a focus of political pressures and social tension than is commonly expected to be true of educational institutions" (Winston 1971, p. 679). Thus black colleges have grappled with the demands of inculcating academic values while not neglecting ethical and moral values, of serving educational goals while serving the community, of being open to all while remaining committed to a specific constituency, of responding to pathology while promoting health, and of combatting social injustice while never swerving in allegiance to American democracy. They have performed this miracle through a strategy based on the complementarity of these processes, on the necessity of including all these elements in a workable philosophy of education, and, most important, on the essential *unity* of what was involved.

Community Service

Companion chapters in this book testify to the dedication of black colleges to academic principles and procedures. The published statements of black colleges disclose their devotion to academic excellence, their belief in the importance of both teaching and research, and the central position of learning on their campuses. In additon, the statements describe another dimension, which overlaps and extends the self-concept apparent in the discussions of academic matters. This is the concept of service, an emphasis singled out in much of the literature on black colleges (Carnegie Commision 1971, p. 2; Drake 1971, pp. 888–890; Harris 1971, p. 731; Henderson 1974, p. 73). Judged by the words of the colleges themselves, the location of the ebony tower, unlike some of its ivory counterparts, is squarely in the community and the society.

Indeed, perhaps the greatest and most distinctive contribution of black colleges to the American philosophy of higher education has been to emphasize and legitimate public and community service as a major objective of colleges and universities. The most superficial perusal of the catalogs and other publications of these colleges reveals how deeply ingrained this mission is in their consciousness. Enter to learn; go forth to serve is a common motto. Service is invariably linked with instruction, research, and learning in descriptions by the colleges of their principal functions.

Service is defined in many ways: extension and adult education programs; responsiveness to the needs of the black community, the local community, or the state or nation; training for leadership; faith in democracy; financial aid to promising students, who otherwise would have little chance of access to higher education; teaching racial understanding or vocational skills; attention to ethics and values and to personal and social health; the contributions of alumni to society. Service is not seen by the colleges as a substitute for strong academic programs or as a threat to them. The black colleges view educational excellence and community service as inextricably intertwined, producing together an appreciation of the relationship between the curriculum and the world beyond the campus.

Service for many colleges is a true outgrowth of their academic programs. Lincoln University (Pennsylvania) believes its strong liberal arts curriculum stresses the "relevance of all knowledge to the problems of the present." Texas Southern University emphasizes "traditional academic characteristics" and at the same time declares that it is "its broad special purpose to apply its total educational resources to help solve immediate and future urban problems." Langston University (Oklahoma) proposes to direct the research conducted on campus "toward solving problems of people in Oklahoma." The educational programs of Clark (Georgia) involve "continuing interaction between the college and the community," while for Howard University (Washington, D.C.) "in a very real sense the District of Columbia is an extension of the University's campus."

Sometimes the nature of an institution's mission of service is described in general terms. Kentucky State University is committed to the "development of a sense of obligation to contribute to the intellectual, cultural, spiritual, and economic growth of the community." Howard University seeks to foster the "knowledge and sensitivity to make a difference in this world." Graduates of Morris Brown College (Georgia) are enjoined to "make socially constructive and culturally relevant contributions to local, regional, and national undertakings." Spelman College (Georgia) promotes "student and faculty involvement in various facets of the social, political, and economic life of the community."

Other black institutions define service more specifically. Knoxville College (Tennessee) sees it as problem solving, telling its students: "The hope of solving the world's problems lies mainly with you. . . . Preparing you for this responsibility is the ultimate purpose of college in general and of Knoxville College in particular." For Central State (Ohio) service is expressed in terms of the marketplace: "high-quality productivity" and "economic self-sufficiency. "On the other hand service is often related to particular communities, as at the District of Columbia Teachers College, which has a "major concern for problems of the urban community, including those facing Afro-Americans, Spanish-speaking and other ethnic minorities in the Nation's Capitol and the nation."

The concept of service is not limited to lofty words. Black colleges engage in a wide variety of social service activities. Miles College (Alabama), for example—neither the wealthiest nor the largest black college—includes programs like Headstart, Upward Bound, Manpower (for retraining industrial workers), the Alabama Center for Elected Officials, workshops for public school teachers, ECHO (an adult education program), Talent Search, a VISTA unit, the Emergency School Assistance Program (to deal with problems of desegregation), and the NAB Cluster Program (to promote community dialogue). In addition, most Miles students remain in Alabama after graduation, following through on the call to reinvest "their knowledge and capabilities to the benefit of their city and state." In recent years, such investment has produced an Alabama state senator and state representative, the first black state cabinet officer, a Birmingham city councilman, and about half of the black teachers in the Birmʲ·ɹgham area public schools.

Service to the community does not reside exclusively in an outreach to surrounding localities. One of the major forms it takes is the provision of access to higher education. Says Federal City College (District of Columbia), "Open admissions and minimum cost are among the many ways in which the College is available and responsive to the needs of the community it serves." The makeup of student bodies resulting from this approach by black colleges presents a perplexing picture, at first glance.

Open Enrollment

A hasty reading of the descriptions of the kinds of students that black colleges are seeking to attract could produce a diagnosis of institutional schizophrenia by those unfamiliar with the missions of the colleges. One set of statements common to most of the colleges suggests that they seek to be cosmopolitan institutions offering a classical education for the leisure class. A separate set of statements from the same colleges leaves no doubt that they see themselves attracting students who are black, oppressed, and most often, needy.

However, these positions are not irreconcilable. It was the absence of open colleges that led to the founding of black colleges after the Civil War. The prominent black educator Daniel C. Thompson has discussed the implications of this historical phenomenon:

> The truth is, Black colleges have always had to practice modified open enrollment . . . [and] this may be an innovation in higher education in which they, with proper funding and improved staffing, can lead the way. This could be these colleges' greatest, most far-reaching contribution in the democratization of higher education in American society and to emerging educational systems in so-called developing countries. (Thompson 1973, pp.65–66)

Most colleges studied in this project state that they are open to students "without regard to race, creed, sex, or national origin." In some cases, the statements are of recent origin, motivated by state or federal requirements or by the spirit of the times. But it would be a serious mistake to conclude that these colleges seek only to fulfill the letter of the law. Rather, they see a varied student body as an important constituent of an education designed primarily to equip black students to face both the challenges and the injustices of a multiethnic society.

Lincoln University (Pennsylvania) has been an outstanding exemplar of this tradition: "Lincoln will actively seek to enroll students of diverse race, color, and national origin . . . since we believe that only by freely living and learning together shall we move to greater understanding of man's personal and collective problems." Fisk University (Tennessee) espouses similar principles, based on the historical dynamic of the institution: "Fisk has a powerful and unique relation to history, and its students are involved in a day-by-day making of history in a way few student communities are in present-day society." Involvement with "the paramount issue of the nation and the world: the universal right of every human being to equal access to the benefits of civilization" will not damage Fisk's capacity to produce graduates who can facilitate the "liberation of black people so that they can become 'free' in the strictest sense, socially, economically, and politically." Fisk's view of education, dating from its charter, rests on two principles: No racial discrimination of any kind is to be tolerated in the life of the school; the school is to measure itself by the highest standards "of American education at its best."

A chorus of similar sentiments greets anyone who delves into the policy statements of black colleges. They are often associated with the institutions' history, philosophy, and even geography. Dillard University (Louisiana), for instance, makes the following statement: "Keeping in mind the diverse backgrounds of the founders and their philosophy of mutual respect for people of all cultures, Dillard makes no distinction as to religion, race, color, or sex in the selection of students, faculty, or administration." Further, "Like New Orleans which surrounds it, Dillard represents a merging of people, a blending of attitudes."

President John T. King of Huston-Tillotson College (Texas) has called black institutions "the most open . . . in the country today." Such a description seems to fit Howard University, which points out that it "has been described as America's most cosmopolitan and integrated educational community." Integration of a student body, however, is not always a requisite for an open college, as Paine College (Georgia) argues: "Historically bi-racial in establishment and leadership,

predominantly black in enrollment, yet open to all qualified students
. . . Paine College continues to work toward mutual understanding and
esteem between Blacks and Whites." A black student body, furthermore, is not necessarily a homogeneous student body. As Bennett
College (North Carolina) explains: "[Our students] represent varied
political ideas, socio-economic levels, religious beliefs, and cultural
backgrounds." Or consider Xavier University of Louisiana, the only
Catholic university in the United States with a predominantly black
student body; one-third of its students are non-Catholic and 10 percent
are white.

The dedication of black colleges to openness and equal educational
opportunity, which is no new development, represents a gamble of the
most audacious variety and at the same time is an expression of the
belief that they can truly serve *their* people and preserve *their* culture
while they offer an education and a unique experience to people of *all*
backgrounds. Many of the same colleges that view themselves as open
to all recognize their distinctive nature. Here are some examples of
statements to this effect:

> While [Howard] was established for youth regardless of their nationality,
> religion, or sex, it has always had a special commitment to the education of
> Blacks and other minorities.

> Although [Lane College's (Tennessee)] doors have always been open to all
> colors and creeds, we've especially learned something about the needs of
> minority students.

> Clark College [Georgia] has as one of its missions a commitment to provide
> education for black men and women.

This focus often takes on an intellectual thrust: Shaw University (North
Carolina) fulfills its "historic role as a black college" by .

> identifying with the aspirations and problems of black people and acting as
> a vehicle for their liberation and base for their intellectual empowerment.

The focus is typically reflected in the curricula of the black colleges. For
example:

> At Morehouse students are deeply interested in urban and Third World
> problems. . . . The College has responded to this interest by establishing
> majors in African studies, Afro-American studies, and Caribbean studies.

There are almost as many individual definitions of this aspect of the special mission that distinguishes a black college as there are colleges. One theme, however, unites all of them: attracting, educating, and graduating men and women who otherwise would not have gone to college. The black colleges are aware that, for many of their students, attending college is not a question of *which* but of *whether.* Although some students may have gaps in their educational background, the colleges aim at much more than compensatory education. They wish to graduate seniors whose diplomas mark the completion of undergraduate education, not simply the removal of educational handicaps. Morehouse epitomizes this philosophy:

> Inferior elementary and secondary schools have often failed to prepare black youngsters for programs of vigorous study. It takes courage . . . for a black college to insist on academic quality. Here is a black college that, despite the crippling circumstances with which it has had to live, dares to demand the best.

Black colleges wish to be open to all, to serve a special group, to attract those whose educational backgrounds or economic circumstances prevent them from going elsewhere, and to graduate individuals prepared to compete on any level with college graduates from around the nation. Are these goals or philosophies in conflict? The colleges do not seem to think so, a fact that emerges clearly in their approach to admissions and to academic achievement.

From Norfolk State College (Virginia), for example, we get the following statement on admissions:

> A person's innate right to improve himself through access to education must never be governed by his socio-economic status or his background, whether these be disadvantaged or not.

From their beginnings, black colleges have recognized the role of social factors in determining access to higher education. Howard University makes this explicit:

> In creating Howard University, the founders fulfilled a compelling need by providing academic opportunities for people who had traditionally been denied access to higher education for reasons other than their intellectual abilities.

These colleges devote their energies to creating opportunities rather than constructing rationales for selectivity. Like many others, Stillman College (Alabama) carries the effort beyond the admissions process:

The dominant assumption . . . is that students who are admitted will succeed, not fail. Programs and schedules which provide students with the opportunity for reaching their potential . . . are essential.

This emphasis permits Stillman College and other schools like it to work productively with students from all backgrounds. Shaw University, for example, offers

an unparallelled opportunity for a student to seek a college education and proceed toward the accomplishment of his educational and behavioral objectives within a period of time commensurate with his background, previous academic preparation, and achievement process.

In sum, the concern of black colleges is not with who gets in but what happens to them afterward. According to Virginia Union University, for instance, "Entering qualifications of the students . . . are important, but they are secondary to the qualifications of the graduating student." In the same vein, Voorhees College (South Carolina) states that it "seeks to meet the student at the level of skill and achievement that he has reached at the time of his entry into the college and to raise these levels of skill and achievement as high as possible." At Elizabeth City State University (North Carolina), the process of a university education is viewed as involving the acceptance of a student "where he is and taking him where he should be."

Realism is the keynote. What Albany State College (Georgia) calls "bridging the gap between actual achievement level and the academic requirements of the institution," Benedict College (South Carolina) sees as "accepting each student at the reality level of his development when he enters the institution and of providing programs which help him move toward the goal of optimum intellectual and social development." This emphasis on *reality* allows the colleges to educate students with superior preparation, students from the weakest educational backgrounds, and the majority, who fall between these categories.

Democracy, Citizenship, and Leadership

Black colleges do not regard themselves as a separate world. The general society is never far from their consciousness, and the literature that they issue contains a profusion of statements about the role of graduates in American society, marked by emphasis on democracy, citizenship, and leadership.

Black colleges could be easily excused if they seemed cynical about this nation after a century of segregation and shabby treatment. In addition, we have been in an era when much academic opinion in America regarding the government and American citizenship has ranged from contempt to lack of interest, with occasional islands of concern over electoral politics surfacing in a sea of despair or disdain. The black colleges, however, have consistently held out to their students a vision of civic participation and even of leadership in democracy; nearly every college that was examined is on record as viewing education for democracy as one of its primary goals.

Some of the colleges clearly regard themselves and their brother and sister institutions as building blocks of American democracy. Spelman (Georgia) sees "democracy in personal and social relations" on campus as a step toward "full participation of blacks in American society" and toward "leadership roles for black women." Academic pursuit figures as a major avenue toward these goals; at Wilberforce (Ohio), for example, students are taught "to become familiar with the origin and development of democratic ideals and institutions." Added to the social and academic definitions of democracy is a personal one, expressed with particular clarity by Livingstone College (North Carolina): "The true Livingstonian is democratic. Snobbishness and class distinction are not characteristic of the . . . consciousness of the Livingstone student."

The vehicle for participation in democracy mentioned most often is "constructive" or "responsible" citizenship. The seriousness with which many colleges take their mission of citizenship training is indicated by Dillard's rhetorical question: "What can surpass responsible citizenship, the development of which is a primary aim of Dillard University? This is the very essence of a just society." It also stands out in Tuskegee's statement that the "high-level citizenry required of our society" is the general aim of its educational efforts. That these colleges have a key role to play in developing good citizens is made explicit in Southern University's (Louisiana) statement of purpose: "To provide opportunity for its clientele to learn how to perform responsibly and intelligently the duties of citizenship."

Leadership is the other side of the coin of citizenship for these institutions. Leadership for the community is sought at Morris College (South Carolina); for "various fields" at Rust College (Mississippi); for "the systems and affairs of the nation" at Shaw University (North Carolina). Howard University has chosen no small goal: educating "outstanding black leadership who will play a major role in America's future." Often it is anticipated that leadership will stem from the triumph of the inherent virtues of the institution; Paine College

(Georgia), for example, discerns leadership training emerging both from its academic activities and from its religious community. Florida Agricultural and Mechanical University is typical of how black colleges view the entire subject: "The institution assumes as its function the development of men and women for productive citizenship, effective service, and responsible leadership."

Historians can surely cite many complex, ironic, and interrelated causes for the seeming obsession of black colleges with democracy and citizenship. Certainly these rights seem the sweeter because they were so long denied to black people. But in addition, repeated public dedication to the principles of democracy and citizenship by the black institutions must have deflected the antagonism of anxious whites, fearful that black colleges would become hotbeds of rebellion. Also, the belief that education is the liberating force that will free black people from tyranny and whites from their own bigotry has surely been a major contributor. Depending on your point of view, this vision seems a naïve and unjustified faith in people and processes that have proved traitorous, a call to the society to live up to its principles, an indication that times really have changed, or a touching reminder that newly enfranchised citizens are often the most fervent. Whatever combination of forces has been at work, its end product is a frequent litany of "education–citizenship–leadership–democracy" that affirms a belief in the democratic process and in the ability of colleges, students, and alumni to influence it.

Social Change

Despite the oft-repeated, almost ritualistic, yet clearly sincere allegiance to the forms and usages of American democracy, the black colleges do not accept today's social order uncritically. They feel that change is needed and plan to contribute to it. President Vivian W. Henderson of Clark (Georgia) recently expressed this position in un- compromising terms: "My colleagues in the black colleges . . . want to continue our historic role of providing a base for challenging the status quo in race relations and social behavior" (Henderson 1974, p. 79) . A generation ago, the noted educator Horace Mann Bond had also called for this sort of base: "The contemporary liberal arts college for Negroes needs to align itself with social forces and derive its mission from them, if it is to make a notable contribution" (quoted in Gallagher 1966, p. 251).

Through most of the statements of purpose by black colleges there runs a theme reminiscent of the blues, "Change is gonna' come sometime." For many black colleges that time is now. For many others, it is not far off. Phrases referring to social change appear over and over: "a rapidly changing society"; "continual social change"; "vast socioeconomic changes"; "an ever-changing social order"; "a dynamic society"; "growing complexity"; and "the new demands of our times." To varying degrees this emphasis may represent faith in democracy, exasperation with an unjust society, and the recogntion of massive technological and social revolutions. By contrast, the catalogs of most of the white colleges that were examined reflect a much more serene and static world order with references to change usually confined to discussion of scientific and technical innovation.

For many black colleges, the dynamic of change in today's world requires a response in vocational directions to prepare students for positions created by equal opportunity employment and for new jobs resulting from scientific and social advances. Thus Clark College (Georgia) asserts that "existing programs should prepare students to become professionally related to the needs of present and future societies. Tougaloo College (Mississippi) announces the goal of preparing graduates for "lifelong innovation related to new information and technologies in their chosen fields." The University of Arkansas at Pine Bluff states that it wishes to instill the "skills and competencies needed for functioning effectively in the modern world." Wilberforce University (Ohio) urges "educational experience relevant to the demands of a complex age."

Many colleges voice a strong optimism about the future that will result from change. President C. W. Pettigrew of Fort Valley State College (Georgia), for example, predicts that his college's graduates will be "in harmony with a more rational social order which we have significantly helped to shape." Changes for the better on his campus are linked to the emergence of a better society. "The feeling of improvement saturates the campus," President Pettigrew says. Indeed, what else could one expect at an institution whose motto is Getting better every day? Saint Paul's College (Virginia), similarly hopeful, believes its graduates will be equipped to "adjust readily to change and to lead rewarding and productive lives in a vibrant society." Also optimistic is Tuskegee Institute (Alabama), which sees its alumni "fully prepared for living and service in an ever-enlarging world."

If some black colleges are not as convinced that society will be better in the future, they are determined to do their part in trying to make it so. Dillard's motto is The goal is a tomorrow far better than today. Howard University conceives its role as developing professionals and scholars to "move this society into closer harmony with a concept of social justice." Knoxville College wishes to be "an urgent and persistent force for justice and constructive change," while Bowie State College (Maryland) hopes to teach "specific knowledge and skills for living more effectively in a changing society." College after college sets its goal at effective living in an ever-changing world.

The espousal of and dedication to social change by the black colleges goes far beyond mere optimism about a better tomorrow, hopes for more career opportunities, or even eradication of the more obvious injustices of our society. The frequency with which references to change and its by-products occur suggests that the process of change itself (both within these institutions and in the society) has become an intrinsic part of the definition of education by black colleges. Thus defined, education becomes in large measure learning to live with change and learning to effect change. Perhaps the black colleges, with a greater experience of social change and a greater stake in a changed society, are in a unique position to teach the rest of the educational world the importance of dealing with this essential aspect of our times.

Nowhere is the commitment to a concept of education that unites academic and experiential understanding more sharply etched than in the dimension of change. According to Clark College (Georgia), "The explosion of knowledge and information, advances in technology, growth in human learning, the rise and pervasiveness of ethnic sensitivity, demographic change, and various syndromes regarding racial identity," have made traditional liberal arts programs insufficient for contemporary black youth. Nor is this concern a new one. Philander Smith College (Arkansas) was founded in 1877 to "help freed men to face the vexing experiences of 'conflict and social change.' "

For Dillard University (Louisiana), no contradiction exists between scholarly dedication and concern with change. Dillard stands for "a consciousness of heritage; an awareness of the truth beyond today; the discipline of a scholar preparing for life in the future; these qualities are essential to the character of the Dillard University students." Like Dillard, Knoxville College sees change as a dynamic which interlocks past and future:

Change . . . is the recurrent theme in the institution's history; the capacity for
constructive change, for recognizing and meeting new needs in the future of
new students is itself the thread of continuity. . . . New methods of teaching,
new areas of study, and new professional goals [are needed].

An educational institution must, says Stillman College (Alabama),
"utilize the best of its heritage as it moves into the future." Only then
will society change and racism be eradicated.

Black educators feel that the black colleges should take advantage of
their unique relationship to social change in this country. Daniel C.
Thompson of Dillard University has suggested that a research and
instructional focus would be fruitful:

In every community where Black colleges are located the issue of social
change in paramount. Sometimes it involves the increase or decrease in
population, the increase of Black voters, school desegregation, equal employment, the use of public facilities, or racial conflict. Studies of these
processes could yield valuable knowledge about the nature of social change
. . .The main object would be teaching and the expansion of knowledge for
the benefit of the students and teachers involved. (Thompson 1973, p. 160)

The "good life" is of course a traditional goal of liberal arts education
but, as Elizabeth City State University (North Carolina) explains, "The
'good life' requires the individual to adjust constantly to changing
socio-economic conditions." Without an appreciation of the necessity
of this vital element in our lives and society, these colleges are saying,
yesterday's progress and today's principles will be lost. Norfolk State
College (Virginia) challenges its graduates to "take a dynamic
approach to understanding traditional values such as freedom, liberty,
and equality and . . . seek to re-define, update, and respond to these
concepts in a manner relevant to the times." Saint Augustine's College
(North Carolina) is "vitally interested in preparing its students to cope
with an ever-changing dynamic society by helping them develop their
powers of critical thinking and distinguish between the real and the
unreal." Spelman College (Georgia), established for the education of
black women, dedicates itself to "recognize and respond creatively to
those unique opportunities and problems which women encounter in
the changing world," and to inculcate an "awareness of the social, economic, political, moral, and religious changes that are taking place in
contemporary life." This awareness, it argues, allows the educated
person to keep history from repeating itself and to ensure that the more
things change, the *less* they will stay the same.

Concern about Health

One of the principal benefits of social change in the view of many black colleges should be improved levels of health, both for students and in society in general. Over one-third of the catalogs studied include a direct reference to health in their general declarations of aims and objectives; very few of the catalogs of white colleges that were examined make any such reference. These pronouncements point to a long-standing focus on health at black colleges and several levels of thinking about it.

Undoubtedly such statements demonstrate a concern for the actual physical well-being of students on the campus, which is more sophisticated than Booker T. Washington's pragmatic emphasis in the early days of Tuskegee but in the same tradition. There is evidence that the concern is well warranted. One recent statistic from Federal City College (District of Columbia) reveals that 46 percent of the students who dropped out of Federal City College in 1974–1975 did so for health-related reasons as opposed to approximately 13 percent who left school for financial reasons (Federal City College 1975, p. 11). If the experience of Federal City College is widespread, and if the general health of black students reflects lack of access to satisfactory medical care in precollege years, then we must broaden our conception of the mission of these colleges and deepen our admiration for them in overcoming yet another disadvantage forced upon them by a racist society.

Some of the statements about health also seem to have been inspired by the Greek ideal transmitted through the Romans of *mens sana in corpore sano,* which is translated exactly by the catalog of Coppin State College (Maryland). Some statements, like that of Voorhees College (South Carolina), no doubt reflect the American ideal of physical fitness as symbolized by Theodore Roosevelt and repopularized by President Kennedy and his fifty-mile hike.

Other statements can be traced to the role of in loco parentis that black colleges often assume. Many white colleges also took on this responsibility in the past, but commitment to it has probably been more intense at black colleges; most of them were clearly compelled to offer a measure of protection to their students since they were located near hostile white communities. This philosophy of in loco parentis together with the influence of the British public school ideal may have produced the statements that recommend "the *acquisition** and maintenance of sound health" (Paine College, Georgia) and encourage "optimum

physical *development* and *safeguarding** of health" (Delaware State)
—as if students come to college to learn how to be healthy and to
employ that knowledge for the rest of their lives.

Morristown College (Tennessee) makes what is perhaps the most
explicit statement about health, advocating "the development of
healthful habits of living" through physical education and recreational
experiences "that will serve throughout life." This statement may express to some degree today's emphasis on "carry-over sports," the "new
physical education," and "lifelong learning." It may also indicate that
black colleges see themselves as islands of health in a society sickened
by segregation and white supremacy.

It becomes clear that many statements about health by black colleges
are not aimed solely at encouraging students to get enough sleep, have
regular checkups, and jog or play tennis to lose excess poundage. For
these colleges, health means far more than physical well-being. In some
statements, the wider perspective takes the simple form of linking
physical health with other kinds; for example, juxtaposing mental and
physical health (Grambling College, Louisiana); relating social,
mental, and physical health (University of Arkansas at Pine Bluff); or
connecting mental, physical, emotional, and spiritual health (Livingstone, North Carolina). Oakwood College (Alabama) ties the concept
of health as a unity to the development of the "whole person," so often
the primary goal of student affairs programs at these colleges and many
others. In Oakwood's words, its philosophy is founded on education for
the "whole being . . . the harmonious development of the physical, the
mental, and the spiritual powers."

Translating this concern for the whole and healthy person from the
individual to the communal level, we quickly realize that the personal
health these colleges wish to instill and nourish is a step—perhaps a
metaphorical one—toward a more general social health, which their
graduates will contribute to the larger community. District of Columbia
Teachers College and Florida Agricultural and Mechanical University
endorse this ideal, the former stating that its program of general
education emphasizes the "ability to maintain and improve both personal and community health" and the latter exhorting its students to
"develop positive attitudes relative to personal and community health."

Health is defined in social as well as personal terms by black colleges;
it is seen as contagious. Fort Valley State College (Georgia) wishes to
produce persons who are themselves healthy and "who know how to

*Emphases added.

keep" both themselves and others healthy "in body and mind." Dillard University (Louisiana) emphasizes that health is contingent on a deep understanding of the "laws of health," which can result in a "consciousness of the importance of health in the community." For individuals, says Lincoln University (Pennsylvania), health includes *full participation in society* and "in all areas of life that promote the health and general welfare of the student." Such participation, says Daniel Payne College (Alabama), includes vocational aspects; therefore the college aims to develop an appreciation for good health and "strength of both body and mind as a necessity for successful careers." Langston University (Oklahoma), stressing the need to balance work and recreation, recommends an appreciation both of "physical health and vigor" and of "the importance of appropriate leisure time activities."

Health, then, is a term with many meanings and great significance for black colleges. A sizable number of them do indeed feel it their duty to nourish the physical as well as mental and spiritual well-being of their students. The effort, however, is expected to have repercussions in the larger society. It is meant to lay the foundations of a multidimensional and productive life for the individual, who, in turn, will restore an ailing community to social health.

Ethics and Values

One expression of the concern for a healthy society is the emphasis on the study of values on the black campus. Recently an article in *The Chronicle of Higher Education* (O'Brien 1976) reported a growing concern about ethical values in American higher education. The lead paragraph stated: "The ethical questions raised by Vietnam, Watergate, and current issues such as abortion and euthanasia have made 'values' one of the most popular topics on American campuses." The article went on to list numerous colleges where the study of ethics and values was part of the curriculum or otherwise emphasized on campus. A quote in the article from President Theodore Hesburgh of Notre Dame put the matter in perspective: "Teaching values is the hardest thing in the world. . . . Values that bear on global justice, professional values, and such personal values as honesty, integrity, justice, and compassion for others are too important for the university to take a chance that the students will not be exposed to them" (O'Brien 1976, p.5).

The article did not cite any black colleges especially engaged with the issue. Nevertheless, half the black colleges in our study express a concern for ethics and values in explicit statements of purpose, a far higher percentage than among the white colleges sampled. Often the concern takes the form of a simple statement that the college wishes to foster or develop "moral, spiritual, and aesthetic values" (as at Alabama State University); to prepare students to make "sound choices and value judgments" (as at Jackson State College, Mississippi); or to "meet a high standard of moral and spiritual values" (as at Morris College, South Carolina).

Some of the colleges link moral and spiritual values and the good life, or at least a satisfying life. Stillman College (Alabama) associates the development of a workable "philosophy of life" with "a sense of values." Delaware State College hopes to aid its students to "adopt . . . values which will be beneficial to them throughout their entire lives." At Barber-Scotia College (North Carolina), the aim of education is to foster "respect for others, a sense of justice, moral and spiritual integrity, and the acceptance of responsibility."

Beyond purely individual ethical development many colleges view the acquisition of sound personal values as an indispensable step toward a more just social order. Paine College (Georgia) emphasizes that ethical and spiritual values will "make individual life meaningful and social life humane." Tougaloo College (Mississippi) sees concentration on ethics and values producing the time-honored social virtues of "fair play, brotherhood, and goodwill toward men." Perhaps the strongest statement of this view is provided by Norfolk State College, which holds that its education will have been effective if its "intellectual training and guidance" give students what is "needed to support . . . the moral, spiritual, and aesthetic values upon which our society rests." Like Norfolk State, Livingstone (North Carolina) links the success of its educational program with sharpening the "keen sense of personal and social responsibility" through emphasis on "high intellectual, cultural, and moral standards." Howard University expresses the ethical imperative forcefully with the statement that it is "a place where ideals are as important as ideas."

Many of the colleges studied are church related, and they frequently speak of their commitment to ethical and moral principles in religious terms, as growing out of their religious faith. Mississippi Industrial College wishes to help students realize that they owe "respect for human and individual rights as gifts of God." Bishop College (Texas) stands for the guidance of "personal and social behavior by the values of the Christian religion." Rust College (Mississippi) feels that "the Christian values in human development are the most crucial . . . of the values to be preserved in society and human relations."

It has not taken Vietnam or Watergate to focus the attention of black colleges on ethics and values. Long before either, they were led to that focus by their religious heritage and daily exposure to a society where moral values were often inoperative—where people denied the humanity of others on racial grounds and thereby lost a good part of their own humanity.

Educational Emphases

Black colleges must solve the problems of welding divergent educational approaches into a working synthesis. The classic confrontation of the liberal arts and vocational emphasis poses one major dilemma. It is being overcome, not by lessening the impact or scope of either approach, but by demonstrating their interdependence. Lincoln University (Pennsylvania) is a liberal arts college; its objective is "a thorough grounding in the liberal arts through a curriculum which, incorporating the heritage of the past, stresses the relevance of all knowledge to the problems of the present." At the same time, it points out that "the liberal arts, which encompass the sciences and mathematics, are the recognized preparation for the learned professions and public service and best equip the student to play a useful role in an increasingly complex yet unitary world." Fisk University (Tennessee) seeks to develop in the student the skills "necessary for application of individual creativity, earning of livelihood, and the concomitant growth of the society." Yet the college also asserts that it is an "accepted principle that the best preparation for professional study in any field is a good liberal arts education." To take another example, Le Moyne-Owen College (Tennessee) offers "quality liberal and liberating education . . . and a wide variety of career-education programs." The black colleges unabashedly wish to prepare young people for specific careers, realizing all the while that education must also be able to take their graduates beyond their careers. In the words of Stillman College (Alabama) "Liberal education is offered in the confidence that truth is ultimately what sets man free." On the conceptual level, anyway, black colleges believe in a liberal arts education, but they also insist on the utility of the liberal arts and do not fear to combine them with career education.

Black Studies

The repercussions of the black studies debate of the 1960s and the 1970s have obviously been felt on black college campuses. Their statements suggest that they have maintained an equanimity on the subject that has eluded the rest of the university community. Many black colleges see as a false issue the argument that focus on a particular culture destroys the ability to see things in a global perspective. For Morehouse College (Georgia) there is no conflict between "introducing students to the history, culture, and problems of mankind" and also acquainting them with the lives of one part of mankind. Stillman holds that "knowledge and understanding of the history and culture of black and other peoples and how they have interrelated through the years are essential to the promulgation of truth" and the recognition and eradication of racism.

One may study black history and culture, these colleges are saying, without being chauvinistic, and one may be fascinated by other cultures without denying one's own. Xavier University of Louisiana, for example, insists on recognition that "the university exists within the larger society" and that there is a "priority of claims from or relating to the Black experience." Shaw University (North Carolina) represents many colleges who see the "concerns and methodologies generated" through an examination of "the black dilemma" as "starting points for research into a variety of problems" concerning "the human dilemma." Morehouse, which prepares students "for successful professional employment in mainstream American life as well as in the black community," proposes to do both by giving students "a better understanding of themselves as human beings and of the world in which they live" and by acquainting them with "the history, culture, and problems of black people." Henry Allen Bullock, who believes that colleges with predominantly black student bodies must change to become true "black colleges," recommends a dual curricular and social emphasis as one means for accomplishing this objective:

A black college must be two schoools in one. First, it must prepare its students for full and efficient participation in a WASP-dominated society from whose overpowering influence they cannot escape; second, it must train them for a world of blackness in which they must live. (Bullock 1971, p. 594)

Other Areas To Be Examined

There are many other areas that should be studied by those seeking to understand the self-concept of black colleges. The image of these colleges that emerges from their alumni magazines is, for instance, somewhat different and perhaps more timely than what is pictured in their catalogs. It is intriguing to note that in some alumni publications graduates who are succeeding in business receive the largest share of attention, although few statements in the catalogs of the colleges refer to business careers as opportunities for graduating seniors or give business careers prominence over other vocational choices.

The role of religion in private colleges is also an area that would repay more detailed attention. So is the role of women. The reader has surely not failed to notice how almost exclusively masculine have been the references quoted from catalogs, even from campuses with a preponderance of women students. Are the catalogs waiting to catch up with campus realities in this regard, or do they indicate a lack of the new consciousness prevalent on many other campuses? Innovation and student–faculty interaction, major concerns on many campuses, are two other important topics. What generalizations can one make concerning differences among black colleges with respect to them? Then, there is the whole area of student services and codes of conduct, which is undergoing many changes. What are the new approaches to student affairs on these campuses, and what constitutes the "whole person" whom many of the colleges are seeking? Finally, what are the most important elements in the "search for truth" that is the ultimate aim of so many colleges?

Today's black colleges visualize themselves as trying to heed what DuBois said many years ago about the function of the black college: "It must maintain the standards of popular education, it must seek the social regeneration of the Negro, and it must help in the solution of problems of race contact and cooperation" (DuBois 1961, p. 87).

Leonard Kriegel, a perceptive critic of the American college, has said:

> We cannot achieve a university that is nothing but intellectual, but we should not surrender to the mixture of certification factory and research institute so characteristic of contemporary American education. There must be a surer ground for a university to occupy, a place that does not ignore

legitimate . . . demands of the day but a place whose fundamental loyalty is to its students. For it is only in the students that the university finds its own liberation. (Kriegel 1972, p. 77)

Black colleges have staked out that surer ground more precisely than any other institutions of learning. We should be watching with interest as they and their students and faculty seek to occupy it fully and to liberate each other while teaching a lesson to the rest of the academic community in the process.

Chapter 4

The Socio-Ethical Role and Responsibility of the Black-College Graduate

Samuel DuBois Cook

Education, at least in its most luminous and creative manifestation, the grand liberal arts tradition, is a powerful and effective instrument of human freedom, happiness, virtue, and justice—in other words, the Good Life and the Good Society. For, at best, education means much more than individual adjustment to social and institutional imperatives; the discovery, application, and transmission of knowledge, values, and cultural norms; and the utilization of technical skills in the job market.

Education means, ultimately, the liberation and cultivation of the human and spirit. It also means self-realization, the becoming, perhaps more accurately the approximation, of our best selves. Thus, according to Jacques Maritain, the Thomist philosopher, "the chief task of education is above all to shape man, or guide the evolving dynamism through which man forms himself as a man" (Maritain 1960, p.2). The aim of education, he went on to say,

> is to guide man in the evolving dynamism through which he shapes himself as a human person—armed with knowledge, strength of judgment, and moral virtues—while at the same time conveying to him the spiritual heritage of the nation and the civilization in which he is involved, and preserving in this way the century-old achievements of generations. The utilitarian aspect of education—which enables the youth to get a job and make a living—must surely not be disregarded, for the children of man are not made for aristocratic leisure. But this practical aim is best provided by

the general human capacities developed. And the ulterior specialized training which may be required must never imperil the essential aim of education. (Maritain 1960, p.10)

Education involves the ultimate issues and concerns of the human enterprise, questions of the purpose, goal, and meaning of human life and destiny and of the improvement of the quality of human experience and aspirations. Leighton said that

> Beliefs are the product of education, by which the innate dispositions of human nature are molded, transformed and given set and direction. Man's innate powers are plastic and, in a broad sense, education is the whole process by which these powers are molded, transformed and set. All life is a process of education. (Leighton 1930, p. 530)

Ignorance and freedom are intrinsically incompatible and mortal foes. "If a nation," said Jefferson, "expects to be ignorant and free, in a state of civilization, it expects what never was and never will be" (quoted in Padover 1946, p. 89). Social progress and cultural change are linked to the acquisition, expansion, and utilization of knowledge and technical skills—as the progress of black Americans demonstrates with clarity and certainty. "I look to the diffusion of light and education," said Jefferson, "as the resource most to be relied on for ameliorating the condition, promoting the virtue, and advancing the happiness of man" (quoted in Padover 1946, p.92).

Education can be and often is a source of radical dissatisfaction and a powerful catalyst of social reform. The slave owners knew what they were doing when they made it a serious criminal offense for slaves to learn how to read and write and for others to teach them. In his monumental *An American Dilemma,* Myrdal asserted prophetically that *"the long-range effect of the rising level of education in the Negro people goes in the direction of nourishing and strengthening the Negro protest"* (Myrdal 1944, p.881). Surely the civil rights movement is, among other things, a monument to the growth, development, and diffusion of education in the lives of black people. Education is a rich and unique contributor to human liberty, equality, and justice. It is a presupposition of free people and free societies.

THE DUAL MISSION OF BLACK COLLEGES

The socio-ethical role and responsibility of the men and women who graduate from black colleges can only be understood within a broad historical and theoretical framework. Before examining this role and responsibility a point of clarification is essential. Are the socio-ethical role and responsibility of the black-college graduate different from those of the white-college graduate? (Both "black college" and "white college" are used here very loosely.) Fundamentally, the answer is in the negative. Do black graduates of white colleges have the same socio-ethical role and responsibility as the graduates of black colleges? The answer is in the affirmative. The social and moral obligations of black graduates of Harvard, Yale, and Duke differ neither in kind or degree from graduates of Morehouse, Saint Augustine's, and Dillard. Commitment to the betterment of the black condition is the same for both.

What I shall assert and elaborate as the socio-ethical role and responsibility of the black-college graduate applies with equal force, perhaps a fortiori, even more so, to the graduates of white colleges. Generally speaking, the alumni of white colleges are the heirs, possessors, and agents of disproportionate power, privilege, and advantage in comparison to the alumni of black colleges. Hence they have greater responsibility for righting the wrongs and eliminating the massive injustices and other social evils of American society. The height of social irresponsibility, and indeed social immorality, would be to exempt the strong from the moral requirements of human justice and place the burden on the weak; or to assign the obligation of instituting a more just, humane, and decent social order to the victims, to the powerless, rather than to men and women of power and privilege who through will and commitment could redeem the promises of the land and make liberty and equality for all an objective reality. The attainment of social justice is primarily a function of power. Therefore the graduates of white colleges have an even greater socio-moral obligation than black-college graduates to bring about social change and reform in race relations.

Moreover, higher education ought to make a creative and qualitative social and moral difference in all our lives—white and black, Jew and Gentile, northerner and southerner—and in the institutions, organizations, and processes we touch. Education should make the graduates of all colleges more sensitive to human needs and aspirations, more compassionate toward human suffering, more intolerant of social injustice and oppression, and more responsive to the bitter cries, agonies, heartaches, and deep longings of others. Human beings belong to each other. The solidarity of all humanity is an urgent social necessity as well as a moral given. Education should enlarge, enrich, and deepen our vision.

The difference between the socio-ethical role and responsibility of the graduate (black or white) of the black college and the graduate (white or black) of the white college is a matter of emphasis, orientation, philosophy, and existential commitment and vision; it is also related to the climate of social morality. At issue, in large measure, are the unique resources, vitalities, and perspectives of black colleges. These special gifts flow not from nature but from fortune and history—from the special experiences and perceptions of black people in the New World. The emphasis and orientation of black colleges also flow from the contradictions, ambiguities, tensions, and ambivalences of black life in the United States.

Ideally, members of the oppressor class would have the same kind of socio-ethical concerns and moral sensibilities as members of the oppressed class, but we know that because of the power and persistence of collective and individual egoism, this is not the case. Members of privileged groups are caught up in all kinds and degrees of moral conceit, hypocrisy, arrogance, self-deception, and what Reinhold Neibuhr might have called "ideological taint" or "distortion" or "egoistic corruption." Hence moral expectations for oppressor and oppressed, realistically speaking, must be quite dissimilar.

The class of phenomena called black colleges is marked by a distinctive philosophy, history, curriculum emphasis, and raison d'être. A central assumption is that students at black colleges, vis-à-vis white colleges, will acquire a set of values, a spirit of social service, social conscience, moral sensitivity, and sense of personal and social responsibility—principally with reference to social and racial justice—that will stay with them and motivate them after graduation. Another way of putting it is that black colleges aim to reinforce, enlarge, and deepen certain socio-moral properties and impulses.

It is hardly an accident that Martin Luther King, Jr., was an alumnus of Morehouse College rather than of Harvard College and that the overwhelming majority of the leaders of the civil rights movement—nationally and locally—are graduates of black colleges. Perhaps the black colleges provided a social creativity, ethical imagination and motivation, a sense of outrage at injustice and oppression, a passion for social justice and righteousness, a will to a better social order. This is why they produced leaders with the socio-ethical vision that Dr. King had. Unlike white colleges, black colleges can hardly foster a love of, and a passion for, the status quo.

If the foregoing contains a measure of validity, one must say something about the mission of black colleges and what they seek to impart to their students and graduates.

In broad strokes, the black college has the same general mission as a white college, but, additionally, the black college has a special and unique purpose. The black college, thus, has a dual mission. It is about human excellence, the superior education and training of tender minds, nourishment of the creative imagination, and reverence for learning; it is also about the development of moral character and the production of better men and women for a more humane, decent, and open world.

Academic Excellence

The first order of business for any institution of higher learning is academic excellence. Black colleges must be profoundly committed to it. To be sidetracked from the pursuit of academic excellence in the name of any rival god or goal would be suicidal for them. Academic excellence is necessary for utilitarian as well as for intrinsic significance. It is necessary because, among other things, it is the chief means of access to the benefits of a highly technological and competitive culture. It is the key to high-level jobs, security, professional advancement, self-confidence, pride, and self-respect.

"Education," said Alfred North Whitehead, "is the acquisition of the art of the utilisation of knowledge" (1947, p.16). Graduates of black colleges must be competitive with the graduates of white colleges for professional positions in the mainstream of American society. Black institutions cannot compete in the broad sweep of American life without being competent agents for the transmission of topflight skills, genuine learning, and intellectual excitement. Black colleges must be more than black; in order to survive and prosper, they must be centers of excellence. Several, of course, already are.

There is no substitute for excellence. Black colleges, therefore, must reject as false all counsel to pursue other priorities in the place of academic excellence, including cheap and vulgar conceptions of "relevance." A decade ago, Howard Zinn (1966), a political scientist and historian, articulated "a new direction" for black colleges. His views have been echoed countless times and have received widespread acceptance. Zinn proposed the following agenda for black colleges:

With work-study programs along the Antioch model, they could have students spend half their time in the poor communities that surround most of these colleges, and half the year in school studying the problems of poverty. Work in the social sciences, the natural sciences, literature, and art, could all be directed toward transforming the lives of the poor. (Zinn 1966, p.81)

This approach, imaginative as it is, must be viewed as a supplement to, rather than a substitute for, the predominant goal of academic excellence. The problem is not one of desirability, legitimacy, or social need but of priorities, resources, and competence. There is also the question of whether black colleges should become social welfare agencies and institutions, primarily designed to rehabilitate black communities. Do black colleges possess the resources—human and material—to be successful in "transforming the lives of the poor"? After all, money is the crowning need of the poor.

Zinn, however, seems to have a sense of futility and irrelevance about the achievement of academic excellence on the part of black colleges relative to their white counterparts. He calls this objective orthodoxy, to be dismissed as a "traditional" goal. He is, by contrast, quite confident of the potentially unique contribution of black colleges through social activism and community involvement and improvement:

> Decisions for such new approaches need to be made soon, before the dominant mood—which is to take over the traditional goals of other colleges—becomes frozen. In the pursuit of orthodoxy, the Negro institutions will probably remain second-best. Thrusting into new directions, they could fulfill a unique function which would not only raise their stature, but be of inestimable benefit to the nation, even the world. (Zinn 1966, p. 81)

The irony is that Zinn, himself, represents scholarship and intellectual discipline par excellence.

A position similar to Zinn's has been taken by the black political scientist Charles V. Hamilton. His article, "The Place of the Black Colleges in the Human Rights Struggle" (1967), implies that social activism and immediate community involvement exhaust the mission of black colleges. Academic excellence is not a priority or concern for him. Instead he argues that the curriculum should be relevant to the lives and experiences of black students and that the black college should get involved in the ghetto. They should do this not only through formal study but also by preparing students from the ghetto to return there for leadership roles and the deliberate inculcation of a "sense of racial *pride* and *anger* and *concern*" (Hamilton 1967, p. 7).

Hamilton advocates "a black college where one of the criteria for graduating summa cum laude would be the demonstrated militancy of the candidate" (Hamilton 1967, p. 7). He then goes on to issue a militant challenge:

> And people will ask: What about accreditation? and I will answer: Our relevancy and legitimacy will accredit us. How creditable can the present system be when it cripples hundreds of thousands of black students annually? (1967, p. 7)

This is the advocacy of self-accreditation or perhaps no accreditation. How will dubious credentials assist black-college graduates to compete in the mainstream of American culture? How will they manage to gain entrance to graduate and professional schools and to get the kind of education and training that will enable them to improve the quality of life in the black community? Hamilton's proposal prescribes a vicious circle; it constitutes a sure recipe for disaster for the black college and the black-college graduate.

The conclusion is inescapable that there is an organic relationship between academic excellence and social relevance, involving mutuality, reciprocity, and reinforcement. A principal socio-ethical responsibility of the black-college graduate is first-rate professional competence. Topflight blacks in the professions and in other key leadership positions, because of their stature, self-confidence, independence, and influence as models, are likely to make a much greater contribution to social reform and community improvement than blacks, whatever their ideology and rhetoric, who represent professional incompetence and failure. Other community or educational goals are no substitute for excellence.

Social Justice

In the social order, nothing ranks higher than justice. In a direct sense, the main mission of the black college and the socio-ethical responsibility of the black college graduate is the pursuit of justice, whose dimensions in the present American context are primarily racial, economic, and sexual. The primacy of justice is the key to the Good Society. "Subjectively," said Reinhold Niebuhr, "the test of an adequate social ethic is the sense of responsibility. Objectively, the test is the concept of justice" (Niebuhr 1960, p. 1085) Niebuhr asserted that establishing justice in "a sinful world is the whole sad duty of the political order"(quoted in Davis and Good 1960, p. 180) and that "the problem of politics and economics is the problem of justice" (Niebuhr 1956, p. 128). Equality is the substance of justice, and the search for a better world is the wellspring of moral and social consciousness.

Black colleges and their graduates ought to be informed and inspired by the great humanistic vision—blending rational humanism, sober idealism, and existential personalism. A good society must be built on the principle of the primacy of persons, not things, the Thou, not the It. The human being, whatever his race, creed, sex, or economic status, is the most precious and unique reality in the world. Martin Buber was right. "Only men who are capable of truly saying *Thou* to one another can truly say *We* with one another" (Buber 1955, p.176). Reverence and respect for persons not in the realm of abstraction but in their concrete particularity are required for the continued existence of every society and culture; it is especially timely in the current American situation.

Affirmation of authentic, universal humanism—not black, white, male, or female—is a moral imperative and an urgent social necessity. The humanistic vision embraces what Martin Luther King, Jr., called the beloved community, meaning all humanity—white and black, Jew and Gentile, Protestant and Catholic, rich and poor, male and female. "Injustice anywhere," said King, "is a threat to justice everywhere. We are caught up in an inescapable network of mutuality, tied in a single garment of destiny. Whatever affects one directly, affects all indirectly" (1963, p. 77). The indivisibility of justice is rooted in the commonality of human nature and destiny.

This social vision closely parallels what Maritain called integral or new humanism. According to him,

> If mankind overcomes the terrible threats of slavery and dehumanization which it faces today, it will thirst for a new humanism, and be eager to rediscover the integrity of man, and to avoid the cleavages from which the preceding age suffered so much. To correspond to this integral humanism, there should be an integral education. . . .
>
> Bourgeois individualism is done for. What will assume full importance for the man of tomorrow are the vital connections of man with society, that is, not only the social environment but also common work and common good. The problem is to replace the individualism of the bourgeois era not by totalitarianism or the sheer collectivism of the beehive but by a personalistic and communal civilization, grounded on human rights and satisfying the social aspirations and needs of man. Education must remove the rift between the social claim and the individual claim within man himself. It

must therefore develop both the sense of freedom and the sense of responsibility, human rights and human obligations, the courage to take risks and exert authority for the general welfare and the respect for the humanity of each individual person. (Maritain 1960, pp. 88–89)

In the struggle for the translation of this humanistic vision, the black college and the black college graduate should be especially sensitive to this country's desperate need to overcome the tyranny of racism. Racism is an evil that is self-devouring. It demeans both whites and blacks, both the oppressors and the oppressed. It makes us all tragic losers. Sexism, too, is a great tragedy. And so is poverty in this land of affluence. As Martin Luther King, Jr., asserted, "In a real sense, all life is interrelated. The agony of the poor impoverishes the rich; the betterment of the poor enriches the rich. We are inevitably our brother's keeper because we are our brother's brother" (King 1968, p. 211).

So, the black college and the black-college graduate have a peculiar moral and social obligation to help sensitize this nation's conscience; to insist on the need for profound changes in social morality and patterns of behavior; to heighten social concern and ethical responsibility. Like religion, perhaps one of the chief functions of higher education in this age is to help create and maintain a sensitive and creatively restless conscience. A morally complacent, easy, and self-satisfied conscience is a deadly foe of social and human betterment. It helps to sanctify, rather than to rectify, social injustice and oppression.

Humanism, social idealism, imaginative realism, and an awareness of the contradictions and accidents of the human predicament should all be a vital and prominent part of the climate of instruction on college campuses. Those who have experienced this kind of education should emerge from it with a passion for social justice, a hunger for social reconciliation and redemption, and a radical ethic of concern for the disinherited and the "least of them."

As Benjamin E. Mays has asserted,

Education is not designed merely to lift one above his fellows, but rather its purpose is to equip men to help his fellows—to elevate the masses, the less fortunate. For if one has a better mind than his fellows, more wealth than his fellows, is more favorably circumstanced than his fellows, has a better opportunity to develop than his fellows, he is obligated to use skills in the interest of the common good. To use education for the common good is mandatory because trained minds are rare—only a small percentage of the total population of the world is college trained. And to whom much is given, much is required.

Furthermore, man can fulfill his true destiny in this life only in proportion as his skills are used in the service of mankind. (Mays 1960a, p. 6)

The prophetic wisdom and sense of justice expressed in these words stoked the fires of creativity for social change in Martin Luther King, Jr., and others. That is why King called Benjamin Mays his "mentor." The charge that Dr. Mays gave to Howard University applies with equal force to all black colleges:

> Howard in the second century should train its graduates to know that we are all a part of mankind and that no man is good enough, no man is strong enough, and no man is wise enough to think that he is better than another man and thus justified in setting himself apart from the man farthest down; for if one man has more intellect than another, is richer than another, it may be luck or fate. We are all what we are largely by accident or God's grace. No one chooses his parents and no one chooses the circumstances under which he is born. I have seen a brilliant mind and a dull mind born into the same family. I have seen beauty and ugliness in the same family. The boy born in the slums has no choice, and the boy born in the midst of splendor and wealth has no choice. The man in splendor and wealth has no right to look down on the one from the slums or the ghetto because he too might have been born in the slums. (Mays 1970, p. 112)

Relevance

Beyond what has already been suggested, what about the relevance of the black college to the black community? What of more direct, comprehensive, and sustained involvement of the black college in community service? "The Negro college," says Charles V. Hamilton (1967, p. 9), "is one of America's few legitimate bastions of relevancy." And later, "Protect your relevancy with a passion" (1967, p. 10). The bitter cry for relevance is heard from the thoughtful and sensitive everywhere in seats of learning. It must be heeded. It is the cry for higher possibilities—for something better and more meaningful. But the vision of relevance is one thing; its particular content quite another. We must be sure that there is harmony and unity between our vision of relevance and the relevance of our vision.

Relevance is a tricky concept; in all too many contexts and quarters, it is a cliché and a substitute for rigorous analysis, rational discourse, and sustained reflection. Relevant to what and for what? What kind of relevance? Vague and mystical answers and glittering generalities will not do. If relevance refers to vocation, life, and culture, then what particular and specific kind of vocation, life, and culture? What are the programs and other means for achieving it? It is not enough to assert that we mean relevance to the black experience, for here, as elsewhere, we must be selective and reflective; the black experience is multidimensional and ambiguous. Relevant to black liberation? Very well. But what kind of liberation? Liberation from, to, and for what? What are the specific and particular methods of its achievement? The term *relevance* is not self-defining and self-applying. Its meaning, application, and dimensions are not self-evident.

My view is that black Americans must take the long and total view of relevance. Nothing, except the persistence of white racism, can be more disastrous for blacks than to be caught up in a narrow and cheap bag of relevance. A relevance that provides therapeutic satisfaction for today but ensures disablement and frustration for tomorrow is self-defeating; it must be rejected as unworthy of rational and moral human beings.

A major responsibility of black colleges is to teach their students the enduring relevance and significance of critical thinking. Critical thinking in this tragic world is a moral and social imperative. Our students must be taught the necessity of weighing alternative possibilities, scrutinizing conditions and operations, examining evidence, and evaluating the probable consequences of various courses of action. They must be taught to be critical and skeptical of proposed roads to and schemes of black liberation, independence, freedom, and the New Zion.

Community Improvement

Black colleges are and will continue to be concerned with a better life for the poor, whatever their race or ethnicity. But they must make their contribution on their own terms and in the light of their unique resources. Their community service must be done primarily through training and sensitizing their students and graduates, motivating them to use their skills for community improvement. Black colleges would be socially and morally irresponsible if they were indifferent to the slums, the ghettos, persons on welfare, the ill-housed, and the hungry. But they would be equally irresponsible if they assumed that their resources are sufficient to solve the day-to-day problems of the black community. Beyond certain responses in terms of curricula and other limited programs, there is not much black colleges can do alone to achieve and sustain genuine community improvement. According to Vivian W. Henderson,

Students expect to experience learning by doing, thus being actively involved in correcting ghetto problems (poverty, community development,
racial discrimination, policical participation). Negro colleges, in other
words, are expected to be involved in solving day-to-day problems of black
people as well as preparing youth for service in black communities and for
the community at large. (Henderson 1971, p. 636)

On the other hand, Patricia Roberts Harris asserts,

It is in allaying fears and in providing security in assuming leadership roles
that these Negro colleges should seek their future community role. Although all institutions of higher learning are in a financial bind today, the
Negro college has always had and will probably always have fewer funds
than needed to meet the requirements of its students. Therefore, expansive
programs of urban renewal, or social welfare, with their attendant demand
for highly trained personnel, should not be the goal of black colleges, even if
funding can be found for them.

Instead, the community service of the Negro college should be an extension of the service provided in the past. The community service programs of
the Negro college should be designed to discover and train individuals with
the ability to evaluate and change their environments. Some kind of credit
or certification ought to be provided in order to convince participants that
the activity is not just busy work.

The activity with and for the community should continue to be essentially
tutorial, but with a wide range of subject matter. (Harris 1971, p. 728)

Preparing young people for service in the community—the black
community and beyond—is the more responsible and rational
approach. Here, again, sensitivity to the masses as well as the classes
and the town as well as the gown is crucial. The black college has a
responsibility to train its students for positions of imaginative, creative,
and innovative leadership, and its graduates have a responsibility to
assume such positions of leadership.

First of all, that leadership should be in the field of human rights and
the struggle for social change and justice. Patricia Harris holds that "the
major contribution of the black college will be in the training of secure
leadership that will assume responsibility for engineering social
changes" (Harris 1971, p. 729). She points out:

From this black middle class, created by the black college, came the core of
the leadership that changed the status of blacks in the United States. . . .
From Martin Luther King to Stokely Carmichael, spokesmen for the black
community have been recruited from among graduates of black colleges.
(Harris 1971, pp. 723–24)

Leadership in Decision Making

Our concern is with the collective not the individual contributions of black colleges and their graduates. In addition to preparing students for leadership in the field of social activism and institutional reform, black colleges must train their students for positions of creative and responsible leadership in business, industry, government, public service, and the professions. Participation in the total decision-making process, character, and direction of American life and culture is indispensable. Leadership is the key to the enlargement and enrichment of human opportunity and the establishment and maintenance of a more humane and just society.

Mack H. Jones contends that the major responsibility of black colleges to the black community is ideological and political—the heightening of political consciousness:

> Black colleges have the power to remake the political consciousness of the black student and ultimately of the black nation. That is their primary responsibility to the larger black community. If it is met, secondary responsibilities such as working with community organizations, participating in community politics, providing staff assistance for community leaders, and so on, will take care of themselves. If the colleges do not meet their primary responsibility, their secondary involvement . . . will be of little consequence anyway. (Jones 1971, pp. 741-42)

With respect to the professions, the unique contribution of black colleges is indeed impressive. Vernon E. Jordan, Jr., properly notes that

> Today, as in the past, the black colleges provide the training and dedication offered reluctantly, if at all, by their more prestigious brother institutions. It is the black colleges that have graduated 75 percent of all black Ph.D.'s, 75 percent of all black army officers, 80 percent of all black federal judges, and 85 percent of all black doctors. These institutions have profoundly influenced the development of black Americans and there is no doubt that they will continue to do so. (Jordan 1975, p. 165)

Models of Integration and Community

Black colleges—especially those that are private and church-related—have been and are models of integration, democracy, freedom, and genuine human community in action. Their faculties and staffs, in particular, represent all races, colors, creeds, and cultures. Historically, in the oppressive South they have been centers of interracial and intercultural contact, fellowship, and understanding. (See, for example,

Mays 1960b, pp. 246-47, and Bond 1960, p. 226.) Looking to the future,
Howard Zinn comments:

> There is too much wistful talk in education circles about how far Negro
> colleges must go to "catch up" with the rest. What is overlooked is that the
> Negro colleges have one supreme advantage over the others: they are the
> nearest this country has to a racial microcosm of the world outside the
> United States, a world largely non-white, developing, and filled with the
> tensions of bourgeois emulation and radical protest. And with more white
> students and foreign students entering, Negro universities might become
> our first massively integrated, truly international educational centers. (Zinn
> 1966, p. 81)

Critical Intelligence: Power, Freedom, and Social Change

The discussion of critical intelligence dramatically reminds us of the
vital kinship of power and freedom. Neither a freedomless power nor a
powerless freedom commends itself to rational men and women. As
John Locke emphasized, power is the central core of freedom; what
liberty means, he asserted, is the power to act or refrain from acting, to
think or not to think, according to one's own preferences (Koch 1961,
p. 29).

The philosopher and educator John Dewey also laid stress on the
inseparable relationship between freedom and power. Liberty, he
asserted, is not merely an abstract idea.

> It is power, effective power to do specific things. There is no such thing as
> liberty in general; liberty, so to speak, at large. If one wants to know what
> the condition of liberty is at a given time, one has to examine what persons
> *can* do and what they *cannot* do. The moment one examines the question
> from the standpoint of effective action, it becomes evident that the demand
> for liberty is a demand for power, either for possession of powers of action
> not already possessed or for retention and expansion of powers already
> possessed. . . .
> In the second place, the possession of effective power is always a matter of
> the distribution of power that exists at the time. (Dewey 1946, pp. 111-112)

Thus understood, there is a necessary distinction between formal and
empty freedom, on the one hand, and empirical and effective freedom,
on the other. In the hard-hitting words of Dewey and Tufts,

> The freedom of an agent who is merely released from direct external
> obstruction is formal and empty. If he is without resources or personal skills,

without control of the tools of achievement, he must inevitably lend himself to carrying out the directions and ideas of others. (Quoted in Mays 1970, p. 111)

That distinction is critical for black people in their quest for freedom and equality. We must have the material as well as the formal, the empirical as well as the legal, freedom as well as equality.

Hence social justice entails economic power as well as political power. One of the most crucial problems confronting black people is how to translate political power into economic gains. Black colleges and black-college graduates have a special responsibility in this context. Without material resources and skills permitting effective action, freedom is empty and powerless.

In broad terms, some of the other socio-ethical responsibilities of black colleges and their graduates are to be critical and skeptical of simplistic and easy social solutions, monistic strategies of social reform and historical change, naive and inflammatory rhetoric of violence and revolution, the failure to count and balance the costs of proposed roads to black liberation, and the failure to make practical, qualitative distinctions amid the infinite complexities of public policy, choice, personnel, and the entire public order and process. There is also the obligation to identify and expose and seek to eliminate the increasingly subtle, covert, and sophisticated forms of discrimination and segregation, which are infinitely more difficult to eradicate than the overt and visible forms.

Black colleges and their graduates have a responsibility to insist on the unity and continuity of means and ends, to recognize the endless complexity of social change, to stress the wisdom of nonviolence and the tragic futility of violence in the struggle for a better life and a more humane existence, and to bring a profound sense of moral and social urgency to the task of social reconstruction and the realization of freedom and equality. Of special significance is the responsibility of blacks to take the initiative and leadership in the quest for equality of citizenship and humanity.

Above all, perhaps, black colleges and their graduates have a grave responsibility to subject all our struggles, issues, and ideological and power encounters to the motive, judgment, and norm of love. All else is tentative and provisional. Love is the ultimate and supreme norm of history and culture. Love is not only relevant but desperately crucial to the structure, process, and struggles of power.

PRESERVATION OF BLACK COLLEGES

By definition, without black colleges there can be no black-college graduates. The preservation and strengthening of selected black colleges is an educational, social, and moral imperative. They are "black" only in the sense that Harvard, Princeton, Stanford, Duke, and other such colleges are "white" and operate within a particularistic historical frame and cultural context. The critical differentia are leadership, control, and historical association and psychological identification.

The preservation and strengthening of black colleges of quality are essential not only to the continuation of the civil rights movement and the struggle for social justice, the enrichment of the professions, the development of creative and responsible black leadership, the enlargement and enrichment of educational opportunity, and the vitality of pluralism and diversity in higher education, but also to the quality of life and human experience in America and to its destiny. As Vernon Jordan has asserted,

> Most crucial to the black community and the nation, is the continued survival of the black colleges. Their doors were open when white colleges would not allow blacks in, much less welcome them. Their doors are open today to masses of black students who cannot afford the high-cost predominantly white institutions. The bulk of them are in the South, where the majority of black people still live. Generally, their students are poorer than those attending predominantly white colleges. . . .
>
> Given the importance of these black institutions to the black community, given the outstanding job they are doing in educating young blacks who have had no other alternative as well as those who prefer such schools, and given their function as a repository of black intellectual, cultural, and educational resources, their preservation and improvement must rank high on the list of national educational priorities. (Jordan 1975, p. 165)

To black colleges and their graduates, the New World owes an awesome debt. But, beyond that, black colleges and their sons and daughters have received meaning, fulfillment, and intellectual and moral justification in the performance of their mission, in the fulfillment of their obligations.

We Are All Responsible

By implication and in reality, ideas concerning black colleges apply not only to American higher education as a whole but also to seminal aspects of the American condition as well. My discussion has centered on the black college and its graduates, but it also involves the socio-ethical role and responsibility of all American colleges and their graduates. Universality is entailed in particularity.

Not only from the perspective of humanism and idealism but also from that of rational or enlightened self-interest, white colleges and their graduates have as much at stake as black colleges and their alumni in the creation of a better society and in desperately striving for the beloved community.

Justice is morally desirable and socially necessary not merely for the sake of blacks but equally for the sake of whites; indeed, for the sake of all Americans. Injustice militates against the unity, vitality, and creativity of the entire nation. It erodes the sense of community and is at war with the common good. Racism, sexism, and poverty impoverish us all and make us all tragic losers. After all, the American Dream and promise are about justice, equality, freedom, democracy, and dignity for all who inhabit this land. In the tragedy and glory of the American pilgrimage, we are all involved, and, ultimately, we are all one. The indivisibility of justice and humanity is the crowning truth of the moral order and of the social adventure.

Chapter 5

History and Goals of Black Institutions of Higher Learning

Jane E. Smith Browning and
John B. Williams

In general, little attention has been paid to the history of education in the South. In the case of the black colleges and universities whatever work has been produced focuses on individual institutions and overlooks many of the relationships among the colleges, their local communities, and the larger society. Furthermore, the characteristic adjustments the colleges made to outside and internal social forces have been ignored.

In this chapter, we describe some of the forces that have had a major impact on the development of black colleges since the 1860s when large-scale efforts were initiated. In particular, we will be concerned with two recurring policy issues: (1) the proper relationship between education and the broader society, and (2) the meaning of racial equality.

One way to tell the history of the black colleges is to show first how ideas about the role of education and the role of blacks in American society have emerged and changed and then to trace the impact of these changes. Our goal is less ambitious. There are undoubtedly other policies that recur and have impact on the colleges as well as those we shall discuss. It is our hope that future efforts to explore the history of black education in the South will proceed through an exhaustive identification of policies shaping the history of black institutions, an analysis of the effects of these policies, and systematic descriptions of various responses.

68

BENEVOLENT SOCIETIES, 1860–1900

Organized attempts to provide education for blacks in the South go back to the start of the Civil War. At this time, of course, almost the entire black population was located in southern or border regions, where laws and strictly enforced social customs prohibited blacks from being taught to read and write. In the North, at least two colleges for blacks had been founded before this, and in many northern states they were permitted to attend white colleges in small numbers.

It was the missionary groups which took the first major step toward a system of schools and colleges for blacks. Following the lead of the American Missionary Association (AMA) in 1861, several religious benevolent societies sent missionaries into the South with the goal of uplifting the freed slaves through religion, education, and programs of physical assistance. The AMA alone was responsible for founding seven black colleges and thirteen normal schools between 1861 and 1870. By the turn of the century, throughout the South other missionary agencies and the Freedmen's Bureau were carrying on similar work (Tappan 1855; 1869; 1873).

By and large, the missionaries tended to mix social, economic, and religious ideas in their dedication to the task of uplifting the freed men and women. They were moved not only by their religious convictions but by the social and economic values that had produced the Yankee Protestant society of the North—particularly in New England. They were in agreement that someone needed to demonstrate that former slaves could be remade into the ideal of a Yankee, Calvinist, American citizen. Their common goals were to save the souls, educate the minds, care for the bodies, and prepare the freed men and women for their responsibilities as new citizens of the South. Education could guarantee freedom for blacks if properly executed (American Missionary Magazine 1863; American Missionary Association 1848; McPherson 1975).

The beginning of the Civil War had witnessed mass migrations of slaves fleeing to areas like Fortress Monroe, Virginia, which was controlled by Union troops. When General William Butler refused to return three slaves who had fled to the federally occupied territory of the Fort, declaring them "contraband of War," he had set the stage for similar escapes throughout the South. With more and more slaves escaping to the increasingly expanded territory dominated by the North, the Emancipation Proclamation in 1863 amounted to a broadscale ratification of Butler's two-year-old policy at Fortress Monroe (American Missionary Association 1861; Engs 1972; McPherson 1964).

Policies aimed at punishing the southern rebels and maintaining the Union and the presence of federal troops enabled northern missionaries and ex-slaves to establish schools and colleges for blacks during the period 1861–1880. This is not to suggest, however, that the work proceeded smoothly. On the contrary, the missionary experiment met with grave difficulties, some of its own creation, others from forces beyond its control.

Pressures from southern whites, lack of support from the North, and disagreements with the army characterized the social drama that unfolded. At times, southern whites attacked the missionaries as well as the blacks. The federal troops committed acts of violence against freedmen; army officials stole supplies and generally undermined the efforts of the missionaries. Furthermore, the characteristically ambivalent posture of northern whites toward the problem of the former slaves, typified by President Lincoln's leadership, undercut attempts to improve their situation (Engs 1972; McPherson 1975; Rose 1967).

Beyond these difficulties, the missionaries themselves disagreed over the fundamental issue of equality. Blatant acts of discrimination against blacks were few among them. They were, nevertheless, indecisive among themselves over how to treat the former slaves while preparing them for new roles as full-fledged American citizens. Some favored a gradual process, arguing that unless relations with the newly freed men and women were tempered, it would be impossible to maintain discipline. By this line of argument, as their pupils began to improve, more responsibility could be offered and equal relations gradually achieved. Others argued that the only way to overcome the characterological deficiencies caused by slavery was to treat the blacks as equal mature human beings from the beginning, commenting upon their mistakes with patience and kindness. There were other points of view, as well. Regardless of the terms of the argument or the perceived poles of the debate, however, it is clear that serious disagreements over this issue led to a conflict that the missionaries themselves never resolved. In this problem, we can discern the rationales for the present-day conceptions of missionaries in their do-good role all over the world (Drake 1957; Engs 1972).

Religious difficulties also entered the picture. Religious training to save the souls of the former slaves was very much a part of the missionaries' work. Problems arose because disputes over religious differences were common throughout the South—between "strict immersionists" and Unitarians, between "new light" Presbyterians and Congregationalists, and ultimately between blacks and the white missionaries. By allowing missionaries of numerous faiths to participate in American Missionary Association projects, the AMA leadership had avoided jurisdictional disputes among the Protestant churches involved in missionary work. But the policy of non-affiliation encouraged religious disputes within the ranks of workers in AMA programs. In an effort to remedy such disputes and purge its own ranks of troublemakers, the AMA allied openly with its major patron, the Congregational church. Consequently, the association was drawn into heightened competition, public debates, chicanery, and political maneuvering in order to gain prominence over the array of denominations involved in missionary work (Drake 1957; Engs 1972; Williams 1976).

The most serious religious conflict occurred over the style of worship favored by the former slaves; typically, they turned their backs on the undemonstrative practices of the New England church, preferring a more animated revivalist demonstration of their faith. The missionaries were dismayed and confused by what they saw in the black congregations. In many places, they simply gave up their efforts to persuade blacks to join the missionary churches. This led to a system of separate religious worship even before the end of the Reconstruction, a pattern that persists today as testimony to the country's lingering failure to create an integrated society (Drake 1957; Engs 1972; Williams 1976).

In addition, the model of classroom instruction, curriculum organization, and school governance instituted by the missionaries often proved to be inappropriate. Initially pleased by the blacks' ability and enthusiasm for schooling, the missionaries soon met with frustration when they tried to develop their notions of a campus with school buildings and dormitories; and when they attempted to impose governing norms for social and classroom interaction. All these preconceived ideas conveyed to the freed men and women a message of continued inferiority, which they rejected. At Berea, Kentucky, among other places, this problem was particularly acute (Peck 1955; Williams 1976).

As a result of these obstacles, the missionaries associated with the AMA began to fight openly among themselves. Their complaints ranged from accusations of laziness and immoral behavior to protestations against the misuse of authority by their leaders and complaints about inadequate support from colleagues in the North. Also, in their negative evaluations of each other, they repeated the need for better organization and standardization of the policies and procedures they used in their work. Missionaries in the field attempted to put pressure on the central office of the AMA for better business management and greater coordination among the highly decentralized missions spread throughout the South. It is interesting that one of the major weapons the central office used to purge the missionary ranks of ineffective field workers was to accuse them of failure to file proper reports or of mismanagement of funds, even if the real shortcomings lay in areas unrelated to efficiency and proper administration. Complaints like these can be found throughout the archives of the American Missionary Association.*

Even if these difficulties characterized the work of the missionaries throughout the latter decades of the 1800s, other more serious events were to follow. What C. Vann Woodward (1951) has called the "unknown compromise of 1877," signalled by the withdrawal of federal troops from the South, ushered in a period of general repressiveness in southern society. One form that it took was the establishment of a system of laws for the disenfranchisement of blacks. Another was the policy to limit the growth of black education and channel it into vocational training, which became general throughout the South in the late 1890s (Bullock 1970). This policy reflected the judgment that blacks deserved and were most able to benefit from an industrial rather than a classical or liberal education. The rewards of an industrial education were now to represent the heights to which blacks could aspire in southern society. Perhaps the most clearcut manifestation of the "unknown compromise" was the *Plessy* v. *Ferguson* decision of the Supreme Court in 1896; it established by law the right to set up separate public institutions for blacks and whites. In the *Gung Lum* v. *Rice* decision of 1927, racial separation was effectively extended to include all educational institutions (*Gung Lum* v. *Rice* 1927; *Plessy* v. *Ferguson* 1896).

Industrial education thus symbolized a new consensus on the inferior status of blacks. It also served to emphasize the role of education as a mechanism of social control, at least for blacks in the South. Through vocational education, blacks and other inferior groups would be

*For example, for complaints about mismanagement by missionaries in Kentucky during the course of one year, see the American Missionary Association Archives (1865).

confined to low-level positions in the economic system. At the same time, they would be available as a disciplined labor force in the anticipated new period of industrial and agricultural expansion.

The compromise policy of industrial education "for life" and the series of court cases that established the policy of racial segregation in the South brought closure to many of the issues with which the missionaries had grappled. Their work continued, however, and some of their more progressive ideas about black equality persisted, among them the importance of a liberal arts education as a liberating force. But it is fair to say that the early contradictory era of black education, in which the missionaries played the leading role, was ended. The compromise of the early twentieth century can be best understood in the light of the successes and failures of the missionaries in beginning a process that they had hoped would lead to a generation of educated black citizens.

BLACK COLLEGE DEVELOPMENT, 1900-1954

Two years after *Plessy* v. *Ferguson*, in June 1898, a group of influential citizens from both the North and South convened the first of several sessions to plan the development of a separate system of education for blacks and whites in the southern states; like the ones to follow, it was held at Capon Springs, Virginia. The participants included people who had been involved in the missionary era of black education as well as newcomers to the field—industrialists, clergymen, humanitarians. Regardless of their real feelings, they agreed that industrial education should be the focus of a system of education for blacks.

The founders of Hampton Institute in Virginia, which was established in 1868, had already developed a successful system of industrial education; by the end of the century, relatively large numbers of black and Indian students had graduated from the institution. Hampton now emerged as the model for the higher education of blacks, and participants in the meetings accepted the apologist explanations for the southern racial situation that it proceeded from. As Hollis Frisell, the white president of Hampton Institute, explained,

> There are those who are bold enough to believe . . . that the world has made some progress . . . that there is no reason . . . why different races of different colors should not dwell together in peace. I believe that in the South today, in spite of difficulties that prevail, that condition of affairs is working out.

We are all agreed that slavery was a curse. . . . Yet, when Indian and Negro are placed side by side in a schoolroom and workshop at Hampton, it is very clear that slavery was a much better training school than was the reservation. (Capon Springs 1899, p. 28)

The notion of social equality and experimentation that had characterized the approach of the missionaries in past years was to be abandoned in favor of a system of separate colleges for the industrial training that had proved successful at Hampton and later would be successful at Tuskegee Institute.

The Capon Springs Conferences were only a small part of the massive planning that went on. Foundations like the General Education Board, the Peabody Fund, the Slater Foundation, and the Phelps-Stokes Fund banded together to establish black schools and colleges on the model of industrial education in what amounted to a coordinated movement.

Political and financial support for the movement that was taking hold of black education was provided by the Morrill Act of 1890, which extended to southern states the opportunity to found colleges based upon the industrial model of education for blacks as well as whites. It complemented the earlier Morrill Act of 1862. The impetus behind both acts was the need to increase the country's productivity in agriculture and farm goods and to educate an essentially rural population as the country extended westward.

Ironically, as a consequence of the Morrill Act of 1890, Hampton Institute suffered a setback despite its position as the model for black higher education. Before, Hampton had quietly received federal funds under the act of 1862 because there were no public colleges in Virginia during or immediately after the Civil War. However, Virginia State College for Negroes was founded in 1882, and funds that for a number of years had gone to Hampton were diverted to the new institution (John 1923, p. 89).

In the broader view inspiring the Morrill acts, industrial education was seen as including whites as well as blacks. The movement in the South, however, implemented a system of oppression that followed from the determination to create through law a new social order with whites on top and blacks on the bottom. The private black colleges, consequently, and those public black colleges that had been founded before 1890 were confronted with a new model of education and a tangible system of competing institutions that were backed by federal money and white political support (Bullock 1970, pp. 117–146; Curry 1894, p. 507).

The Continuing Debate

Disagreement grew, however. In the first place, there was no consensus on the true meaning of industrial training; at the college level, its meaning continually changed during the period from 1900 to 1954. In the purest sense, industrial education implied training in manual skills, instruction that would inculcate a familiarity with tools and machinery appropriate for agricultural and industrial production. This definition provided the foundation for the vocational instruction at public black colleges during this period. The catalogs for most public black colleges describe separate agricultural, mechanical, and industrial art divisions during the early stages of their history. In some cases general education courses are also described. One could infer from reading the catalogs that industrial education varied depending upon the purposes, resources, and particular history of a college or university, and on the extent to which leaders of the college actually intended to limit curriculum to courses in industrial education (Browning 1975, p. 54).

It is also clear that the industrial education movement met with mixed feelings in the black academic community and among some northern philanthropists, who subscribed to the missionaries' model of instruction and continued contributing funds to the private, missionary-founded, liberal arts colleges. In most cases, blacks saw the new industrial colleges as an opportunity to gain control over the education offered to black youth, even though it was not intended to equal the education provided to whites; this was, for example, the case in Arkansas and Virginia. In some places, however, the new colleges seemed to fulfill the thwarted ambitions of blacks for full equality (McPherson 1970).

In the long run, disagreements and the continued existence of two general styles of curriculum, often in the same institution, created an arena for a widespread debate over the definition, purpose, and needs of the traditionally black colleges in preparing students for careers and life in American society. By 1900, approximately thirty-five public and private black colleges had been founded. Before the Morrill Act of 1890, the primary goal of black colleges for the most part had been to produce educated leaders for the black people. They were established to train teachers, preachers, and other key community figures, equipped to remedy the despairs arising from slavery. From their beginning, these colleges included character building through the teachings of the Christian faith, lessons in personal cleanliness, and instruction in both liberal and industrial subjects. Because of the existence of such schools in various places in the South, there remained some room for a choice between liberal or industrial education or a combination of both into the 1900s. Among those involved in the debate that ensued were two men recognized for their historic contribution to the course of black higher education. One was Booker T. Washington, advocate of industrial education; the other, W. E. B. DuBois, ardent proponent of liberal education.

The two men did not differ in their definitions of the status of black colleges in the American higher education system; they both recognized the separate but unequal status of the black colleges. Nor did they differ in their desire to see the black colleges teach a type of cultural idealism; both saw them as black and American, with a contribution to make to the welfare of humanity. They did differ, however, in their approach to the task of educating black leaders of moral character. Washington advocated vocational training appropriate for the masses. DuBois advocated the development of an elite group, a "talented tenth" to teach and lead other blacks. The positions of these two men, expressed through their activities, their speeches, and their writings, formed the poles of a continuing debate over the curricula of the black colleges (Pugh 1974).

Booker T. Washington, a graduate of Hampton Institute, wrote with reference to his work at Tuskegee Institute:

> In our industrial teaching we keep three things in mind: first, that the student shall be so educated that he shall be enabled to meet conditions as they exist now, in the part of the South where he lives—in a word, to be able to do the thing which the world wants done; second, that every student who graduates from the school shall have enough skill, coupled with intelligence and moral character, to enable him to make a living for himself and others; third, to send every graduate out feeling and knowing that labour is dignified and beautiful—to make each one love labour instead of trying to escape it. (Washington 1974, p. 17)

Since most black people depended upon agriculture for their living, Washington believed that they should be educated in keeping with the requirements of an agricultural society. He instructed blacks "to cast down their buckets in agriculture, mechanics, in commerce, in domestic service, and in the professions." Washington also believed that the introduction of industrial training at the black colleges established a "united and sympathetic interest" between blacks and whites in the South and between the whites in the North and the whites in the South. This common involvement was for Washington a basis for mutual faith and cooperation between the black and white races across the country (Washington 1974, p. 144).

W. E. B. DuBois argued that a liberal arts education provided blacks with the resources for attaining intellectual, social, and political equality. He feared that industrial education would foreclose their chances for upward mobility in American society. DuBois described Washington's philosophy of industrial education as "tacit acceptance of the alleged inferiority of the Negro." For DuBois, industrial education required blacks to give up political power, abandon their insistence on civil rights, and withdraw demands for the education of black youth (DuBois 1961, p. 48).

As DuBois defined it, the problem with industrial education was rooted in the "actual situation of American Negroes"; it did not prepare students for changes in industrial techniques and economic organization. DuBois said that black students needed a college training that is "broader and more universal . . . so that they can apply the general principle of knowledge to the particular circumstances of their condition" (quoted in Walden 1972, p. 180).

In his autobiography, *The Souls of Black Folk,* DuBois examined the role of the Negro college and of the college-bred black in the future development of the South. He believed that the Negro college should be a place for the development of a black "talented tenth" and that "the American Negro problem is and must be the center of the Negro American University" (quoted in Walden 1972, p. 178). The talented tenth were described by DuBois as "exceptional men," the "best of the race." "Men we shall have," DuBois wrote, "only as we make manhood the object of the work of the schools—intelligence, broad sympathy, knowledge of the world that was and is, and of the relation of man to it" (quoted in Lester 1971, p. 385).

Despite the long-term effect of the arguments by DuBois, government officials, philanthropists, and school administrators endorsed and applauded Washington's industrial education programs. At the turn of the century, his philosophy was incorporated in schools across the South (Bullock 1970, pp. 147–166).

An example of the tone of the support that was given to Booker T. Washington can be seen in the writing of T. Thomas Fortune, a black journalist of the early 1900s. Fortune wrote:

A thorough acquaintance with the conditions which now rule in the Southern states, where a majority of Afro-Americans reside, convinces me that

what the masses most need at this stage of their development is skilled captains of industry. We have been making teachers and preachers and professional men for three decades . . . but a close observer sees plainly that they are in danger of starvation unless more attention shall be given to the industrial and commercial side of life (quoted in West 1972).

Grambling College in Louisiana provides an example of how one black public college was influenced by Washington's philosophy. Grambling is the outgrowth of Lincoln Parish, a member school in the North Louisiana Negro Farmers' Relief Association. In 1900, the association wrote Washington asking him to send someone from Tuskegee Institute to help them start an industrial school. On August 4, 1901, Charles P. Adams appeared as Washington's representative. The college then set up programs of instruction in methods of farming; preparing and preserving food; improving health and sanitary conditions; buying land and building houses; and living in harmony with other people. These programs carried through directly from the principles that Adams brought to Grambling. Students who wished to enter were accepted with the understanding that all who entered had to work as well as study (Wilson 1972).

Surveys of Black Higher Education

Yet debates over what the black colleges should become, it was discovered, were not grounded in objective facts about them. The growth of black colleges had been impressive but there was scant information about what they were actually doing. At the beginning of the twentieth century, few of the colleges were accredited, and they had received little recognition beyond the communities where they were located—certainly very little among whites. All concerned wondered about the content and the quality of the education that was being offered.

The foundations needed to know about the quality of education in black colleges in order to justify the continued expenditure of funds; essentially, it was a question of whether the schools they had founded were producing results. Many groups wanted an answer for different reasons, depending upon their views on the issue of industrial versus liberal arts education. Some, like the federal Office of Education, defined quality education as industrial training. They were concerned about the impact of the industrial education policy and the extent to which it was becoming the norm at black institutions. Others, like

W. E. B. DuBois and his supporters, sought evidence that liberal arts education was surviving despite the dominance of the industrial education approach.

Few knew the extent of the disparities. In some schools, the curriculum duplicated what was being offered in the fast-growing elementary and secondary public school system of the South;* in others, it resembled the courses of study at the New England colleges. Furthermore, the significance of the degrees that were awarded was uncertain. What did a college degree from Arkansas Agricultural, Mechanical, and Normal mean in terms of the recipient's qualifications? How did it compare with a high school diploma or a degree from other colleges in the North and South? In the first decades of the twentieth century, pressures for the standardization of curricula, organization, and certification were beginning to have the same impact on black colleges that they had exerted on white systems of education earlier. Adding to the pressures was the fact that black education was separate, industrial, and admittedly inferior in the South (Bullock 1970, pp, 117–146; Tyack 1975).

In order to deal with these and other issues, seven major surveys were undertaken during the period from 1900 to 1954; each set out to assess the quality and variety of education offered by the black colleges. In addition, some of them proposed specific reforms. One of the seven was sponsored by a large foundation, two by a research component of a private black university, and four by the Office of Education of the United States government. In the end, these surveys brought national recognition to the black schools .and eventually led to official acceptance by state and national accrediting associations. Many would argue, however, that accreditation came at the expense of the character, diversity, and vitality of the black colleges (Bowles and DeCosta 1971).

The DuBois Reports

W. E. B. DuBois undertook two surveys of black higher education, covering the period from approximately 1890 to 1910. The first investigated the social and economic situations of a sample of black-college graduates in the South (DuBois 1900); the second examined the content and quality of the education offered by the black colleges (DuBois 1910). Both studies found relatively small enrollments at the college

---

*See Chapter 6 of this volume for a detailed analysis of primary, secondary, and college-level enrollments in black institutions during the period under discussion.

level in the black schools. They were conducted under the auspices of the Fifth Annual Conference at Atlanta University for the Study of the Negro Problems.

The first survey by DuBois dealt with the years 1889 to 1899. It defined as a college any institution that had a course of study amounting to at least one year beyond the curriculum at the ordinary New England high school. Students who had completed such a post-high school curriculum or one more advanced and who had received a bachelor's degree were considered graduates of the college. On the basis of these criteria, thirty-four collegiate institutions for blacks were identified, divided into five groups: three antebellum schools; thirteen Freedmen's Bureau schools; nine church schools; five schools of Negro church bodies; and four state colleges.

In the second investigation, DuBois ranked a sample of black colleges into three groups according to the quality of their curricula and the number of college-level students enrolled. Schools classified as First Grade Colored Colleges had 14 or more units of entrance requirements and more than twenty students of college rank. Second Grade Colored Colleges had 12 to 14 units of entrance requirements and over twenty college-level students. In the last category were schools classified as Other Colored Colleges, with lower entrance requirements and fewer than twenty students.

In his summary of the two surveys, DuBois asked "What type of education is best and will continue to fit the needs of the American black?" Based on his findings with respect to students, college entrance requirements, and curricula, he urged changes at the colleges that he had investigated. Consistent with his talented-tenth position, DuBois's recommendations were for a liberal arts curriculum (DuBois 1910).

The Phelps-Stokes Report

In 1932 the Phelps-Stokes Fund, an influential foundation established in 1910 to support education, reported the results of a large-scale survey of black colleges that it had sponsored (Phelps-Stokes Fund 1932). The most significant feature of the report was a set of recommendations strongly endorsing industrial education and calling for cooperation between the races in the implementation of black higher education. The recommendations were specific and far-reaching. They proposed:

1. An immediate increase in the financial contributions by southern municipal, county, and state governments to Negro public schools

2. Strengthening industrial and agricultural education at black state institutions, particularly land-grant colleges
3. Improved teacher training and equal pay for black and white teachers with equal training
4. Revision of curricula away from liberal arts models emphasizing the classics, and increased attention to the natural and social sciences
5. Eliminating inefficient private black institutions that lacked facilities to merit foundation support
6. Close coordination among foundations and church boards involved in Negro education
7. Closer association between southern white educators and government officials in planning Negro education

These recommendations clearly carried mixed implications for black higher education. On the one hand, they urged increased financial support from local, state, and federal governments, the revision of college curricula, and a movement toward equal salaries for black and white teachers—efforts aimed at strengthening the black colleges. At the same time they called for the elimination of "inefficient private black institutions" and a closer association of southern white educators and government officials in planning the future of black education, which would decrease opportunities for schooling for blacks. Clearly the writers of the report intended control of black higher education to be placed more firmly in the hands of whites in the South.

Government Surveys

Between 1916 and 1942, four surveys sponsored by the federal government made major contributions to the accumulating fund of information about the black colleges as well as producing recommendations for strengthening them.

THE 1916 REPORT *Negro Education: A Study of the Private and Higher Schools for Colored People in the United States* (Jones 1920) reported on an extensive study of black educational institutions that was conducted in 1916. It included individual reports, giving the names of school presidents or principals, student enrollments, teacher profiles, and evaluations of future plans; it concluded with recommendations for each school studied.

Like the Phelps–Stokes report, this survey is best known for its recommendations, which called for changes in student living conditions and activities; changes in finances and accounting, administration, and governance; improving personnel quality and working conditions; and the modification of curricula. In general, in response to the need for trained teachers in the black public schools, the recommendations advocated teacher training. They also encouraged industrial and agricultural training for bettering the economic, intellectual, and spiritual condition of blacks. The report drew data from visits and interviews at the schools, from reports of state departments of education, and from the United States census.

Despite the diversity of goals, approaches, history, and environments of the institutions, the recommendations of this initial government survey were essentially the same for all of them. Teacher training was encouraged; the agricultural and mechanical departments were to become "more organized"; private colleges were advised not to permit foreign language instruction to hinder the development of other courses; and gardening was strongly suggested as a course of study in all of the schools. The introduction to the report stated that for a people 73 percent rural, the theory and practice of gardening should be of first importance because of its economic and educational value. The report's position on the mission of the black colleges was quite clear.

REPORT ON AGRICULTURAL AND MECHANICAL COLLEGES   The Bureau of Education's report, *Agricultural and Mechanical Colleges, 1917–1918* (John 1920), provided information on the scope of specialization in the main divisions of instruction in agricultural and mechanical colleges. It illustrated the variety of courses offered at the colleges and the distribution of students in them. All of the colleges enrolled students in agriculture and carpentry; all but two of them enrolled students in sewing courses; all but one in cooking courses; and all but three in laundering courses. Agriculture was defined to include instruction in agricultural education, agricultural engineering, agronomy, animal husbandry, dairy husbandry, rural economics, soil and fertilizers, and veterinary science.

PROGRESS REPORT, 1928   The Klein survey of 1928 (Klein 1969) was undertaken as a reexamination of the black colleges and universities that had been included in the government's 1916 report. The 1928 report also gave individual accounts of the colleges and universities and, like the 1916 report, recommended teacher, agricultural, and industrial training for all black colleges; the land-grant colleges were encouraged to strengthen their agricultural and mechanical departments. By 1935, one researcher was able to report 80 percent to 87 percent of the colleges had implemented the recommendations contained in the 1916 and 1928 surveys either fully or partially (Eells 1935).

NATIONAL SURVEY, 1942   In 1939, the Congress charged the United States Office of Education with the task of conducting a study of higher education for black people. It had been requested to do so by the Association of Colleges and Secondary Schools for Negroes. The 1942 report (U.S. Office of Education 1942) is the result of that study. Like the 1916 and 1928 reports, it compiled information on the students, staff, income and expenditures, and curricula of the black colleges and universities. For example, the objective of Volume 3 of the study, *Intensive Study of Selected Colleges for Negroes,* was to "assemble and interpret such social, economic, and educational data as will indicate needed programs of education and the nature of the educational services now rendered to meet those needs."

The findings revealed that all of the colleges in the study provided general education, advanced education, and professional and technical education, but, in comparison with accredited institutions, they ranked low in quality. In order to improve their quality, the black colleges were reported to be making significant changes that reflected faculty opinion and student needs. The study did not go on, unfortunately, to specify the content of the curricula or the opinions and needs expressed by the faculty and students.

The Consensus Changes

The DuBois, Phelps–Stokes, and government reports made two contributions to knowledge about black colleges and to their development during the period from 1900 to 1954. First, they provided individual colleges with recommendations which facilitated their acceptance into the mainstream of American higher education, albeit on a segregated basis. Second, the findings of the reports drew attention to the issue of quality in black colleges and began the process of approval by national and regional accrediting agencies. The Southern Association of Colleges and Schools, the accrediting agency for institutions in the southern region, was founded in 1895 but paid no attention to the black colleges until after the government's 1928 report (Bowles and DeCosta 1971).

As far as assessing the level and kind of college work offered before 1954, the surveys all gave a fairly equal emphasis to teacher and industrial education throughout the period from 1900 to 1954. In cases where these areas were weak, the surveys recommended strengthening the industrial and teacher education courses, a reflection of Booker T. Washington's philosophy of industrial education. Until the 1942 Office of Education survey, however, there was little evidence comparing the black colleges with a national sample.

The appearance of this new information by no means resolved the issue of industrial versus liberal arts education. It served only to support the opinions of the researcher, the sponsor of the research, or the constituency served by the sponsor. The surveys made clear, however, that during the first decades of the 1900s both types of education coexisted. This was so despite the force of law and public policy, which prescribed industrial education for blacks, placed control of black colleges in the hands of southern whites, and reflected a basic belief in black inferiority; as a consequence, the black colleges suffered from discriminatory allocations of funds by federal and state government and by foundations and from other official discrimination during this period. Black educators may have disagreed over the best response to make to these circumstances, but in most cases they maintained liberal arts programs at the colleges they controlled, suggesting an unwillingness to accept black inferiority as a standard for black higher education (Schuck 1972).

The existence of liberal arts programs at even industrial colleges was one indication that black leaders did not agree with the public policy on black education and the education of blacks. In addition, the later survey showed that patterns of differentiation existed within the system of black institutions. Some of the private liberal arts schools were judged superior to most of the state schools, not only by objective criteria but, more importantly, in the eyes of the black community. A ranking order had arisen, with colleges like Fisk, Morehouse, and Spelman having more prestige than the newcomers with primarily industrial curricula.

By 1942 when the Office of Education undertook the last important survey of the period, it was obvious that liberal arts education and industrial education had both become acceptable to whites in the South. Although the states and the federal government continued to discriminate in funding practices, beliefs had changed about the impact of higher education on racial equality; the fears of whites had subsided. Even though many still wished to maintain a system of containment for black aspirations, there was now emerging a consensus that recognized and accepted a college-educated class of blacks in the South.

Moreover, in the 1930s and early 1940s education was less closely related in people's minds to social and economic success than it had been earlier. The reasons lay in the Depression and in the international events leading up to World War II. The progressive school of education, for example, began to call for education for the reconstruction of social values to combat the threat of totalitarianism emerging in Europe.

This period also includes the antecedents of a renewed struggle over the issue of racial equality. The new ideas of education for social reconstruction eventually expanded. It was obvious by 1954 that the events of prior decades and altered views of schooling would introduce profound changes in the American educational system of public schools and collges, particularly with respect to racial equality.

THE *BROWN* DECISION AND ITS AFTERMATH, 1954-1975

In 1954 the Supreme Court's decision in *Brown* v. *Board of Education* declared that racial segregation in public schools deprives black students of equal protection of the law under the Fourteenth Amendment of the Constitution. Reversing the *Plessy* v. *Ferguson* decision of 1896, it stated that "in the field of public education the doctrine of separate but equal has no place" (*Brown* v. *Board of Education* 1954).

In general, blacks accepted the *Brown* decision, speculated on its implications for areas other than education, and interpreted it as the beginning of further acceptance of blacks and their institutions (Cohen 1974; West 1972). Some educators, however, were cautious. Even before the *Brown* decision, in April 1952, Martin D. Jenkins, the president of Morgan State College, had pointed out that for most of the black colleges integration would mean participation in state systems reorganized to offer services to the majority (Jenkins 1952). The danger was, he warned, that services designed specifically for black students would disappear and existing patterns of discrimination could be perpetuated under the guise of equality. The National Conference on the Courts and Racial Integration in Education at which these fears were expressed suggested that state education boards and white universities should make adjustments that would accommodate black teachers, administrators, and students and that the black community should organize to apply political pressure to make sure, on the one hand, that the new law was enforced and, on the other, that enforcement did not result in a similar system of discrimination. The confer-

ence also encouraged blacks to enlist the support of liberal white sup-
porters and of organizations like the National Association for the
Advancement of Colored People (NAACP) and the Urban League
(Jenkins 1952; Johnson 1954).

Despite the doubts of many black educators and officials and although the implications of the new decision were unclear, there were
immediate benefits for the black colleges as a result of it. Funding for
physical improvements became available and many black colleges initiated building programs despite the strong possibility that the new
riches may have been intended, at least in the case of state funding, to
prevent the speedy implementation of the new desegregation order.
College enrollments also grew as a result of the increased financial aid
for students (National Center for Education Statistics 1972; Southern
Education Foundation 1972).

In order to correct past injustices, officers at a policy-making level in
government and higher education once again needed more information
about the black colleges: one reason was that their needs had been long
ignored. The federal government and private philanthropic organizations commissioned fact-finding reports, and studies were undertaken
by individual academicians. For the most part, these reports offered
general information about physical plants, curricula, students and
faculty, and financial characteristics. Typically, they also included
recommendations for strengthening the colleges, and they documented
patterns of discrimination, particularly in funding black colleges. These
critiques of the black colleges were instrumental once again in
dramatizing the problems that they confronted and outlined the
governmental support needed. Much of the financial assistance of the
late 1960s and early 1970s was based on the findings of these studies
(Jaffe 1968; LeMelle and LeMelle 1969; Thompson 1973).

While these actions proceeded on the basis of the somewhat
ambiguous desegregation policy outlined in the *Brown* decision, civil
rights groups across the country pressed for a clearer definition of their
victory. Demonstrations spread as attempts to integrate public facilities
were accelerated. Students in the black colleges were an important
force in the civil rights activity of the early 1960s (Meier and Rudwick
1968, pp. 221–252).

In February 1960, four black-college students from North Carolina
Agricultural and Technical State University sat down at a segregated
lunch counter in Greensboro, North Carolina, and refused to leave
until they were served. This sit-in was the first highly publicized direct

action in which college students participated. Direct-action protests exploded across the South after the Greensboro sit-in. During 1961 alone, over 50,000 people, including many black-college students, demonstrated against segregation in a hundred cities, an action that resulted in over 3,600 arrests (Thomas 1973; Zinn 1965).

As a consequence of the self-esteem they had gained from direct-action protest, black students began to change their hair styles, their names and their dress. Black student organizations were formed on campuses throughout the country, talk of avowedly black universities began, and black studies programs entered college curricula. By the late 1960s, black students all over the nation were making it clear that they wanted decision-making participation and that desegregation had to mean more than assimilation.

After experiencing humiliation and violence in their attempts to desegregate public facilities, black-college students pressed for continuing the policy of separating black colleges from white systems of higher education. This new thrust reversed the goal of integration that black colleges had cautiously pursued before the middle 1960s. The new view, increasingly advocated by black leaders, complicated the work of federal officials, administrators at black colleges, and young civil rights groups who marched under the banner of integration (Haskins 1973; McWharter 1968; Wright 1970).

Public policy officials responded in two ways to the civil rights protests and the black power demands for equality. One response was a renewed attempt to achieve a more precise and comprehensive definition of the policy of desegregation through judicial and legislative channels. Another was to extend funding programs aimed at correcting past practices of discrimination against the black colleges.

Changing Policies and Goals

Many of the curricular, administrative, and faculty development programs of the late 1960s, supported mainly through Title III of the Higher Education Amendments of 1968, were an outgrowth of the federal government's response to the separatist and black power challenges of the black students. Title III provided grants to "developing institutions" for cooperative programs with prestigious colleges and universities that had a reputation for academic excellence. Other programs that it funded included assistance to low-income students, curriculum reform, faculty retraining, and management and planning services (Howard 1967; Miller, Gurin, and Clark 1970).

Attempts to achieve a better definition of the integration policy through the courts and Congress resulted in the passage of several civil rights laws—the first was the Civil Rights Act of 1964—and a series of court desegregation orders in public school systems. The Civil Rights Act of 1964 removed the responsibility for implementing school desegregation from the courts and passed it on to the Commissioner of Education of the Department of Health, Education and Welfare (HEW). Title VI of this act prohibited institutions that receive federal funds from discriminating on the basis of race in hiring, promotion, and admissions policies.

In 1969, in compliance with the 1964 act, HEW's Office of Civil Rights required ten states to submit plans for achieving racial equality in public colleges and universities. The ten states were Alabama, Arkansas, Florida, Georgia, Louisiana, Mississippi, North Carolina, Oklahoma, Pennsylvania, and Virginia. Federal officers had completed investigations that revealed the existence in these states of separate dual systems of public higher education (Winkler 1974). There were reasons for the delay in dealing with segregation in higher education after the *Brown* decision. Public elementary and secondary education were viewed as much knottier problems to resolve, requiring the immediate attention of law enforcement officials in Washington. Also, the provisions of law, as they had been refined since 1954, applied more directly to public school education and provided more of an opportunity for initial success in this area. It became clear by 1969, however, that the Nixon Administration's integration efforts in higher education amounted to even less appeasement, and further steps were needed in the judgment of some leaders (Bishop 1971; Southern Education Foundation 1974).

Displeased with the federal government's progress in enforcing the provisions of desegregation orders, in 1970 the Legal Defense Fund of the NAACP and the Washington law firm of Rauh and Silard filed a class-action suit in a federal district court suing HEW for failure, in the case of public higher education, to obtain state plans for desegregation and at the same time failing to withhold federal aid to ten designated states. The lawyers for the plaintiffs argued that HEW's failure to carry out the 1964 civil rights ruling ensured racism and a dual system of public higher education that was both costly and wasteful. In the spring of 1973, the NAACP Legal Defense Fund finally won its case over an appeal by defendants of the earlier district court decision in 1972. The court ordered HEW to obtain desegregation plans from the ten states and to notify the states of HEW's acceptance or rejection of the plans by April 30, 1974. The deadline was later extended to June 30 (*Adams* v. *Richardson* 1973).

By June 1974, nine of the ten states had submitted plans for desegregating their public colleges and universities. Louisiana refused to comply, and Mississippi's plan was rejected. HEW accepted the other eight plans, describing them as projecting "notable progress" in the areas of recruitment and retention of students from minority groups, of equal-resource allocations to all state colleges and universities (with additional funds to make up for past injustices), and of hiring faculty members from minority groups (Winkler 1974).

The eight plans approved were not uniform; different states adopted different strategies. Overall, however, HEW required that the plans be "comprehensive and statewide, that they enhance through equalization rather than threaten the existing black colleges, and that they provide substantial desegregation of all institutions." These criteria, as well as individual specifications for the ten states, were aimed at developing an "adequate remedy for segregation and discrimination in public higher education" and were concerned with maximizing the capacity of black colleges to provide an education of good quality and with increasing the black presence throughout higher education. These concerns had been recommended to HEW by the attorneys and staff of the Legal Defense Fund of the NAACP and the firm of Rauh and Silard. In accepting the plans HEW agreed also to monitor the implementation process of dismantling the dual systems (NAACP 1973).

In the 1973 appeal of *Adams* v. *Richardson*, the National Association for Equal Opportunity in Higher Education, an organization of 110 presidents of public and private black colleges and universities, had asked for a negative finding by the court. The association argued that access to public higher education for black students and the survival of the black colleges would be threatened by a unitary system. They further pointed out that total desegregation would compromise the identity of the black colleges and displace black administrators and faculty. Their belief was that, until equal opportunity for blacks is achieved in all aspects of education and employment, the black colleges must remain viable alternative institutions for entrance into a society that discriminates against blacks (*Adams* v. *Richardson* 1973; Egerton 1974; Southern Education Foundation 1974).

Thus the period from 1954 to 1975 was beset with many contradictions when it came to adopting policies aimed at achieving racial equality or integration. Notions of black equality changed from goals of assimilation to demands for black power and black control. One result of confusion over the policy of integration has been a new-found freedom and independence for black colleges. This freedom is also a consequence of changes in ideas about the relationship of education to society. Underlying the assimilationist ideal reflected by *Brown* was the notion that education is a channel for passage into mainstream American society: black children could learn to compete successfully in the American social and economic systems, despite the history of discrimination against their parents. On the other hand, black separatist ideals carried with them the idea that education was for social action—to change the society, not to gain access to and support its existing institutions.

The compensatory policies, like Title III, seemed to reflect a similar belief in education for social reconstruction, sometimes rejecting, at other times acquiescing in, the more radical ideal of black control and separatism. In the *Adams* case we seem once again to find a vision of education as a major force for assimilation into the mainstream. While the guidelines of the new policy for dismantling dual systems of higher education now take into account the need for black participation at all levels of the system, integrated educational business as usual seems to be the goal of this new assault on the problem.

ASSESSING THE HISTORY OF BLACK COLLEGES

The development of black colleges in a sense turns on the issue of racial equality and the role of education in achieving or preventing attainment of it. Historically, the direction taken by the colleges was determined in large part by agreements in these two policy areas.

During the missionary era of the late 1860s, ambivalence on the issue of racial equality from the outset compromised attempts to educate the former slaves. The missionaries themselves suffered from indecision; their problems were exacerbated by the actions of the military and northern whites; their work became overwhelming as organized problems, religious disputes, and internal dissension mounted. Education in the liberal arts was, for the missionaries, a means of remaking blacks into the image of the ideal American citizen, so it was not offered without some penalties for them. What distinguishes the missionaries' work from other social reforms of the period and from that which followed was a belief, at least stated, that blacks were equal to whites but for the debilitating effects of slavery.

The period from 1900 to 1954 witnessed a retreat from stated beliefs in black equality as a basis for educational policy. The century began with a consensus on the limits of blacks' aspirations. In education, industrial training was the means agreed upon for the achievement of a tightly constrained end. As with any policy consensus, however, there was room for disagreement. Although the black colleges were pressed to adopt industrial education and, in doing so, to acquiesce in second-class citizenship, debates among leaders of the black educated class, assessments of the industrial education policy, confidence in the strength of the new southern order, and a variety of social and economic forces—including the impact of World War II—led to acceptance of more than one model of education at the black colleges. From the viewpoint of history, the end of the debate over liberal arts and industrial education and steps toward acceptance of the black colleges into the mainstream during the first decades of the 1900s were hints that the basic issue of racial equality might indeed reemerge and higher education might play a role in achieving it.

The period from 1954 to the middle of the 1970s was a particularly confusing twenty years because notions of equality and ideas about the impact of education changed so quickly. The black colleges benefited, especially financially, from a new confidence among both blacks and whites in the equality of black Americans. Like most social institutions, however, black colleges during the period suffered from internal and external conflicts. The vagaries of the desegregation policy led to direct action against segregation policies that no longer were supported by the force of law, bringing black colleges into direct confrontations with whites in the South. Participants in the direct-action campaigns, particularly black college students, grew cynical about the responsiveness of existing social and economic systems and began to demand changes in them. Federal policies, vaguely proposed and variously enforced, eventually called for the achievement of conflicting goals for black colleges—on the one hand, survival as separate institutions through programs for strengthening the black colleges, on the other, assimilation through designs for integrating the races.

While the policy for racial equality seems to have evolved from desegregation to separatism and back again and as the political strength of various groups has grown and diminished, ideas about the role of education have vacillated back and forth between noninvolvement to social reconstruction. In its most extreme forms at the black-college campuses, noninvolvement in the struggle for civil rights has been interpreted to mean traditional liberal arts education amplified to the level offered at the best white colleges. At the other extreme, social reconstructionists have called for programs based upon the black experience and presented from the perspective of the black scholar that ideologically and practically are concerned with solving the basic problem of racial discrimination in all its forms in American life.

Although voices representing the most extreme poles of the dilemma over racial equality have died down and even though few students are demanding more black studies courses, the problem remains. Black colleges live today with these ambivalences. Some wonder if, having existed so long under similar conditions of ambivalence about the notion of equality and its proper educational antecedents, the black colleges will at this point disappear. Implied in the question, posed in this manner, is our judgment that they should not.

In the meanwhile, black colleges continue to survive, and most college graduates who are black still receive their degrees from the schools that are classified as "historically black." These are the four-year colleges and universities founded specifically for the higher education of blacks before 1954, the year of the *Brown* decision. At the present time, 105 historically black colleges are in existence, performing the function for which they were established. In addition there are approximately twenty-nine two-year and four-year colleges with student bodies that are predominantly black, although the schools were not necessarily founded to serve a black population.*

The situation presents an anomaly. The proportion of college-age blacks attending institutions of higher education has increased. According to the Census Bureau, 12 percent of the young black adults eighteen to twenty-four years of age were enrolled in college in 1975, most in schools that are not classified as predominantly black (U.S. Bureau of the Census 1976, p. 121). In fact, the proportion enrolled in predominantly black colleges went down from 58 percent in 1970 to 40 percent in 1973. Yet the majority of black college graduates in the 1970s have earned their degrees from the historically black colleges, as the study reported in Chapter 7 of this volume indicates.

---

*The source of this information on the current number of historically black and predominantly black colleges is unpublished data furnished by the Research Department, Institute for Services to Education, Washington, D.C.

One obvious reason for the discrepancy is the fact that nearly one-third of black college students are enrolled in two-year colleges (U.S. Bureau of the Census 1976, p. 142). Linked to that is the limited access of blacks to predominantly white four-year colleges and universities, a situation that continues despite the changes which have taken place. However, there is a third—and possibly critical—factor that must be considered; that is, the distinctive character of the black colleges, themselves.

Part II   Administration, Financing, and Governance

Chester M. Hedgepeth, Jr.,
Ronald R. Edmonds,
Ann Craig

The ability of the black colleges to endure hardship during their turbulent history reflects in large measure the aggressive and pragmatic leadership of their presidents. The single most perplexing problem confronting black-college presidents has been the attempt to provide a sound education with only marginal resources available. Hence the leaders of these institutions have been forced to be ingenious in the development of their faculties and in finding aid for students of limited means, according to Charles Willie and Marlene MacLeish.

Today, black colleges are multimillion dollar enterprises and constitute a major source of employment in their communities. It is a credit to the leadership of these colleges that financial stability, community service, and quality education are top priorities on the agenda of presidents and trustees. "Among the educational priorities of black-college presidents," write Willie and MacLeish, "are the initiation of cooperative education programs, the inclusion of career-oriented courses, the development of preprofessional programs in medicine and law, and the creation of endowed professorships."

Of prime importance in stabilizing black institutions are the management and planning skills demonstrated by their major administrative officer. Prezell Robinson notes in his discussion, "The welfare and well-being of the college require that its resources be managed in such a way that maximum effectiveness is achieved." The maintenance of tight budgetary controls to maximize scant resources has been misunderstood by some investigators of black higher education. "Black-college presidents have remained visibly in control," say Willie and MacLeish, "but their control has been for the sake of preserving their institutions." The mission of the black colleges is complex, and uncommon demands are made on the administration to keep the institutions afloat financially. This has resulted in a style of governance that has typically combined hard-headed financial management and transcendental spiritualism.

Deriving support largely from government and a handful of philanthropic foundations, black colleges specializing in manual training attracted more financial support in the second half of the nineteenth century than schools that emphasized the liberal arts. Sherman Jones and George Weathersby also report that in the first two decades of the twentieth century private black colleges, unlike public institutions, depended heavily upon gifts and contributions from churches and private citizens. Later, however, northern white philanthropists, like the Rockefellers and the Rosenwalds, recognizing the role that black colleges could play in uplifting the black race, provided financial support to carry them through the 1920s and 1930s. Most recently independent black colleges, including those emphasizing the liberal arts, have received increased federal and state support for curriculum and faculty development. Student financial aid, providing indispensable support for enrollment at black colleges, is also derived from programs funded by the federal government; in addition, the colleges themselves set aside a portion of their income for student aid.

Black colleges should not forget their basic role when they are in financial difficulties; this note of caution is sounded by Charles Merrill, trustee of a black college. He says, "I feel that obtaining money, no matter how crucial it is, has to be a number two priority for both the board and the president. The number one priority is still the intellectual and moral quality of the college." Trustee Merrill criticizes tight presidential control over affairs at black institutions, but he also shares with us his experience of mob rule and shows that it is no substitute for a rational, flexible, and bureaucratic organization. Most black colleges appear to follow the bureaucratic model, with the president firmly in charge.

Herman Branson states in effect that the proof of the pudding is in the eating. There is no arguing with the hard fact that black colleges in the North as well as the South continue to graduate a higher proportion of their black students than do other schools. Branson points to the black college-educated leadership in major metropolitan communities like Philadelphia as evidence of the effectiveness of the black colleges.

During the present financial crisis experienced by most American private colleges, the black institutions of higher education, like others, must look increasingly to the federal and state governments for the financing of current and capital operations. In the final analysis, to understand the financial stresses that underlie the functioning of the black colleges, one has to perceive fully the almost Sisyphean task undertaken by their administrators and trustees. The chapters of this section show that they no longer intend to suffer silently. The leaders of the black colleges have assumed a vocally aggressive stance that projects the positive image of these institutions that is rightfully theirs. "Despite the obstacles that confront the predominantly black colleges today," says Robinson, "they will continue as strong and viable institutions, providing this nation with a source of leadership."

Chapter 6

Financing the Black College

Sherman J. Jones and
George B. Weathersby

Throughout their history, the historically black colleges have had to satisfy the often conflicting objectives of the philanthropists who financed them, the students who attended them, and a society that offered only limited opportunities to their graduates. Yet many of these institutions have survived for over a century. They have long been financed at a minimal, barely adequate level of support. At the present time, the financial crisis affecting higher education in general is probably more acute at the black colleges because most of them started with less.

This chapter reviews how the historically black colleges—both independent and state-assisted—have obtained their funds and how they have used them. The topics discussed are (1) financing the historically black colleges when they were founded and shortly thereafter; (2) financing them in the early twentieth century; and (3) recent trends in financing.

FINANCING THE BLACK COLLEGE
IN THE NINETEENTH CENTURY

College education was not an important factor in the affairs of the nation during the 1800s. For example, the 19 American colleges and universities that awarded bachelor's degrees during the seventeenth and eighteenth centuries had only 9,144 graduates ьy 1800. As late as

100

1870, there were only 2,500 seniors in 153 American colleges and universities that awarded the bachelor's degree (U.S. Dept. of Interior, 1872). Similarly few blacks had obtained college degrees before 1861. Only 28 acknowledged Negroes had graduated from American colleges before 1861, the first two from Bowdoin and Amherst in 1826 (Bowles and DeCosta 1971, p. 12).

Black colleges in the literal sense of that term did not really exist until the 1920s. True, in the middle of the 1800s there had been many institutions that called themselves colleges. In fact, however, most of these institutions devoted only a limited portion of their resources to educating young people at the college level; their activities were concentrated on their elementary and secondary departments. Before the turn of the century, a few students had always been enrolled at the better private institutions dedicated to the education of blacks, but they accounted for only 10 percent of the total enrollment. With one or two exceptions, public black colleges did not get into the business of educating college students until after 1916 (Bowles and DeCosta 1971, p. 33).

During the nineteenth centruy, the recurring question in black education was whether colleges were needed; if the answer to the question was yes, then how and in what manner could they be adequately financed?

Enrollment of Blacks in Higher Education

Many colleges and universities in the United States, white as well as black, had little choice before 1900 but to support subcollegiate instruction to ensure both current and subsequent enrollments in their college departments. For example, as late as 1895 all of the white colleges in Alabama except the university reported students at the elementary and high school levels. Even in Massachusetts, Boston College and Tufts reported precollege enrollments in 1895.

As we have noted, many of the educational institutions founded for blacks after the Civil War had included the words *college* or *university* in their titles, although this represented their long-term aspirations rather than the current realities. The fact of the matter is that as late as 1916 a national survey found that of approximately 92,600 students in Negro schools offering college-level work only a little over 2,600 (or less than 3 percent of the enrollment) were pursuing the college curriculum (Holmes 1934). As Table 6–1 shows, the college-level enrollment in

Table 6-1
Enrollments in Negro Colleges, 1921-22 to 1931-32

YEAR	INSTITUTIONS	ENROLLMENTS COLLEGE	HIGH SCHOOL	ELEMENTARY	TOTAL
1921-22	70	5,231	15,361	13,692	34,284
1923-24	82	7,641	18,706	11,938	38,285
1926-27	99	13,197	18,387	10,325	41,909
1931-32	106	22,609	8,859	4,321	35,789

SOURCE: Holmes (1934, p. 191).

Negro colleges did not exceed their elementary and secondary enrollments until around 1930.

Only three black institutions in 1900 reported more than 100 students of college level in their programs—Lincoln in Pennsylvania, Wilberforce in Ohio, and Biddle University in Charlotte, North Carolina (Johnson 1938, p. 281). In that year only 3 percent of the nation's total undergraduate college and university enrollment was black—about 700 to 800 students (Pifer 1972). Even in 1917, of the 900 students at Hampton Institute, 44 percent were in the elementary grades and 56 percent in the secondary; by 1922 there were still only 21 college students at the school.

Furthermore, the limited opportunities for a higher education available to blacks were almost wholly confined to the black private colleges until well into the twentieth century. It has been estimated that between 1863 and 1890, about 200 blacks in all had graduated from northern white colleges, 75 of them from Oberlin. In 1899, W. E. B. DuBois (1903a) prepared a survey of Negro college graduates, the results of which are presented in Table 6-2. By 1899, according to DuBois, 2,329 black people had received college degrees, 83 percent from Negro colleges and 17 percent from white schools.

As to publicly supported black schools, none of the black land-grant institutions that resulted from the Morrill Act of 1890 offered college work until 1916. Of the seventeen publicly supported black schools founded before 1890, only two were listed as colleges in 1890. One of these had a college enrollment of 4 students, and the other had 86 in

Table 6–2
Negro College Graduates up to 1899

YEAR	NEGRO COLLEGE	WHITE COLLEGE	TOTAL
Before 1876	137	75	212
1875–80	143	22	165
1880–85	250	31	281
1885–90	413	43	456
1890–95	465	66	531
1895–99	475	88	563
Unknown	57	64	124
Total			2,329

SOURCE: DuBois (1903a).

1890, according to a survey published in 1894 by the United States Department of the Interior. In the years before the 1930s, virtually all of the graduates at the collegiate level of the Negro colleges had been enrolled at the private black institutions. Of the 1,683 college-level students in black institutions in 1916, for example, 1,467 or 91 percent were in the private institutions.

It is not until 1932 that a change becomes apparent. By that year, the black land-grant institutions were enrolling 7,294 college-level students (Holmes 1934, p. 152), and 58 percent of the black students in black institutions were at the private colleges as against the 91 percent reported in 1916.

Evolution of the Black College

The South lagged behind the rest of the nation in developing a public school system. Except for North Carolina and Kentucky, the southern states had nothing that even remotely approached a system of public schools before 1860 (DaBrey 1936, p. 114). The greatest success of the Freedmen's Bureau lay in planting the free school among blacks and the idea of free elementary schools among all groups in the South. It was not until the early 1900s, however, that the South actually began to develop a public school system.

Northern missionary groups had begun to establish Sunday and elementary schools through the South for the newly freed black people during the Civil War. As the war progressed, they received increasing support for their efforts from northern philanthropists. During the Reconstruction period, the incipient free-school movement for blacks expanded geographically and continued to grow in enrollment. The end of the Reconstruction period in 1877, however, checked its expansion, and subsequently both governmental and private contributors to its support became quite limited. Somehow, though, the system of education survived in a reduced status, supported by a trickle of private funds and by black religious denominations; white teachers from the North who left were replaced by blacks.

In 1890 the funds from the Morrill Act of that year gave seventeen Negro public institutions a new lease on life and made public support of Negro education possible once again. As noted earlier, these were essentially boarding schools for elementary or secondary students (or both) until about 1916 when they began to offer college instruction.

After 1900 there was an increase in public support for Negro schools from state legislatures and from various foundations broadly concerned with improving education in the South. By the time of the 1916 survey of Negro education by the United States Office of Education (USOE), 1,175,500 Negro students were attending the public schools of the South, and there were sixty-four Negro high schools (Jones, 1920)*

Generally negative about the programs at the Negro colleges, the USOE report did note that "the development of the Negro race in the United States depends more directly on elementary school teachers than on any other group" and that "so far as teachers are trained they come largely from the private institutions." This report went on to forecast the need for at least 600 new black teachers each year. Clearly there was a role for the private black colleges in teacher training.

As a direct result of the influence of this USOE survey and with a renewed sense of their particular mission, the black colleges entered a period in which they found it somewhat easier to obtain financing for their educational programs. It was during this period that the academic legitimacy of the black colleges was firmly fixed. They would emerge from it as colleges.

*See Chapter 5 for a discussion of the USOE's survey of Negro education, in connection with the development of black colleges from 1900 to 1954.

The Impact of Industrial Education

The intense debate among black educators over the merits of an industrial versus a liberal arts education for the victims of slavery and their descendants has been discussed in Chapter 5. One of the strongest assets of the industrial education movement was its appeal for southern whites, who feared the prospect of racial equality, and for northern capitalists, who desired an end to the disorders of the Reconstruction period and the creation of a stable and trained labor force. Industrial education, with its paternalistic thrust and its emphasis on the Yankee virtues of industriousness and thrift, was the ultimate compromise between the South and the North with respect to black education and the education of blacks. During the latter part of the nineteenth century generous philanthropic support was available for schools emphasizing manual labor and industrial education for blacks.

The model for black industrial education was Hampton Institute, founded in 1869 as an alternative to the classical education of other black college programs. Hampton's first principal was Samuel Chapman Armstrong, a white retired army general from New England, who had fought in the Civil War and had been involved in the activities of the Freedmen's Bureau; he had attended Williams College in Massachusetts. Armstrong established Hampton Institute with the help of the American Missionary Association and various individuals in New York and New England. The program he instituted emphasized moral uplift, economic self-help, and character development. It featured a highly regimented daily life and the extensive use of student labor.

Armstrong's view of the appropriate education for the newly freed blacks emerges with stark clarity in a paper presented to the National Education Association in 1872. Armstrong's position is summarized by the historian Louis Harlan, thus:

> He noted that surely black people were "in the early stages of civilization," lower on the evolutionary scale, not so much racially inferior as backward. They were children who must crawl before they could walk, must be trained before they could be educated. Their moral training was much more important than their intellectual instruction, for not until the backward people, as individuals and as races, put away childish things, stilled their dark laughter, and learned self-discipline through external discipline would they be ready for the intellectual and spiritual peak of the pyramid. Armstrong would not discourage a bright young dark man from higher education and higher aspirations, but he believed that the whole black race should abstain

from politics and civil rights agitation until industrial education had done its work. And it was the work of a lifetime. (Harlan 1972, p. 61)

Hampton's success in obtaining philanthropic funds led many other black institutions to establish similar programs. Booker T. Washington, a graduate of Hampton Institute, built on the Hampton model to establish Tuskegee and became the kingpin of this widely admired and emulated approach to Negro education.

Industrial education was a movement that had emerged during the Jacksonian era with the purpose of enabling poor youths of all races to learn economically useful trades or mechanical skills. During the late nineteenth century many white industrial schools, responding to the changing requirements of an increasingly technological economy, shifted their emphasis to engineering. The Negro industrial schools, however, took a more humble, less ambitious line of development. They continued to concentrate on agriculture and the simple trades; to dignify labor through doing the common things of life uncommonly well remained their credo (Harlan 1972, p. 64). One of the ironies of history, observes August Meier, is that neither Hampton nor Tuskegee took the first steps toward offering blacks the advanced technical training necessary for effective competition with whites in an industrial age (Meier 1966, p. 93). It was Howard University in Washington, D.C., noted as a high-quality liberal arts institution, that introduced engineering at a Negro school on a college level in 1915.

Organizations Supporting Education for Blacks

Payments from students and their parents were a negligible factor in financing the black schools of the postbellum period. One significant source of support were the benevolent societies established during and shortly after the Civil War to uplift the emancipated blacks; sixty-five were founded between 1846 and 1867 (Leavell 1930, p. 47). These groups not only provided financial support to the schools but teaching and administrative staffs as well in many cases.

The Freedmen's Bureau was set up by the federal government in 1865 to oversee the movement of the emancipated slaves into freedom. Although it failed to deliver forty acres to each of them as it was initially charged to do, the Bureau did help the former slaves in many ways; its most lasting contribution was in the area of education. According to Leavell, from 1866 to 1870 the Bureau gave just over $3.5 million to black schools (Table 6–3). In 1868, 1869, and 1870, it gave over

Table 6-3
Number of Teachers and Pupils and Expenditures in Black Schools
That Received Aid from the Freedmen's Bureau and from Benevolent
Societies, 1866-1870

| | | | MONEY EXPENDED BY | |
YEAR	TEACHERS	PUPILS	FREEDMEN'S BUREAU	BENEVOLENT SOCIETIES
1866	1,045	90,778	$ 123,650	$ 82,200
1867	2,087	111,442	531,345	65,087
1868	2,295	104,327	965,897	700,000
1869	2,455	114,522	924,182	365,000
1870	3,300	149,581	967,853	360,000
		Totals	$3,512,375	$1,572,287

SOURCE: Leavell (1930, p. 50). Used by permission of George Peabody College for Teachers.

$900,000 each year, a sum which supported more than 100,000 students. This financial assistance from the federal government immensely aided the efforts of the benevolent societies.

The two most important foundations supporting black schools in the 19th century were the George Peabody Education Fund, established in 1867, and the John F. Slater Fund founded in 1882. The Peabody Fund gave its major attention to building permanent systems of public education in the South for both blacks and whites, to scholarships for students preparing to teach, and to normal schools. Upon terminating its activities in 1914, it turned over $350,000 to the John F. Slater Fund, to be used for the industrial and scientific education of blacks in county training schools (Leavell 1930).

The Slater Fund had been established specifically to benefit black education. During its first thirty years the fund's resources were used extensively to assist the private denominational colleges in the training of teachers and to assist public schools in industrial and vocational training. In 1937 it merged with the Negro Rural School Fund to form the Southern Education Fund, which is still in existence.

Table 6–4
Sources of Income for Black Colleges, 1896

SOURCE	AMOUNT	PERCENTAGE OF TOTAL EXPENDITURES
Private	$ 610,946	54.7
State and municipal	289,845	25.9
Tuition and fees	124,481	11.1
Endowment	92,297	8.2
Totals	$1,117,569	99.9

SOURCE: Data from U.S. Dept. of Interior (1896).

Sources of Income for the Black Colleges

In 1896 (U.S. Dept. of Interior 1896) the United States Commissioner of Education issued a report that identified 178 schools for Negroes, enrolling some 40,127 students; 3.6 percent were receiving college-level instruction. The income distribution of these 178 schools is shown in Table 6–4.

FINANCING THE BLACK COLLEGE
IN THE EARLY TWENTIETH CENTURY

Between 1890 and 1925 many black colleges and universities made the transition from being primarily elementary and high schools to being colleges in fact. Their problems of financing did not necessarily improve with their change in status.

Financing private higher education has always been an uncertain affair in the United States. Financing private *black* higher education between 1890 and 1915 was made even more difficult by the increasing interest of philanthropists in industrial education. Although sources of financing were more reliable for state-supported and land-grant institutions, their actual financial condition was not much better than that of the private institutions. Throughout the period from 1890 to 1915 black colleges were continually in search of funds that would allow them to exist.

Sources of Income for Black Institutions

Private black colleges, unlike the public institutions, depended heavily on contributions and gifts to meet their expenses. Table 6-5 shows the distribution of the sources of income for 652 black institutions surveyed by the federal government in 1915. The table shows that tuition income played a minor role in the overall financing of both public and private institutions. The table shows, for example, that tuition income accounted for only 12.4 percent of the total income of all the schools, ranging from 8.8 percent at the government-supported institutions to 19.7 percent at the institutions maintained by the colored denomination boards.

Table 6-5 further highlights the fact that the federal government was a relatively minor source of financing for these institutions. Only 9.1 percent of the total income for all schools came from the federal government (and Howard University in Washington, D.C., got almost one-half of that). Indeed, government funds were received by only

Table 6–5
Sources of Income for Negro Institutions, 1915

| TYPE OF SPONSOR | PERCENT OF INCOME FROM VARIOUS SOURCES | | | | | TOTAL INCOME (100%) |
	FEDERAL LAND-GRANT FUNDS	STATE APPRO-PRIATIONS	DONATIONS AND OTHERS	CHURCH	TUITION	
Public (27)	37.4	50.0	3.7	0	8.8	$ 963,611
Independent Boards (118)	0	0	88.7	1.0	10.2	1,099,224
White denominational boards (354)	0	0	26.8	59.2	14.1	1,546,303
Colored denominational boards (153)	0	0	12.5	65.6	21.9	342,030
Totals	9.1%	12.2%	37.1%	29.1%	12.4%	$3,951,168

SOURCE: Data from Jones (1920).

twenty-seven institutions. State appropriations to the schools amounted
to 12.2 percent of their income.

During the first decades of the twentieth century, financial support
for almost all of the black educational institutions rested on the gener-
osity of the church denominations and private citizens. These two
groups contributed from 70 percent to 90 percent of the income for each
category of private institution included in the 1915 survey (Table 6-5).
Over 90 percent of the enrollment in the Negro schools at this time was
in private institutions.

Table 6-6 shows the sources of income for eleven selected black
private institutions in 1915. Overall these schools received 84.2 percent

Table 6–6
Sources of Income for Selected Independent Black Institutions, 1915

SCHOOL	TOTAL INCOME	DONATIONS	TUITION	OTHER SOURCES	CHURCH
St. Augustine's	$ 25,929	$ 5,398	$ 00	$ 3,204	$ 17,417
Biddle	17,121	00	379	4,222	12,520
Tougaloo	26,169	4,132	3,236	3,873	14,928
Talladega	39,822	7,282	5,965	1,000	25,575
Shaw	31,973	2,250	9,573	4,990	15,160
Morehouse	17,560	1,185	2,860	1,050	12,465
Spelman	39,566	3,625	6,186	20,255	9,500
Hampton	291,484	104,292	00	187,192	00
Fisk	54,305	20,362	14,408	11,065	8,500
Tuskegee	265,960	134,094	15,055	116,811	00
Lincoln	48,063	11,176	2,394	31,993	2,500
Totals	$857,952	$293,796	$60,056	$385,655	$118,565
Percentage distribution		34.2%	7.0%	45%	13.8%

SOURCE: Data from Jones (1920).

of their income from donations and other sources (investments, gifts, and contributions). Tuition accounted for only 7 percent of the income at these eleven rather typical—and certainly, at the time, best-known—black colleges. During this period Hampton received all of its income and Tuskegee 94 percent of its income from donations and other private sources; few other black institutions were so well supported by outside donors.

The best-financed black colleges were those that emphasized the industrial arts. For example, by 1915 Hampton and Tuskegee had become the two most heavily endowed schools by far with endowments of $2,709,344 and $1,942,112, respectively. Overall, black institutions were endowed to the sum of about $9 million, 51.5 percent of which was held by Tuskegee and Hampton. The best-endowed liberal arts college, by contrast, was Lincoln University with an endowment of $700,000.

Table 6–7
Black Schools with Most Current Income, 1915

SCHOOL	INCOME
1. Hampton Institute	$291,484
2. Tuskegee Institute	265,960
3. Howard University	172,257
4. Ohio, Combined Normal and Industrial Department	77,000
5. Fisk University	54,305
6. Prairie View State Normal College	49,985
7. Lincoln University	48,063
8. Alcorn Agricultural and Mechanical University	47,774
9. West Virginia Collegiate Institute	46,499
10. Oklahoma Agricultural and Normal University	46,400
11. Atlanta University	44,794
12. South Carolina Normal, Industrial, Agricultural and Mechanical School	44,216

SOURCE: Data from Jones (1920).

The top twelve schools in terms of current income in 1915 are listed in Table 6-7. Again, Hampton and Tuskegee were better financed than all other black institutions.

Financial Problems of Liberal Arts Colleges

Based on the financial backing they received, the type of education offered at both Hampton and Tuskegee clearly was approved by the philanthropists. Since private black institutions of all kinds depended quite heavily on outside philanthropy, many of the black colleges were tempted to offer industrial education and deemphasize their academic programs in order to be in a better position to compete for outside funds. For example, Fisk University, short of money in 1906, offered to establish a department of applied science in the university. With the aid of Booker T. Washington, Fisk then obtained funding from the John F. Slater Fund, the General Education Board, and citizens of Nashville. Fisk proposed to give courses in agriculture, mechanical arts, animal husbandry, rural engineering, plant breeding and the domestic arts. DuBois called the program a poor imitation of those offered at Hampton and Tuskegee; it was dropped in 1909 (DuBois 1973).

Other liberal arts institutions flirted with industrial education from 1880 to 1915, including Atlanta, Clark, Morehouse, and Spelman. Many black colleges had to close their doors during this period because of lack of support. A few discontinued their programs in law and medicine.

According to Harlan (1972), Booker T. Washington wielded enormous influence in the awards made to black education by the Carnegies, Rosenwalds, the General Education Board, the John F. Slater Fund, the Phelps–Stokes Fund, and the Jeanes Fund. As one example, black schools that received funds from the Carnegie Foundation to build libraries got them on Washington's recommendations (DaBrey 1936, p. 114).

A better day for the support of the black liberal arts colleges was soon to come as the role they could play in uplifting the black race became more generally appreciated by northern white philanthropists. The General Education Board, a foundation influential in the development of the black colleges during the 1920s, expressed the changed attitude in reviewing its activities from 1902 to 1914:

> These schools have, with varying degrees of success, rendered a large service, particularly in the training of teachers for the public schools and in the training of colored ministers. In some cases, they have developed colleges

which will form the nucleus of a system of schools for the higher education of the Negroes. Any discussion of Negro education must recognize the disinterested motives of these organizations and the importance and value of schools maintained by them. (General Education Board 1920)

Similar sentiments on the part of other foundations and of wealthy individuals would lead to better financial prospects for the private and public black colleges in the 1920s and 1930s

The Big Educational Foundations

The financial position of the black private colleges and universities, in particular, improved dramatically after 1915 as a result of the increasing interest and financial support of the big educational foundations. The two with the greatest impact in the period under discussion were the General Education Board and the Julius Rosenwald Fund.

The General Education Board

John D. Rockefeller established the General Education Board in 1902 and by June 1919 had contributed $53 million to it. From 1902 until 1964, when its funds were exhausted, the foundation contributed $324.6 million to promote a variety of educational activities in the United States. Approximately $63 million (almost 20 percent) went to black education, most of it to higher education.

Before 1920, the General Education Board had contributed to both the public and private sectors of black education; after that year, almost all of its funding for black education was concentrated on the private institutions. The rationale for the shift was indicated in the foundation's 1914 annual report, which stressed the urgent need for better institutions of higher education for blacks. The report argued that if "primary and secondary Negro schools are to have good teachers, principals, and supervisors" (General Education Board 1914), some adequate provision would have to be made for their training. Private black colleges had long been the major supplier of black teachers, and a number of them now were granted increasingly substantial financial assistance by the foundation.

The Julius Rosenwald Fund

Incorporated in 1917, the Julius Rosenwald Fund had expended a little more than $22 million in the areas of health, education, fellowships, and race relations by the time it was liquidated in 1948. The fund gave approximately 22 percent of its income ($4.7 million) directly to black colleges for such purposes as endowment, operating expenses, buildings, and new programs. Another $1.1 million was awarded for fellowships and scholarships for black students.

RECENT TRENDS IN FINANCING

The financing patterns of the black colleges from the 1920s through World War II were fairly well set by conditions and trends established earlier. After World War II, the federal government began to play a larger role in financing higher education. This had a tremendous impact on the subsequent financing of the black colleges and undoubtedly will greatly influence their future viability. Income and expenditure patterns of the black colleges for selected years from 1970 through 1975 are analyzed in this section. The analysis is based primarily on information from the Higher Education General Information Survey and from applications submitted by institutions for funding under Title III of the Higher Education Act of 1966.*

Income and Expenditures for Operations

An institution's expenses are broken down into two primary categories: capital expenses and current operating expenses. Capital expenses are those made for long-term investments. Building programs, endowment accumulation, and major repairs and renovations that require large sums of money not ordinarily available to an institution are examples of capital expenditures.

Current operating expenses refer to educational and general expenses and expenses for auxiliary enterprises. Educational and general expenditures are operating expenses for the basic program offerings of a college, including such items as the academic program, the library, the institution's contribution to student financial assistance, the physical plant, and general administrative support.The other major category that comes under the heading of current operating expenses

---

*The Higher Education General Information Survey is an annual statistical survey covering all colleges and universities in the United States, conducted under the auspices of the U.S. Office of Education. Title III of the 1965 Higher Education Act, as amended, is a program of institutional support to so-called developing institutions of higher education. Most of the historically black colleges fall in this category.

covers what is referred to as auxiliary enterprises. These include programs not directly related to the basic purposes of the institution, but important to its functioning: dining halls, athletics, dormitories, a bookstore.

Sources of Revenue

Tables 6-8 and 6-9 show in conventional form the amounts and sources of income received by black private and public institutions of higher learning for educational and general expenses in 1970 and 1975. A review of the two tables shows the following:

1. State and local governments accounted for 69.7 percent and 56.9 percent of the educational and general income at black public institutions in 1970 and 1975 respectively (Table 6-9). In contrast, state and local government accounted for only 3.6 percent of the income for operations at independent institutions in 1975 and only 1.5 percent in 1970 (Table 6-8).
2. Tuition and fees, on the other hand, are an important source of funds for the independent sector and less important for the public sector. They accounted for 52.2 percent and 39.6 percent of the educational and general income at independent black colleges and universities in 1970 and 1975 respectively, compared to 19.8 percent and 16.9 percent at the public institutions in the same years.
3. The major sources of financing educational and general expenditures at the state-assisted institutions in 1975 were state and local governments (56.9 percent), tuition and fees (16.9 percent), and the federal government (12 percent).
4. The major sources for financing educational and general expenditures in the independent sector in 1975 were tuition and fees (39.6 percent), gifts and grants (23 percent), and the federal government (20.7 percent).
5. The percentage of income for operations coming from the federal government increased over this five-year period for each sector of black higher education.

The categories used in Tables 6-8 and 6-9 are not as useful for identifying the actual sources of financing at the black colleges as the breakdown used in Tables 6-10 and 6-11, which takes into account the

Table 6–8
Mean Income by Source for Independent Black Colleges and Universities

SOURCE	1970 (45 INSTITUTIONS) AMOUNT	% OF E & G[a]	1975 (49 INSTITUTIONS) AMOUNT	% OF E & G
Tuition and fees	$ 866,441	52.2	$1,267,354	39.6
Federal government	207,951	12.5	664,025	20.7
State and local government	25,290	1.5	116,437	3.6
Endowment	112,247	6.8	130,786	4.1
Private gifts, grants	448,827	27.0	737,150	23.0
Sponsored research	0		120,248	3.8
All other income for E & G	0		163,695	5.1
Total E & G	$1,660,756	100.0%	$3,199,696	99.9%
Gross income for auxiliary enterprises	589,966		816,403	
Student aid	289,292		526,086	
All other income	0		22,431	
Total incomes	$2,540,014		$4,564,613	

SOURCE: Higher Education General Information Survey, 1970–75, U.S. Office of Education.
[a] E & G = educational and general income.

fact that between 75 percent and 85 percent of the students at black colleges receive financial assistance. A recent study by the College Entrance Examination Board found the parents of black college students paying 20 percent of the costs of their children's higher education. Furthermore, according to the National Commission on the Financing of Postsecondary Education (1973), the federal government provides the funds for almost 90 percent of all student financial aid. Tables 6-10 and 6-11 adjust the financial data regarding income from tuition and fees to take account of these facts.

After these adjustments have been made, the following important points can be made about financing the current operations of the black colleges:

Table 6-9
Mean Income by Source for Public Black Colleges and Universities

SOURCE	1970 (31 INSTITUTIONS)		1975 (29 INSTITUTIONS)	
	AMOUNT	% OF E & G[a]	AMOUNT	% OF E & G
Tuition and fees	$ 750,407	19.8	$ 1,322,196	16.9
Federal government	369,195	9.7	939,931	12.0
State and local government	2,637,986	69.7	4,456,105	56.9
Endowment	1,658	0.0	2,048	0.0
Private gifts, grants	28,114	0.7	100,641	1.3
Sponsored research	0	0.0	240,185	3.1
All other income for E & G	0	0.0	765,428	9.8
Total E & G	3,787,359	99.9%	7,826,535	100.0%
Auxiliary enterprises	1,023,289		1,501,753	
Student aid	228,674		591,655	
All other income	0		189,211	
Total incomes	$5,039,320		$10,109,156	

SOURCE: Higher Education General Information Survey, 1970–75, U.S. Office of Education.
[a] E & G = educational and general income.

1. In 1975 the federal government accounted for 38 percent of the total income of independent institutions (Table 6-10) and 21.5 percent of the total income of the state-assisted institutions (Table 6-11). Stated in another way, the federal government directly and indirectly accounted for 46.3 percent of the educational and general income of independent black institutions and 27.7 percent of the educational and general income of public institutions.
2. The contribution of the federal government has increased in this five-year period for both groups of institutions.
3. In 1975, tuition and fees paid by students and their parents accounted for only 2.6 percent of total income at state-assisted institutions and 5.5 percent of total income at independent institu-

Table 6–10
Revised Format for Sources of Income at Independent Black Colleges, 1970 and 1975

SOURCE	1970 AMOUNT	% OF TOTAL	1975 AMOUNT	% OF TOTAL
Federal government		33.8		38.0
Student aid (75% of tuition & fees)	$ 649,831		$ 950,515	
Aid to institution	207,951		664,025	
Sponsored research	00		120,248	
State government		2.7		3.9
Student aid (5% of tuition & fees)	43,322		63,368	
Aid to institution	25,290		116,437	
Tuition and fees from student's & parents	173,288	6.8	253,471	5.5
Endowment	112,247	4.4	130,786	2.9
Gifts and grants	448,827	17.7	737,150	16.1
All other income for E & G	00	0.0	163,695	3.6
Auxiliary enterprises	589,966	23.2	816,403	17.9
Student aid	289,292	11.4	526,086	11.5
All other income	00	0.0	00	0.0
Totals	$2,540,014	100.0%	$4,564,615	99.4%

SOURCE: Higher Education General Information Survey, 1970–75, U.S. Office of Education.
[a] E & G = educational and general income.

tions—in both cases less than in 1970 but consistent with the contribution to financing black colleges by this source of income in the past.

4. In passing, it should be noted that the independent sector has significantly more of its income allocated to the student aid account than do the state-assisted institutions, 11.5 percent compared to 5.8 percent.

5. Sponsored research accounts for less than 3 percent of the total income at each group of institutions, in part because of the undergraduate, teacher-education orientation of many of the colleges.

Table 6–11
Revised Format for Sources of Income at Public Black Colleges and Universities, 1970 and 1975

SOURCE	1970 AMOUNT	1970 % OF TOTAL	1975 AMOUNT	1975 % OF TOTAL
Federal government		18.5		21.5
Aid to students	$ 562,805		$ 991,647	
Aid to institutions	369,195		939,931	
Sponsored research	00		240,185	
State government		53.1		44.7
Aid to students	37,520		66,110	
Aid to institutions	2,637,986		4,456,105	
Tuition and fees paid by students	150,081	3.0	264,439	2.6
Endowment	1,658		2,048	
Gifts and grants	28,114	0.6	100,641	0.1
All other income for E & G[a]	00	0.0	765,428	7.6
Auxiliary enterprises	1,023,289	20.3	1,501,753	14.8
Student aid	228,674	4.5	591,655	5.8
All other income	00	0.0	189,211	1.9
Totals	$5,039,322	100.0%	$10,109,153	99.0%

SOURCE: Higher Education General Information Survey, 1970–75, U.S. Office of Education.
[a] E & G = educational and general income.

Patterns of Expenditures

Complete expenditure data were available at this time for only 1975. Table 6-12 shows mean expenditures for a sample of forty-eight independent institutions; Table 6-13 gives mean expenditures for a sample of twenty-eight state-assisted institutions. When the data in the tables are compared, we find:

1. The state-assisted institutions spend, on the average, about twice as much as the independent colleges. This is not so surprising since the

average public black institution is about three times larger in enrollment than its private counterpart. On a per-student basis, the independent sector spends about one-third more per student on educational and general expenditures.

2. However, the pattern of expenditures at the state-assisted institutions is significantly different from that at the independent institutions in two important areas: instruction and student aid.

Public black colleges spend a greater percentage of their funds on instruction than do those in the private sector—70.2 percent compared to 62.7 percent. The reason for this may well be that the public col-

Table 6–12
Mean Expenditures for 48 Independent Black Colleges and Universities, 1975

TYPE OF EXPENDITURE	AMOUNT	% OF TOTAL
Instruction	$1,190,078	26.1
Libraries	139,888	3.1
Contract research and services	175,128	3.8
All other educational and general expenditures	1,358,182	29.7
Total for educational and general	$2,863,276	62.7
Auxiliary enterprises	765,919	16.8
Student aid	723,411	15.8
All other expenditures	215,233	4.7
Total expenditures	$4,567,836	100.0%
Expenditures per student		
Educational and general expenditures per FTE[a] student	$3,105	
Total expenditures per FTE student	$4,954	

SOURCE: Higher Education General Information Survey, 1970–75, U.S. Office of Education.
[a] FTE = full-time equivalent.

leges tend to be larger and can achieve certain economies of scale, which allow them to spend less money on overhead and more on primary activities like instruction; however, this cannot explain all of the difference.

What seems to be happening is that the public institutions can spend more on their instructional programs because on a percentage basis they spend less on student financial aid—7.9 percent compared to 15.8 percent, almost the total difference between what the two sectors spend on instruction. Both sectors of black higher education spend a considerable amount on student aid, but the independent schools spend much more in this area than the state-assisted institutions. Some data will be presented later suggesting that these expenditures act as a drain

---

Table 6–13
Mean Expenditures for 28 Public Black Colleges and Universities, 1975

TYPE OF EXPENDITURE	AMOUNT	% OF TOTAL
Instruction	$3,303,690	34.7
Libraries	407,908	4.3
Contract research and services	340,165	3.6
All other educational and general expenditures	2,622,347	27.6
Total educational and general expenditures	$6,674,109	70.2
Auxiliary enterprises	1,651,126	17.4
Student aid	756,042	7.9
All other expenditures	425,708	4.5
Total expenditures	$9,506,984	100.0%
Expenditures per student		
Educational and general expenditures per FTE[a] student	$2,351	
Total expenditures per FTE student	$3,349	

SOURCE: Higher Education General Information Survey, 1970–75, U.S. Office of Education.
[a] FTE = full-time equivalent.

on more adequate financing of other programs of the colleges. For example, such expenditures directly affect the salary level that the institutions can afford.

In summary, then, the independent sector spends less on instruction but more on student aid than the public sector of black higher education. Except for the differing amounts spent on student aid and instruction, the two sectors are similar in their spending patterns for operating purposes.

Overall Financial Status

The independent sector of black higher education is in a far more serious financial condition than the public sector. In our sample of twenty-eight public institutions, only one had an operating deficit ($65,000) in 1975. By contrast, of the forty-eight independent institutions, eight (16.7 percent) had an operating deficit; the average deficit of these eight institutions was $943,250 out of an average income of $5,261,750. Thus the deficit was 17.9 percent of the total income of these

Table 6-14
Comparison of Income and Expenditures in Black Colleges and Universities for Educational and General Functions, 1975, and for Auxiliary Enterprises, 1970 and 1975

TYPE OF INSTITUTION	INCOME	EXPENDITURES	SURPLUS (DEFICIT)
Educational and General			
1975			
Public	$7,826,535	$6,664,109	$1,152,426
Independent	3,199,696	2,863,276	336,420
Auxiliary			
1975			
Public	1,501,753	1,651,126	(149,373)
Independent	816,403	765,919	50,484
1970			
Public	1,023,289	1,112,448	(89,159)
Independent	589,966	564,905	25,061

SOURCE: Higher Education General Information Survey, 1970–75, U.S. Office of Education.

institutions. Overall our sample of independent colleges had a slight deficit balance, on the average $3,223, while the public institutions had an average surplus balance of $602,172.

Table 6-14 compares income and expenditures for auxiliary enterprises in 1970 and 1975 and for educational and general categories in 1975. The table shows that both sectors ran surpluses in their educational and general accounts and that the private schools, but not the public, ran a surplus in their auxiliary accounts.

Table 6-15
Capital Funds Loans Received by All Institutions of Higher Education and by Historically Negro Colleges by Source and Fund, Fiscal Year 1965-66 (Thousands of Dollars)

SOURCE OF FUNDS	PHYSICAL PLANT FUNDS	STUDENT LOAN FUNDS	TOTAL FUNDS	% OF TOTAL FUNDS
All United States institutions				
Total capital funds borrowed	$1,587,004	$205,091	$1,792,094	
Other funds of institution	77,556	6,365	83,920	4.7
Private sources outside of institution	687,981	1,103	689,084	38.4
Local government	58,354	116	58,470	3.3
State government	336,527	2,349	338,876	18.9
Federal government	426,586	195,158	621,744	34.5
Black colleges				
Total capital funds borrowed	24,824	11,878	36,702	
Other funds of institution	264	140	404	1.1
Private sources outside of institution	6,689	4	6,693	18.2
Local government	00	—	00	0.0
State government	4,771	54	4,825	13.1
Federal government	13,100	11,680	24,780	67.5

SOURCE: Bowles and DeCosta (1971, pp. 164-165). Used with permission. Copyright © 1971 by The Carnegie Foundation for the Advancement of Teaching.
NOTE: To the amounts of money presented in this table, add 000—thus, $1,587,004 in the table represents $1,587,004,000.

Financing Capital Assets

Table 6-15 shows the capital funds loans received by all institutions and by black institutions in 1965-66. Although the data are old, the conclusions to be drawn from them would be the same with current information because these kinds of data tend to be rather stable over time; an institution does not alter its structure of capital financing rapidly. The table shows a clear distinction between the two categories of institutions with respect to loans for long-range needs.

1. The federal government was the main source of capital funds loans received by black institutions of higher education, accounting for 67.5 percent of capital funds loans. Private sources and governments were far less important sources of such loans.
2. In contrast, the federal government accounted for only 34.5 percent of capital funds loans made to all institutions of higher education. Private sources were the leading sources of capital funds loans at 38.4 percent.

These data confirm the important role played by the federal government in financing black colleges. Not only is the federal

Table 6-16
Percent Allocations of Capital Funds Receipts at Independent Black Institutions, 1970 and 1975

ALLOCATION	45 INSTITUTIONS, 1970	49 INSTITUTIONS, 1975	% CHANGE
Physical plant	66.6 ($5,728,695)	62.8 ($7,918,863)	38.2 ($2,190,168)
Endowment	26.0 ($2,274,146)	19.9 ($2,502,750)	10.0 ($228,610)
Scholarships	—	.8 ($96,975)	— ($96,975)
National Defense Loan	8.3 ($726,832)	7.9 ($996,270)	37.1 ($269,438)
Other	—	8.6 ($1,085,823)	— ($1,085,823)
Totals	99.9 ($8,729,672)	100.0 ($12,600,687)	44.3 ($3,871,014)

SOURCE: Higher Education General Information Survey, 1970-75, U.S. Office of Education; Title III applications.

government an important source of funding for current operations at these institutions, but for longer term needs as well.

Tables 6–16 and 6–17 show the distribution of capital funds receipts in 1970 and 1975 for both state-assisted and independent black schools. These two tables reveal the following facts:

1. Independent colleges and universities compared to the public institutions place a greater percentage of their capital funds receipts in endowment, scholarships, and student loan accounts. In 1975, for example, 28.6 percent of the capital funds receipts of the independent schools went into these categories as against 4.7 percent at the public institutions.
2. The public institutions invest a larger proportion of capital fund receipts in their physical plants than do the private institutions, allocating 92 percent in 1970 and 85.6 percent in 1975 compared to 65.1 percent and 62.8 percent for the independent black colleges and universities.

In addition, when black institutions are compared to all colleges and universities on the distribution of capital funds receipts, both sectors of black education well exceed the average in the proportion allocated to

Table 6–17
Percent Allocations of Capital Funds Receipts at Public Black Institutions, 1970 and 1975

ALLOCATION	30 INSTITUTIONS, 1970	29 INSTITUTIONS, 1975	% CHANGE
Physical plant	92.0 ($10,823,969)	85.6 ($20,643,902)	90.7 ($9,819,933)
Endowment	.3 ($38,041)	.3 ($68,315)	79.6 ($30,274)
Scholarships	—	.2 ($56,190)	—
Student loan funds	7.6 ($899,236)	4.2 ($1,011,737)	12.5 ($112,501)
Other	—	9.7 ($2,331,101)	—
Totals	99.9 ($11,761,246)	100.0 ($24,111,245)	105.0 ($12,349,900)

SOURCE: Higher Educational General Information Survey, 1970–75, U.S. Office of Education.

student aid loans and scholarships. The distribution of capital funds receipts for all institutions is somewhat as follows: physical plant, 75 percent; endowment, 22 percent; student loans, 1 percent; annuity and trust funds, 2 percent.

Student Aid Income and Expenditures

Student financial aid, whether provided by the institutions themselves or through a third party, is an indispensable support for enrollment at black colleges. Without extensive financial aid programs, many black colleges—both public and private—would not have enough enrollment to support their continued operation. With 75 percent of the students attending black colleges receiving financial aid, this means that over 120,000 students are being assisted.

Financial aid for students attending a black college typically covers tuition plus a part of their living expenses. As Table 6–18 shows, the federal government provides $3.9 billion of the $4.4 billion (88.6 percent) in financial aid provided to all students in higher education. Thus one may reasonably hypothesize that the vast majority of the

---

Table 6–18
Major Sources of Income for Postsecondary Education in Billions of Dollars, 1971–72

SOURCES OF INCOME	INSTITUTIONAL SUPPORT	AID TO STUDENTS	TOTAL SUPPORT	PERCENT OF TOTAL
Student payments for tuition and other fees	$ 5.9	$0.0	$ 5.9	20.0
State and local government	9.0	0.3	9.3	31.6
Federal government	4.2	3.9	8.1	27.4
Private philanthropy and endowment income	2.5	0.2	2.7	9.1
Auxiliary enterprises and other income	3.5	0.0	3.5	11.9
Totals	$25.1	$4.4	$29.5	100.0%

SOURCE: The National Commission on the Financing of Postsecondary Education (1973, p. 69).

Table 6-19
Comparison of Revenues and Expenditures at Black Colleges and
Universities for Institutional Student Financial Aid, 1970 and 1975

INSTITUTION	EARMARKED REVENUES	EXPENDITURES	SURPLUS (DEFICIT)	PERCENT OVER EARMARKED REVENUES
1970				
Independent	$289,292	$389,552	$(100,260)	135%
Public	228,674	232,320	(3,646)	102%
1975				
Independent	526,086	723,411	(197,325)	138%
Public	591,655	756,042	(164,387)	128%

SOURCE: Higher Education General Information Survey, 1970–75, U.S. Office of Education.

students receiving financial aid at black colleges get it through programs funded by the federal government.

The institutions themselves, however, also set aside part of their income for student financial aid. Table 6-19 shows the revenues and expenditures earmarked for student financial aid in 1970 and 1975 by the average black independent and public institution. Both sectors spent more for their student aid programs than they had earmarked for such purposes. The independent institutions spent on the average 35 percent more in 1970 and 38 percent more in 1975. Such deficits in student aid accounts have been financed in two ways: long-term borrowing and diverting funds from instructional programs.

Tuition at Black Colleges

In their study of black higher education, the political scientists Frank Bowles and Frank DeCosta (1971) conclude that the black colleges are underpricing their services, which is to say that they are charging insufficient tuition—especially the private colleges. Bowles and DeCosta observe that, since the black colleges enroll fewer students than they can accommodate, they are compelled to (1) underprice their tuition to achieve a competitive advantage and (2) provide large grants for student aid, which they supported by borrowing (Bowles and DeCosta 1971, pp. 179; 181).

A comparison of the tuition and fee charges at independent black colleges and at all four-year independent colleges supports this conclusion. The average tuition charged in 1971–1972 at thirteen black private colleges selected on a random basis proves to be $400 less than that charged by all four-year private institutions, as indicated by government data—$1,283 compared to $1,652. Further it appears from the financial data presented in Tables 6–8 through 6–11 that income from tuition and fees decreased in both sectors from 1970 through 1975, going from 52 percent to 40 percent at private institutions and from 20 percent to 17 percent at public institutions.

Historically, tuition income has been relatively unimportant as a source of funds for public colleges as a whole but very important for independent institutions. For example, at many white private institutions today tuition income accounts for 60 percent to 95 percent of educational and general income. This has never been true at private black colleges. Their tuition levels have always been kept low because black parents could not afford to pay much for educating their offspring and others were willing to underwrite such costs.

Table 6–20 shows by race the percentages of income received from various sources to pay the costs of college in 1969–1970. In that academic year, black parents contributed only 21 percent of the costs of

Table 6–20
Percentages of Income Received from Various Sources to Pay the Costs of College, by Race, 1969–70

SOURCE	BLACK STUDENTS	WHITE STUDENTS
Aid from parents	21	45
Educational Opportunity Grants	11	2
Scholarships and grants	18	8
Loans	21	8
Jobs	15	15
Money drawn from assets	9	15
Social security and veteran's benefits	3	2
Other	2	5
Totals	100%	100%

SOURCE: Haven and Horch (1971, p. 10).

educating their offspring, compared to the 45 percent contributed by white parents. Further black students used loans to pay another 21 percent of their costs of education, compared to the 8 percent borrowed by white students. The table also shows that in 1969–1970 black college students used government and private sources (Educational Opportunity Grants, scholarships and grants, loans, benefits) to pay 53 percent of their educational costs, while white students used such sources for only 20 percent of their educational expenses.

In recent years federal government policies on student financial aid and institutional aid have had a strong impact on the financing of black colleges and universities, especially in providing the funds (either in grants or loans) to enable increasing numbers of low- and middle-income black students to afford the costs of a college education. Typically, a low-income student might reasonably expect to receive financial assistance of $3,000-$4,000 (almost all from the federal government in one way or another). For example, such a student attending an independent black college might receive a grant package of about $1,000, a job related to the grant of $500, and a loan of between $1,000 and $1,500.

If the federal subsidy program were better funded, the typical financial aid package would be increased. State governments could be another source of indirect funding for the independent sector, but, to date, very few states have implemented such programs to provide financial assistance to students attending private institutions. Since there are limits to the amount of student aid that the government has been willing to provide, there are also real limits to the levels of tuition that the black colleges can charge; the schools cannot ask for much more than the student can obtain in financial aid.

Outputs and Attainments

The financial factors affecting both the private and public sectors of black higher education have had an effect on the attainments and outputs of the institutions during the years from 1970 through 1975. Table 6–21 presents a few selected measures of attainment and output for both sectors. The data show that, on the average, the public institutions have gained in a number of the measures over this period.

1. Full-time faculty with doctorates at the average institution increased from 39.3 to 66.2.
2. Library volumes increased from 103,815 to 128,305.

3. The average full-time-equivalent enrollment increased from 2,384 to 2,839.
4. The percentage of graduating seniors accepted at graduate schools increased.

In contrast, the independent sector did not do nearly as well during this five-year period: Full-time faculty at the average private institution decreased from 25.6 to 23.5 and enrollments declined about 10 percent.

Table 6–21
Comparison of Outputs and Educational Attainments at Average Black Educational Institutions, 1970 and 1975

| | STATE-ASSISTED INSTITUTIONS | | INDEPENDENT INSTITUTIONS | |
| | 1970 | 1975 | 1970 | 1975 |
OUTPUTS AND ATTAINMENTS	32 SCHOOLS	31 SCHOOLS	48 SCHOOLS	49 SCHOOLS
Full-time faculty with Ph.D.	39.3	66.2	25.6	23.5
Volumes in library	103,815	128,305	67,267	79,791
Undergraduate FTE[a] enrollment	2,262	2,680	1,030	922
Total FTE enrollment	2,384	2,839	1,089	922
Graduates accepted by graduate school	37.4	75.9	32.9	38.8
Total graduates	359	432.1	171.9	173.2
Percent graduates accepted at graduate school	10.4%	17.6%	19.1%	22.4%
Percent freshmen completing first year	64.2%	41.6%	75.1%	35.1%
Educational and general expenditures per FTE student	—	$2,351	—	$3,105

SOURCE: Higher Education General Information Survey, 1970–75, U.S. Office of Education.
[a] FTE = full time equivalent.

CONCLUSIONS

A key question is whether the historically black college, public and private, can survive given the current and emerging patterns of financing and given the fact that the colleges no longer have a monopoly on black enrollments in higher education. The independent institutions are now in financial trouble in ways that their public counterparts are not. State and local governments may take care of the public black colleges, but who will come to the aid of the private black colleges?

The federal government plays an increasingly important role in financing both current and capital operations of black colleges, especially in financing students. At federal and state levels, government may be the best future source for financing all black colleges, through both expanded student aid and institutional aid.

Chapter 7

The Priorities of Presidents of Black Colleges

Charles V. Willie and
Marlene Y. MacLeish

> Nobody knows the trouble I see;
> Nobody knows but Jesus.
> Nobody knows the trouble I see;
> Glory, Hallelujah!

The words of an old spiritual. They were developed in response to the circumstances of a slave, but could have been written for a president of a black college. "Nobody knows the trouble I see" expresses a feeling of aloneness and despair. "Glory, Hallelujah!" is affirmation of hope. Between these two moods hangs the administrative practice of presidents of black colleges. The problems they deal with are severe. The support they receive is scant. Their success has been sure but unsteady. In the words of Langston Hughes, life for the president of a black college "ain't been no crystal stair." Yet they—and their schools—have managed to endure, overcome, and survive because they have faced adversity with ingenuity and continued to hope.

The famous Fisk Jubilee Singers were the creation of a black-college administrator. Shortly after Fisk University was founded in 1866, lack of money was a perplexing problem for the administration; the school's closing seemed inevitable. It was the ingenious idea of the treasurer to organize a singing group of students. He predicted that its inspiring renditions of slave spirituals would attract the public's attention and stimulate help for the new school. In October of 1871 the Jubilee Singers left the campus for a tour of the United States and Europe.

They returned in 1878 with the money necessary to save the school and, according to John W. Work, "created over the world interest in [black] education and in the spirituals" (Work 1940, p. 17).

To this day, black college administrators have been similarly ingenious, pragmatic, and hopeful. They take what they have and use it well to do what they must. In his autobiography, Benjamin E. Mays describes his stewardship of twenty-seven years as president of Morehouse College with the words, "so much with so little and so few" (Mays 1971, p. 170).

Notwithstanding their historical endurance, Mays has said that he saw "a subtle move afloat to abolish black colleges" at the beginning of the 1970s. He has charged that "numerous critics have a crusade of tearing the black college apart (Mays 1971, p. 192). Black college presidents have been the targets of critical scrutiny and ridicule in this attack. Christopher Jencks and David Riesman, for example, have charged that many black colleges are run "as if they were the personal property of their presidents" (Jencks and Riesman 1967, pp. 48–49). Ann Jones, a white professor who taught at a black college only two semesters, describes the president of her institution as a "paternalistic dictator" (Jones 1973, p. 119). However, Tobe Johnson, a black professor of political science acknowledging that "black college presidents probably resemble the autocratic officials," has explained that such a chief executive, "serving as the mediator between the college and the threatening environment, found it necessary to consolidate and maintain personal control over his organization" (Johnson 1971, p. 801).

Thus the hostile, threatening, and nonsupportive environmental conditions surrounding black colleges are related to the administrative styles of their executives. It is a principle of political science that the more hostile and threatening the environment, the easier it is to legitimate the centralization of power. Indeed, Johnson states, "it can be argued that strong personal authority was essential to . . . survival" (Johnson 1971, p. 801). In addition, another factor enters in: The resources of black colleges have been so meager and their margin for error so small that administrators of black colleges cannot risk mistakes.

The presidents have remained in control, but not for self-serving purposes. Albert Dent, former president of Dillard University, has emphasized the fact that the presidents of black colleges "are constantly seeking means by which to improve the effectiveness of their faculties" (Wright et. al., 1967, p. 464). Benjamin Mays, upon becoming president of Morehouse College in 1940, extracted a promise from the board of trustees (apparently a condition of his accepting the presidency) to raise the salary scale of the faculty (Mays 1971, p.171). Black-college presidents have remained visibly in control. But their control has been for the sake of preserving their institutions. Johnson reminds us, moreover, that they had good role models in "the autocratic officials who presided at the prestigious white schools during the nineteenth century" (Johnson 1971, p. 800).

Profile of Black Colleges

In 1967 when Jencks and Riesman published their study "The American Negro College" in the *Harvard Educational Review,* they stated that black colleges tend to be small—only one or two enroll more than 1,000 students, and most have fewer than 500. As a result, they operate with a faculty of 20 or 30 . . . and a budget of perhaps half a million dollars" (Jencks and Riesman 1967, p. 48).

We can now report on a study, conducted by us less than ten years later, which reveals quite a different picture. The purpose of this research was to provide black-college presidents with an opportunity to speak for themselves. It produced data supplied by presidents of 21 of the 88 four-year schools in the National Association for Equal Opportunity in Higher Education.* From 15 we have hard statistical information about their institutions, plus information in narrative form; the other 6 confined their responses to narrative explanations. In all, one-fourth of the total sample responded. Table 7–1 lists the institutions participating, their locations, and the names of the college presidents.

Here is what the statistical data shows (Table 7–2). The average size of the student body in these 15 black colleges is 2,800. Only 5 of the 15 schools have student bodies under 1,000, and all of these have enrollments of over 500. The average size of the full-time faculty is 154; only 3 of the 15 colleges have faculties with fewer than 50 members. The total budgets for the schools range from $1.8 million to $28.6 million, with an average of $9.9 million. Their average instructional

*The National Association for Equal Opportunity in Higher Education is an organization of public and private colleges and universities with student bodies that are predominantly black. It is based in Washington, D.C. This association of two-year and four-year colleges and professional schools coordinates the response of these institutions to proposed federal laws and public policies.

Table 7–1
Institutions Participating in Investigation of Status of Black Colleges, 1976

INSTITUTION	LOCATION	PRESIDENT
Schools sending statistical data and narrative explanations		
Cheyney State College	Cheyney, Pa.	Wade Wilson
Florida A & M University	Tallahassee, Fla.	Benjamin L. Perry
Florida Memorial College	Miami, Fla.	Willie J. Wright
Federal City College	Washington, D.C.	Wendell Russell
Fort Valley State College	Fort Valley, Ga.	Cleveland Pettigrew
Huston-Tillotson College	Austin, Tex.	John T. King
Knoxville College	Knoxville, Tenn.	Robert H. Harvey
LeMoyne-Owen College	Memphis, Tenn.	Walter L. Walker
Morgan State University	Baltimore, Md.	Andrew Billingsley
North Carolina A & T State University	Greensboro, N.C.	Lewis C. Dowdy
Paine College	Augusta, Ga.	Julius Scott
Paul Quinn College	Waco, Tex.	Stanley E. Rutland
Prairie View A & M University	Prairie View, Tex.	Alvin I. Thomas
Rust College	Holly Springs, Miss.	W. A. McMillan
Saint Augustine's College	Raleigh, N.C.	Prezell R. Robinson
Schools sending narrative explanations		
Bennett College	Greensboro, N.C.	Isaac H. Miller
Delaware State College	Dover, Del.	Luna L. Mishoe
Elizabeth City State University	Elizabeth City, N.C.	Marion D. Thorpe
Tuskegee Institute	Tuskegee, Ala.	Luther H. Foster
Morehouse College	Atlanta, Ga.	Hugh M. Gloster
Spelman College	Atlanta, Ga.	Albert E. Manley

budget is $4.1 million. None has a total budget, or even an instructional budget, of less than $500,000.

The black colleges and universities in our study are multimillion-dollar educational enterprises and the major sources of employment in their communities. Their full-time employees range in number from 100 to 2,000; the median is 213. Many of these multimillion-dollar organizations are presided over by presidents of humble origin. They

Table 7-2
Data on Students, Faculty, and Finances for Fifteen Black Colleges, 1976

INSTITUTION	STUDENT BODY			BUDGET		FACULTY			TUITION AND FEES
	BLACKS	NONBLACKS	TOTAL	TOTAL	INSTRUCTIONAL	FULL-TIME	WITH DOCTORATE	FULL-TIME EMPLOYEES	
Cheyney State College[a]	2,185 (81)[d]	515 (19)	2,700	$13,000,000	$ 8,000,000 (62)	188	68 (36)	401	$ 750
Florida A & M University[a]	4,934 (92)	470 (8)	5,404	13,763,292	5,715,864 (42)	399	155 (38)	2,092	476
Florida Memorial College[b]	600 (100)	0 (0)	600	3,000,000	508,312 (17)	52	12 (23)	114	1,200
Federal City College[a]	7,552 (92)	650 (8)	8,202	23,800,000	12,400,000 (52)	387	125 (32)	1,100	N.D.
Fort Valley State College[a]	1,800 (90)	200 (10)	2,000	7,000,000	4,000,000 (57)	152	65 (43)	395	460
Huston-Tillotson College[b]	584 (85)	104 (15)	688	3,157,303	2,646,403 (84)	46	17 (37)	141	N.D.
Knoxville College[b]	1,029 (98)	16 (2)	1,045	N.D.[c]	N.D.	57	23 (40)	182	930
Lemoyne-Owen College[b]	1,100 (99.3)	8 (0.7)	1,108	2,514,000	1,260,000 (50)	58	25 (43)	155	975
Morgan State University[a]	5,532 (87)	829 (13)	6,361	16,710,000	5,889,676 (35)	281	100 (36)	753	200
North Carolina A & T University[a]	4,970 (91)	475 (9)	5,345	11,842,000	6,123,979 (52)	307	134 (43)	1,009	798
Paine College[b]	767 (99.3)	6 (0.7)	773	3,978,942	1,089,628 (28)	51	19 (37)	120	1,250

Table 7-2 (cont)

INSTITUTION	STUDENT BODY			BUDGET		FACULTY			TUITION AND FEES
	BLACKS	NONBLACKS	TOTAL	TOTAL	INSTRUCTIONAL	FULL-TIME	WITH DOCTORATE	FULL-TIME EMPLOYEES	
Paul Quinn College[b]	520 (99.6)	2 (0.4)	522	1,849,506	627,138 (33)	37	0 (0)	95	N.D.
Prairie View A & M University[a]	4,749 (85)	845 (15)	5,594	28,641,272	5,505,329 (19)	250	94 (37)	500	N.D.
Rust College[b]	800 (100)	0 (0)	800	4,144,029	1,570,533 (38)	41	21 (51)	130	2,725
Saint Augustine's College[b]	1,529 (100)	0 (0)	1,529	5,933,463	1,068,046 (18)	78	34 (45)	213	1,150

[a] Public   [b] Private
[c] No data; information not received.
[d] Figures in parentheses represent percentages.

were born in such places as Eatonville, Florida; Middlesex County, Virginia; Telfair County, Georgia; Lumberton, Mississippi; Marion, Alabama; Eastover, South Carolina; Marsh Branch, North Carolina. Some could not have conceived of a million dollars in the days of their youth. Now they are overseeing sums of this magnitude, and their stewardship has been excellent, as the facts show.

How could the black colleges and universities change so rapidly in a decade if they were indeed "academic disaster areas" when Jencks and Riesman wrote about them in 1967 (Jencks and Riesman 1967, p. 26)? Very simply, that assessment was off the mark then and now. Black colleges and universities, quite to the contrary, are a vital national resource. They have pioneered in providing higher education for young people outside the mainstream of American life and have developed unique and extraordinary methods of instruction for students with special needs.

Unique Functions of Black Colleges

We asked the black-college presidents to tell us what their institutions do that is unique. These are some of the responses:

Bennett College, Greensboro, North Carolina
Bennett College provides career-oriented education in a liberal arts context, primarily for black and other minority women . . . from a broad range of secondary school preparation and economic background.

Delaware State College, Dover, Delaware
This college can and does succeed in reopening the doors which have been closed to so many students whose potentials have been judged by instruments developed for the majority culture

Elizabeth City State University, Elizabeth City, North Carolina
We pride ourselves in the Basic Education and Enrichment Program (BEEP) . . . which . . . gives supportive service to those students whose academic backgrounds reflect low levels of achievement . . . and which . . . provides an environment where any student can receive additional assistance in his respective field.

Florida Agricultural and Mechanical University, Tallahassee, Florida
We . . . emphasize the academic programs offered in our School of Pharmacy and School of Architecture . . . not found in many of our predominantly Black institutions.

Fort Valley State College, Fort Valley, Georgia
We have "catch-up" academic programs for underprepared freshmen.

Huston-Tillotson College, Austin, Texas
We take the time necessary and provide the faculty required to reach students where they are when they come to College and help to prepare them for successful productive participation in an expanding American society.

Knoxville College, Knoxville, Tennessee
Knoxville College takes significant numbers of students who have deficiencies and assists them in graduating, with competitive competencies.

LeMoyne-Owen College, Memphis, Tennessee
We enroll students who are not typically thought of as college material and convert them in four years into people who can compete for jobs or in graduate or professional schools.

Federal City College, Washington, D. C.*
FCC enrolls a large number of full-time and part-time students who have been out of the mainstream of formal education for 10 years or more; . . . many of our students are the first generation in their family to attend college.

Morgan State University, Baltimore, Maryland
Morgan has been geared for many years to develop, and improve, programs for instructing in the basic skills in mathematics, reading, writing, and speech.

North Carolina Agricultural and Technical State University, Greensboro, North Carolina
North Carolina A and T State University provides an important opportunity for higher education for blacks and other minorities who otherwise would be denied such an opportunity. The black college or university president or chancellor, professor, department chairman, etc., are needed models of success that are achievable in the eyes of black youth.

Paine College, Augusta, Georgia
Paine College . . . is small enough to identify students to give them the kinds of inspiration and goading they need to maximize their potential. For a decade, Black institutions have taken students who might not be admitted to

*Since the study was conducted this school has been renamed. It is now the University of the District of Columbia.

other institutions, and in four or five years have produced individuals who go on to graduate school and who make significant contributions to society.

Paul Quinn College, Waco, Texas
There are few traditionally minority schools offering special curricula in the areas of undergraduate social work, medical technology, and recreational leadership. Paul Quinn College offers all three of these.

Rust College, Holly Springs, Mississippi
I consider these programs unique at Rust College: The Freshman Inter-disciplinary program which develops self-concept, motivation and rapid achievement among students whose backgrounds are less than favorable; The Summer Study Skills program which provided four weeks of intensive training for all new students prior to enrollment at Rust.

St. Augustine's College, Raleigh, North Carolina
Some of the unique things that we do here at Saint Augustine's College are: The Talent Search Program and the Cooperative Education Program. The primary purpose of [the talent-search] program is to identify, counsel, and assist talented youth, who might have been overlooked by traditional means, to pursue post-secondary courses of study. The cooperative education program provides an opportunity for the students to actually get "on the job" experience.

Tuskegee Institute, Tuskegee Institute, Alabama
Tuskegee is sensitive to the needs of the students we serve in the classroom and of the community we touch in many ways.

University of Arkansas at Pine Bluff, Pine Bluff, Arkansas
The school has always used its resources to get an education for every student that could be reasonably brought within its fold. This included the underachiever, the penniless, and those who, based on standardized conceptions, could never make it.

In summary, these presidents of black colleges believe the unique aspects of their programs to be (1) the career orientation of the curriculum; (2) admission of students at whatever level of preparedness they find them; (3) individualized attention, tailored to meet the academic needs of each student; (4) outreach programs and concern for the local community.

Priorities for Black Colleges

Despite their unique educational programs, the contributions of black colleges and universities to our national life have yet to be fully

Table 7-3
Priorities of Fifteen Presidents of Black Colleges, 1976

PRIORITIES	NUMBER OF PRESIDENTS	% OF TOTAL PRIORITIES
Educational	41	50
Financial	28	33
Physical plant (4)		
Operating funds (24)		
Management	12	17
Totals	81	100%

recognized. The belief that black colleges should be abolished, expressed covertly at the beginning of the decade, is now being openly advocated. This threat has influenced the priorities of black college presidents. Survival is the order of the day.

Although committed to educating any and all who are willing to work diligently for a college education, presidents of black colleges now must give as much attention to refurbishing or expanding the physical plant and to finding funds for student aid, faculty salaries, library, and teaching materials as to other educational matters. In our study, the median annual tuition is $1,175 for the private black college and $476 for the public black college. Since the annual income of blacks continues to be one-fourth to one-half that of whites, increased tuition is not the most promising source of new revenue. The black college presidents recognize this fact. They indicated, as Table 7-3 shows, that the fulfillment of approximately 35 percent to 40 percent of their priorities depend on resources external to their institutions.

The presidents participating in the study listed eighty-one priorities for the future development of their schools, as seen in Table 7-3. Some indicated as few as two priorities; others cited as many as eight. The average was four. About half of the priorities dealt with educational matters such as curriculum reform, faculty development, improving the system for advising students, innovations in career education including the design of new graduate programs, and undergraduate concentrations in the professions.

About one-third of the priorities had to do with finances, including capital improvements in the physical plant and increased funds for student aid, faculty salaries, support staff, research, library acquisitions, and other academic materials. It should be noted that refurbishing or adding to the physical plant was not mentioned frequently as a priority. Most of the financial priorities had to do with student aid, faculty salaries, and basic operating support.

Management Priorities

In recent years, foundations and other agencies have been interested in helping black colleges and universities improve their management skills. As a consequence, workshops and institutes for business managers and other key officers have been held with their support. This is an example of assistance that meets the priority needs of the giver rather than those of the receiver, however. Improvement in management procedures was scarely a top priority for the presidents in our survey; it was listed about one-sixth as frequently as other concerns. Among the management concerns of the presidents were recruitment of students, public relations, long-range planning, establishment of an efficient decision-making process, improving the registration and record-keeping system, and developing a uniform pay scale for full-time employees. Of them all, the recruitment of students was the most pressing matter.

Recruitment of Students

The competition experienced by black colleges from predominantly white schools for the enrollment of black students is severe. In his response to our survey, President Hugh Gloster of Morehouse College stated that the private black colleges are handicapped in the competition because they have received no support to launch a similar campaign to attract white students. He said:

> In the South while students attend predominantly black colleges in significant numbers only if there are no predominantly white colleges in the community or if the predominantly black colleges are public institutions with low tuition rates, we try to recruit white students but are unsuccessful. In a country where foundations and corporations have provided millions of dollar to predominantly white colleges to recruit black students, we have sought funds to recruit white students but have been unsuccessful. As a matter of fact, I know of no predominantly black college that has received a large grant providing scholarship money to attract white students.

Educational Priorities

The characteristic that has probably contributed most to the survival of black institutions of higher education is their flexibility. They tend to change in accordance with what the situation requires. The historic controversy between W. E. B. DuBois and Booker T. Washington as to whether black colleges should provide a liberal arts education or vocational training has been resolved and synthesized. In the words of one administrator participating in the study, "Bennett College provides career-oriented education in a liberal arts context." Bennett College is a women's college in North Carolina. Its student body is predominantly black.

The vision of this president points the way for all institutions of higher education in the United States. The flexibility of black colleges that has enabled them to combine the classical and the contemporary, the liberal arts and the vocational, illustrates what can be done and how it may be accomplished. There are lessons in this synthesis for all of higher education as indicated by the growing number of black and white students who are demanding vocationally oriented college courses. Rather than being backward, the black colleges, in this instance, have been in the vanguard. Indeed, the DuBois–Washington debate dealt with a major issue in higher education in America but was not recognized as such because of the race of the participating parties.

Characteristically, black colleges have responded to current national economic and labor pressures in a pragmatic fashion; many, for example, are placing increased emphasis on new career pathways. Some of the new career options being offered to black college students are undergraduate social work, medical technology, and recreational leadership. One president stated that his school has adopted a mandatory cooperative education program with a view toward using the world of work and its potential rewards to motivate and train students as well as provide earned income to lessen dependence on federal and state financial aid and to establish the college as a place where people of top-quality education are produced.

Among the educational priorities of presidents of black colleges are the initiation of cooperative education programs; changing the curriculum to include professional courses; the development of preprofessional programs in medicine and law; and the creation of endowed professorships.

Several of the predominantly black state universities are developing new graduate programs at the doctoral level that will enhance their capacity to meet the competition of the predominantly white public institutions. In his article, "Presidential Perceptions: Administrative Problems and Needs of Public Black Colleges," John Hill, a college administrator who has worked in predominantly black and predominantly white institutions, has said that "white land grant colleges offer diversified graduate curricula . . . (and) must have more funds in order to maintain their academic programs, to attract quality faculty members, and to compensate persons who have research expertise" (1975, p. 50). Black public colleges have learned this, too, and are apparently following suit. The move to develop new graduate programs, therefore, is a pragmatic response to a racist environment, a way of justifying, in terms that the funding agencies can understand, their reason for being.

In days gone by, black public colleges were deliberately created to be different from other schools. They were assigned the mission of undergraduate education, usually teacher training. Now they are penalized financially for not being like other state supported schools—graduate research centers. This accounts for the haste with which black public universities are developing graduate programs at the doctoral level. Otherwise, they are denied certain federal funds.

Racial Composition of the Student Body

In the light of the *Adams* v. *Richardson* decision of the Supreme Court in 1973, which requires unitary school systems for higher education, questions are frequently raised about the racial composition of the student body of black colleges and universities. In our study, we asked the college presidents:

How do you feel about racial integration in higher education? Do you have nonblack students in your student body? If so, what is the size of your student body, and how many nonblacks are on campus? Did they come on their own initiative, or did you recruit them?

The facts of the matter are these: Of the 15 schools for which we have data, 3 recorded no white enrollment, and 12 reported white enrollments varying from 2 to 845 students. The average number of white students attending these schools was 275, 9.6 percent of the combined student populations. Hugh Gloster, president of Morehouse College, pointed out in his response that white students tend to enroll in public institutions with low tuition. In our study, 7 of the 8 private institutions had a white student enrollment of fewer than 20. On the other hand, the state-supported schools had white students in their populations ranging from 200 to 845. The latter figure represents 15 percent of the total enrollment of Prairie View A & M University in Texas, the largest white enrollment of any of the southern schools participating in the study. The picture is quite different in some of the predominantly black colleges in the North, such as Delaware State, which has a 40 percent white enrollment.

The presidents of black colleges explain that although their schools may be segregated, they have never been segregating institutions. Most predominantly black schools indicate that their faculties are diversified and offer this fact to support the claim that they are open schools. The philosophy and policy of the predominantly black schools is to accept students of all backgrounds. One president emphasized, however, that "government actions to reverse the consequences of centuries of racial desegregation must not be used as an excuse to dismantle or change the ethnic orientation of the black public colleges of the country."

Black colleges are a classic illustration of being damned if you do and damned if you don't. For black colleges and universities, antinomies appear to be eternal. These schools have a philosophy of what they would like to do. But they also are pragmatic, ingenious, and hopeful. These are the sources of their salvation. Their presidents have risen to meet the occasion in the priorities they have identified and presented.

An Apology for Harvard

Presidents of black colleges have been gravely offended by negative characterizations of their institutions, expecially the one emanating from Harvard University. Stephen Wright, Benjamin Mays, Hugh Gloster, and Albert Dent gave spirited rejoinders to the Jencks–Riesman article (Wright et al. 1967, pp. 451–67), but, in general, the administrators of black institutions of higher education have suffered silently. First, the presidents of black colleges were offended that Harvard academic colleagues with outstanding reputations would write such an article. Second, they were disappointed that a prestigious scholarly journal like the *Harvard Educational Review* would consider the article to be as a contribution to knowledge and worthy of publication. Stephen Wright, former president of Fisk University, commenting on the Harvard connection of the professors who wrote the article and the periodical that published it, has charged that if it had not been "written by men of considerable reputation and published in a reputable journal, it would have . . . attracted little attention" (Wright et al. 1967, p. 452).

In correspondence with the presidents of black colleges during the course of our study, we gained insight into the depth of the distrust and hostility toward Harvard. One black college president said:

> I am writing in response to your letter . . . in which you refer to an earlier
> unanswered communication. Forgive my bad manners. I did not respond
> because I do not know the answers and am convinced that there are opin-
> ions [from other college presidents] which should not be watered down by
> any superficial comments from me.
>
> In addition, I am told that things which have come from your school in
> the past have been uncomplimentary to black scholars and black institut-
> ions. I am therefore afraid to be a part of your study. . . . Thanks for your
> understanding.

Another put it this way:

> This is in response to your letter . . . requesting certain detailed
> information about our institution and for nominations to participate in your
> Conference.
>
> I regret that we will be unable to provide you with any information or to
> participate in your Conference.
>
> Those of us who work in the historically black colleges feel that we have
> been studied enough, too often by persons who know least about these
> institutions and their contributions to American Higher Education and to
> the American Society. The reports and writings flowing from these studies
> have been too often hyper and unfairly critical of our institutions, showing
> little sensitivity and even less understanding.
>
> You have my very best wishes for meaningful and constructive endeavor.

Still another black college president refused to answer our inquiry
until he had been assured by one of his faculty members, a recent
graduate of the Harvard School of Education, that the principal
investigator was black. Having been abused once by Harvard
researchers, many black college presidents were reluctant to risk the
possibility of a second coming without extraordinary reassurances.

The irony is that in the spring of 1967, the same year in which a
Harvard-based publication announced to the world that black colleges were "academic disaster areas," Harvard University at its
Commencement awarded the honorary Doctor of Laws degree to
Benjamin Elijah Mays, the retiring president of Morehouse College, for
his outstanding accomplishments as head of a black college for nearly
three decades. 1967 was a banner year for Harvard in terms of the
contradictory signals it gave out about black education and the
education of blacks. A redeeming fact is that Harvard does not recoil
from being contradictory. For some, this would be a vice. For Harvard,
it may be a virtue.

It was in this tradition and spirit that the director of the Black College Conference at Harvard apologized on behalf of the institution at the opening session for the distorted characterization of black colleges published a decade before. No one has taken exception to that apology or disassociated himself or herself from it. The apology, therefore, stands as stated. It should also be noted that during the Black College Conference, David Riesman disavowed his earlier position, informing a reporter with the *Evening Bulletin* of Philadelphia that he had "rethought" it (Pressley 1976).

Judging Black Colleges

One thing we learned in our survey is that black college presidents will no longer suffer silently. Black colleges are not self-sufficient. They are as much dependent on others for their survival as any college or university in America. Despite their dependence (or maybe because of it), they have decided to fight back. Indeed our study reveals that the administrators of these institutions are in an aggressive mood.

This time around, they intend to participate in the assessment of their situation and in the definition of their future. They are insisting that black colleges should be judged in terms of the unique mission of these schools and not by some measuring device that uses Harvard and other Ivy League schools as ideals.

This time, the black college presidents are fighting back; this is what they answered to the questions, "What else ought the nation to know about black colleges?" One college president said:

> The nation should know that the . . . Black Colleges are and have been a critical national resource. They prepared the multi-culture in the nation. In the past 20 years, these colleges have produced a quarter of a million graduates and continue to turn out 30,000 graduates per year. Though more than 60 percent of black college youth are enrolled in white colleges, less than 40 percent of black college youth graduate from white colleges. Black colleges have the expertise and climate conducive to all youth. They have had an open door policy for all ethnic groups for more than a century and have administered specifically to black youth through these years. As a national asset, they need national support.

Another declared:

> The nation ought to know: that the "4 p's": the past, the present, the purpose, and the product of black colleges, provide a unique, essential and

priceless ingredient to American society that the nation can no longer do without nor afford to neglect or defer.

Still another put it this way:

> First of all, the nation must know that quality Black Colleges do exist on a level commensurate with (and in some areas higher than) comparable white institutions. It is incumbent upon Black Colleges to make themselves known by the quality of their leadership, the scholarship of their faculty.

Finally a black college president made this statement on what the nation should know about black colleges:

> The nation ought to know that all higher education institutions exist on a continuum ranging from excellent to terrible and that black and white institutions alike are arrayed all along it. There is only one Harvard; there are many good, fair, mediocre, and bad schools. They all try to serve the same purpose. Black colleges have as much right to persevere in this as others. The numberless mediocre and incompetent white colleges go on and on; if their existence is threatened, the threat has a purely economic basis—no one says they must close because they are inferior institutions. Black colleges that are no worse and possibly better, on the other hand, are threatened with closing because they are inferior. Clearly, this is more than slander; it is rank discrimination and blatant racism. We who support black higher education must fight it with all our power.

The National Association for Equal Opportunity in Higher Education offered the following information:

> During the past 10 years, some eighty-seven historically black colleges have graduated more black students with baccalaureate degrees than all of the other American higher education institutions combined. Therefore, educators need to look beyond the mere enrollment of blacks in white schools and, specifically, at the number of blacks who graduate.

The black college presidents who marshalled sufficient faith to risk participating in one more study by a Harvard professor did so, we believe, because they trusted that our purpose was to help set the record straight. Specifically, one president said, "This letter is written from the valley to the mountain in the forlorn hope that communicating our aspirations will do us some good. We can only hope."

We appreciate the assistance of all, are grateful for their faith, and hope that this study has not betrayed their trust. We have tried to make an accurate assessment of the situation—to be a reliable medium for the transmission of the message of black college presidents.

Chapter 8

Black Colleges of the North

Herman R. Branson

An old map of the United States will show the Mason–Dixon Line between Pennsylvania and Maryland, the former boundary between the North and South. Moving west along this line you will find the states with the first three black colleges of the United States— Pennsylvania, the location of Cheyney and Lincoln, and Ohio, where Wilberforce was founded.

Cheyney was formed in Philadelphia in 1830 as an elementary and high school; it went out of existence briefly in the 1920s. Cheyney thus claims to be the oldest black college in the country, since Wilberforce was not formed until 1856 and Lincoln until 1854. Wilberforce, however, justly claims to be the oldest predominantly black college organized by blacks. It split into two separate institutions in the 1940s; one became Central State University, and the other retained the name of Wilberforce and its church affiliation. As to Lincoln, it was started under the name of Ashmun Institute by a white Presbyterian and in 1866 became the first college in America to be named after President Abraham Lincoln. Years ago, Lincoln had a medical school, law school, and a school of theology. Approximately twenty years after it was founded, its law and medical schools closed as a result of an unstable economy.

Why did black colleges come into existence? Shortly after the Civil War there were roughly 4 million black people in the United States; about 400,000 were free; only about 28 had had a college education. There was an urgent need to educate the former slave population, so

149

that its members could participate in society. In the period between 1865 and 1900 a considerable number of predominantly black colleges were established—Tuskegee in 1881, among others. By 1900 the national census recorded 21,268 black teachers, 15,530 black clergymen, and 1,734 black physicians and surgeons—an astounding accomplishment in a period of thirty-five years.

Between 1900 and 1975, however, the achievement was not nearly as impressive. Of the 300,000 physicians in the United States, fewer than 2 percent are black, despite the fact that Howard and Meharry have been turning out black physicians for more than a hundred years. The same small proportion of blacks is found in law. In 1974, there were 41,409 engineering degrees awarded; only 756 were received by blacks. There should have been at least six times that number to equal the present population ratio.

Even more depressing statistics are those for people who hold doctorates. A study reported by the National Science Foundation shows that of the 207,500 people in America who earned doctorates in engineering and science in 1972, fewer than 1 percent were black; the number should have been nearly 12 percent, or about 30,000 people. In 1974, there were 3,362 doctorates awarded in engineering, and only 12 went to blacks.

Some commentators now hold that too many people are going to college. In similar vein, many years ago a distinguished gentleman from one of the Ivy League schools said that Harvard was ruining young people for our society. One can respond with the answer that blacks, too, want to be part of their society; if Princeton, Harvard, and Yale are ruining white youngsters, black youngsters should have the chance to be ruined also—if they are. That is, young blacks have the right to advanced training; the results can speak for themselves.

The Value of Northern Black Colleges

Let us characterize the four black public colleges in the North and then examine the societal needs that they meet. These four schools are Cheyney State, Lincoln, Central State, and Wilberforce. Collectively they enroll about 7,000 students; they are not large schools. Central State and Cheyney have about 2,500 students each; Lincoln and Wilberforce each enroll 1,200. The four schools have a total faculty of about 500, and their combined annual budget is probably between $30 and $50 million—the cost of a medium-priced airpl. ie. The campuses are valued at between $50 and $70 million. They have a combined alumni of perhaps 10,000.

There are those who contend that these schools should not be in existence. The only criterion for any institution's existence is whether or not it is making a unique contribution to society. The question is, then, what are these northern schools doing at the present time that is of special value?

Because of the availability of data for Pennsylvania, let us examine this state. Of the more than 400,000 students in higher education there, 28,000 are black. The number should be 10 percent of the total figure since that is roughly the proportion of blacks in the population. In higher education, Pennsylvania is running a deficit of 12,000 people as far as blacks are concerned.

Pennsylvania has a good system of higher education. Three categories of schools receive money from the state: fourteen teacher colleges, one black college (Cheyney), and four state-related schools have an average enrollment of 30,000. With reference to the state-related schools, one could say that there are three killer whales followed by a mackerel (Lincoln), but that the mackerel is snapping everything it can get hold of.

The state-related schools in Pennsylvania awarded 12,231 bachelor's degrees in 1975; of this total, 797 went to blacks, and 206 of these came from Lincoln. In other words, more than one-fourth of the blacks receiving bachelor's degrees in Pennsylvania's state-related universities earned them at Lincoln. They did not graduate from Penn State with its 100,000 students; they did not graduate from Temple with its 40,000 students; they did not graduate from Pittsburgh with its 30,000 students; they graduated from Lincoln. The state-owned schools (East Stroudsburg, Indiana University of Pennsylvania, Cheyney, and West Chester) awarded 14,204 bachelor's degrees, of which only 533 were to blacks. Of those, 350 were from Cheyney. If Cheyney and Lincoln did not exist, there would be far fewer blacks in that state with college degrees. This is the situation now.

I am afraid that the high level of concern for blacks is past. In the future one may expect even fewer blacks to graduate from the predominantly white institutions. It should be kept in mind that Cheyney and Lincoln are doing something for a segment of the American population that clearly would not be done were they not present. That is what is important. The total number of bachelor's and graduate degrees awarded in Pennsylvania was 68,837; only 2,816 of those were received by blacks. On the basis of the state population, there should have been 7,000. Pennsylvania has a very good state system of higher education; it includes Cheyney and Lincoln. Yet it is doing only about 50 percent of what it should.

Let us examine some specific fields. Agriculture and natural resources are a good example. It would be an excellent field of specialization for young people who want to help in the development of black Africa. Leaders in Africa express a need for economists, industrial management personnel, and senior research fellows familiar with computer systems. They need competent and skilled people in the fields of agriculture and natural resources, people knowledgeable in agricultural economics, people who could assist in controlling worms that are destroying the crops.

In 1975 in Pennsylvania only 562 people took degrees in agriculture. Of those, only one was black, amazing evidence of neglect and inattention: one black in the entire state of Pennsylvania was learning something about agricultural and natural resources. It does not make sense to talk about a healthy society if 10 percent of its people are not involved in basic training for the management of natural resources. Looking at the biological sciences, 3,477 degrees were awarded; 347 should have been awarded to blacks, but were not. Of the 3,211 engineering degrees, 57 went to blacks; there should have been 320. Of the 1,614 degrees in mathematics, 41 went to blacks; there should have been 161. Of the 3,105 degrees in psychology, 118 went to blacks.

When a survey of higher education was conducted in Pennsylvania recently only one showed overrepresentation by blacks, a category entitled "undecided." Of all white college students 19 percent are undecided with reference to their major subject; 38 percent of blacks in higher education have undeclared majors. They may be in college, but they do not know why they are there.

What Needs To Be Done

The education of black youth has been judiciously and effectively lobbied for, but little has been actually achieved. To comprehend why, one must view society as a whole and then scrutinize its effect on individuals. Two agencies that really focus on the young are the family and the school. To facilitate discussion, let us use a simplistic model. The young people who concern us have not had the type of family experience in this society that would give them the p.oper background for success. Their school experience is tragic. In spite of the efforts of many good and dedicated people, the public school system in America seems to have abandoned hope of educating young blacks. A slow, persistent erosion of concern for the intellectual development of black youth has taken place. When New York City made a survey of the blacks already in higher education who had gone through the secondary system of that city, 72 percent were reading or performing in mathematics at or below eighth-grade level.

A predominantly black college must transcend its locality and look at the youth of America to decide how best to help them. To accomplish what needs to be done will require sophistication and the expression of outrage. Let us define outrage. Blacks are seldom taken seriously. Blacks who are sensitive to the cause of education in America are needed in order to change this damaging situation, but they are not available. There should be black intellectuals in predominantly black colleges or other institutions working on the problems of blacks and doing something about them—in the humanities, the arts, and especially in the sciences. For one thing, people who understand genetics and can respond to scientifically disguised racism are needed to protect the black population.

The predominantly black college in the North will certainly not die. More predominantly black colleges will be coming into existence in Chicago, Detroit, New York, and elsewhere. There is a serious need for people of integrity, understanding, and goodwill to aid these institutions in doing what needs to be done.

On the faculty of Lincoln is a young man with a great enthusiasm for engineering. As a result of his efforts, in two years a genuine rebirth of the engineering program has occurred; it cooperates with Drexel, Lafayette, and Penn State. The forty-two blacks enrolled in engineering at Lincoln would never have known about engineering if that young teacher had not transmitted his enthusiasm to black youngsters in Philadelphia and Wilmington. He holds meetings at Lincoln to motivate minority students toward careers in engineering and science and conducts one-day workshops for high school counselors.

Much is being done, but many more persons and programs of this type are needed. The black college in the North should be strengthened and given increased opportunities to aid young people. Perhaps no other institutions in America are as socially significant as the black colleges in the North because they are doing a job that no other institutions perform or would be able to perform.

If America is genuinely sincere about the elimination of racism, there will come a time when every institution in America will be just an institution, neither black nor white. The predominantly black college should move toward being an American institution irrespective of race. Indeed, we are far from racially distinctive institutions, now. That fact along with the figures which have been given, show a great need for much basic work to be undertaken in the immediate future.

Chapter 9

Effective Management of Scarce Resources: Presidential Responsibility

Prezell R. Robinson

Thinking about effective college management brings two different images to mind. The first is a factory turning out specific products. One sees long assembly lines of busy and tired employees, both men and women, while in the front office managers pore over charts, systems, and procedures and worry about making the largest return on investment possible. The second image that effective management evokes is that of money, people, and materials as scarce and diminishing resources, although not necessarily in that order.

Good people and talented people are in short supply, and those of us who have them in our institutions should nurture and support them. Obviously, I refer here to men and women who can become or who are committed to the institution, people for whom Old Hilltop College is not just another job but a career opportunity. The problem of people raises interesting and important questions that we often neglect. For example,

How much effort is put into developing people in the positions that they now hold?

How deep is their knowledge and understanding of the college's goals and objectives?

How well do administrative officials know and understand the mission of the college?

To what extent have they differing objectives for the Office of Financial Affairs, the Office of Academic Affairs, or the Officer of Development and Public Relations?

Does each administrative officer know about the other?

While these may not appear to be difficult questions, it could take many months to reach an agreement on the answers.

About the matter of money, let us acknowledge that there simply will never be enough of it to meet the need for human services. To some degree we are all conditioned to this kind of scarcity. With regard to materials, it may be said that good, workable, reliable equipment and materials are vital for the attainment of a college's goals. What does it take to help the college perform its job? This is the question that we should ask. Clearly none of the three components—money, people, or materials—will ipso facto lead to the effective management of scarce resources.

Let me ask another question that concerns what might be called the business side of the college. Is there a kinship between operating a college and operating a business corporation? For some, merely to suggest the possibility is to commit heresy. Many commentators in the recent past have urged academics to recognize that our institutions, like our students, have distinct needs. They argue that some of the needs are financial and that college finances should be regarded in the same way as the finances of a corporation.

Upon closer examination, however, one discovers that colleges and universities are dissimilar from corporations in substantive ways. The collegial or shared responsibility, the nonquantitative nature of the product, the dependence upon voluntary group effort, the broad participation in decision making and tenure—all of these are distinctive to the academic enterprise. Furthermore, some college functions resist the efficiency demanded by business. Because there are many users, for example, how does one share costs for expensive laboratory equipment when so much depends upon making adequate equipment accessible to students? Thus there are differences between business and higher education. About all we can conclude here is that the welfare or well-being of the college requires that its resources be managed in such a manner that maximum effectiveness is achieved.

However, something more might be concluded. If we are to be persuaded by the many dire predictions about the state of the economy for the immediate future, our colleges for some time will remain in the dual grip of declining and shrinking resources. We are not, however, relieved of our responsibility for preserving the quality of postsecondary education through the bimodal approach of better management of resources and the allocation of funds to high-priority objectives.

How does one begin? Is there a formula for success? These are my suggestions:

1. Establish the mission and goals of the institution.
2. Develop strategies that will successfully guide the institution toward these stated goals.
3. Develop a strong commitment by faculty to the goals and strategies.
4. Design an organizational structure to implement the strategy, taking into account the primary leadership role of the academic vice-president.
5. Develop a strong committed cadre of trustees.

Management Priorities

Against the background of the above suggestions, the management priorities of the black college may be articulated. As an illustration, Saint Augustine's College top-management and middle-management personnel have participated in a series of workshops sponsored by the American Management Association in Hamilton Grove, New York. The workshops were participatory. Every member of the team was exposed to rigorous experiences related to tough-minded management, including process and action. As a result, some new practices were introduced, existing ones modified, and old practices abandoned. The management team consisted of the president of the college, the vice-president for academic affairs, vice-president for financial affairs, vice-president for administration, vice-president for development, director of planning, one faculty member, one student trustee, and the president of the Student Government Association. Before this experience, the team had been introduced to management workshops at the colleges and at professional seminars presented away from campus under the auspices of the Phelps–Stokes Fund, the United Negro College Fund, the Institute for Services to Educational Development. Consequently, the team members were ready for this new challenge in management.

Black colleges were born in a state of economic deprivation and grew into adulthood malnourished educationally. From their inception until now, they have lacked sufficient funds to support expanded admistrative services, curricular changes, and physical plant improvement.

Because of these conditions, a larger proportion of black students than white students require extensive academic and counseling services. Similarly many students come from homes where the gross income is less than $5,000 per year. Yet the black institutions with their meager resources have historically provided undergraduate education for the vast majority of blacks holding baccalaureate degrees in this country.

The tragedy of the inequity is that the American public, at large, seems to expect black colleges to produce more with less than any other segment of American higher education. The truth of the matter is that far from being "disaster areas" as two Harvard scholars have charged, black colleges have been the most productive institutions in America, given their resources, their personnel, and the general attitude of the public toward them. It seems, however, a paradox that these disaster areas have produced the overwhelming majority of black leadership in America today: about 85 percent of the black doctors, approximately 80 percent of black lawyers, more than 70 percent of black elected officials, and over 80 percent of the black military officers.

Some idea of the scarcity of funds available at the black colleges is evident in the fact that the gross combined endowments of the forty-one member colleges of the United Negro College Fund is about $100 million (United Negro College fund 1974). This is much less than the endowment of most of the white so-called prestigious institutions.

It is interesting to note that, as outlined in the proceedings of the fifty-third annual meeting of the North Carolina Association of Colleges and Universities in November 1973, the corporate sector in 1970 gave $390 million to predominantly black colleges. The federal government during the same year gave $4 billion to higher education and $120 million or 3.5 percent of the total to predominantly black institutions (Robinson 1973).

Somehow, many knowledgeable people in the field of higher education seem to have the impression that the black colleges can prepare graduates with less money and with fewer qualified faculty than other more favored institutions. To paraphrase Shakespeare in his *Macbeth*, This is a tale told by an idiot, full of sound and fury and signifying nothing. It is true that the black colleges have performed what are almost miracles, but they are not administered by magicians (Robinson 1973, p. 23).

Private colleges and universities appear, on the whole, to have made substantial progress in some instances during the late 1950s and 1960s. Around 1969, however, the educational tide seemed to have turned. A time of rough sailing set in. The resulting financial dilemmas have been documented fully by Cheit (1971, p. 72) and Jellema (1973, pp. 3-11). Following the first shock of widespread deficits in 1969 and 1970, the private colleges and universities tightened their belts. However, the new phase is a situation described by Cheit as one of "fragile stability." He is by no means optimistic about the long-range outlook.

The Management of Scarce Resources

Having engaged in some rather broad and sweeping generalities, I hesitate to get into the precarious situation of prescribing. However, the temptation is too great not to dispense some academic pills, though I quickly add that their toxic effect may be as bad as the disease itself.

As president of a black college, I wish to set forth four areas of concern that in my judgment are related to the management of scarce resources—the role and place of trustees, presidential responsibility, planning, and inter-institutional cooperation.

The fact has been established that black colleges were born educationally undernourished and that since their founding, they have lacked a sustaining financial diet. I am acutely aware that somehow we must manage more effectively the human, fiscal, and material resources that we consider valuable. Clearly we must establish some fairly sound means for initiating more effective management of scarce resources on our black college campuses.

An Effective Board of Trustees

At Saint Augustine's College, we have a truly enlightened and dedicated board of trustees, an aggressive and intelligent faculty, and an inspiring student body with a team approach to management, all of which have performed far above average. These positive factors have enabled us to operate for nine consecutive years with a balanced budget that has increased from approximately $1 million in 1966 to about $6 million ten years later.

Among the most important advantages a black college can possess is an active, enlightened, and influential board of trustees. I am suggesting, therefore, that our colleges need able board members who bring to bear one or more of the traditional three Ws—wisdom, wealth, and worth. Historically, the private black colleges and black colleges in general have suffered greatly at the hands of paternalistic boards;

oftentimes they have been saddled with people who had no genuine interest in the college beyond a personal satisfaction in holding power. Most often these people were lacking in affluence, worth, or wisdom, which they frequently compensated by holding tight reins on intellectual growth and many times becoming increasingly involved in the day-by-day operations of the college.

When I became acting president of Saint Augustine's College in 1966, I soon realized that one of the most challenging tasks confronting the institution was a renewal and revitalization of its board of trustees. Consequently top priority was given to the selection for membership on the board of interested individuals of varying backgrounds: bankers, corporation executives, lawyers, philanthropists, alumni, and women. Through institutional and personal contacts, we sought board members who would see their trusteeship as an opportunity to serve the college and to help elevate America by assisting an important and neglected segment of its population.

We were able to attract trustees with outstanding managerial skills—corporate executives, who were flexible enough to translate their expertise into college management—others, who were people of affluence; outstanding educators and scholars; alumni representatives, who were enthusiastic and interested in interpreting the college to sundry sectors, including our own graduates. It was the first time in the history of the college that this kind of effort had been made to build a broad base of trustee representation. In addition, we were able to establish a board rotation policy. Clearly, the complete restructuring of the board was a significant factor in helping the college to make a 180-degree turnaround.

It is my opinion that among the most important functions of a board of trustees at a black college are the following:

1. To select and sometimes dismiss the president
2. To establish the principal objectives and broad policies of the institution, consistent with its charter
3. To preserve and invest assets of the institution (Burgess 1958)
4. To work diligently to assist in providing funds for the institution
5. To bring a sincere and high degree of commitment as partners in the educational enterprise, rather than a degrading form of paternalism

The Importance of Planning

A good trustee board can make the difference between a strong, viable institution or a weak anemic one.

Alvin C. Enrich, the former president of the Academy for Educational Development, in an article entitled "Plan or Perish," has said, "The key to survival [of the small college] is good planning. This means a realistic look at where your institution is and the setting of personal goals that are to be managed" (Enrich 1970).

Planning is a must for the black college. In the words of Enrich, we "plan or perish." Some of our colleges are literally perishing because of poor planning or no planning. The rapidity of change makes planning essential. As Enrich says, "Planning is a tool for dealing with rapid change, a way of coping with the unexpected" (1970, p. 55). A plan provides a means for determining and measuring the validity of prior decisions; in the case of faulty decisions, a sound plan increases the chances for corrective measures before events run out of hand. A plan helps to put the college on course. This is especially true for the black colleges, which, because of their desperate financial plight are inclined to accept any and all funds from foundations, corporations, and donors regardless of the purpose the funds might serve. Far too many black colleges have been caught unwittingly in the bind of accepting funds only to find that their purpose bore no relationship to the plan, purpose, or mission of the college.

An adequate plan that includes the essential elements of management is delineated here:

1. Prepare a description of the college as it now exists. These facts often cover characteristics of the student population, faculty salaries, academic ranks, publications, the status of the physical plant environment, and the nature of the endowment. These facts should be readily available. The acid test, however, is the extent to which the information has been systematically collected, codified, and analyzed. Develop a plan that inevitably forces the institution to look and learn about itself. This can be tremendously helpful, provided that appropriate corrective measures are taken and that concealed strengths and weaknesses are revealed.
2. Prepare a clear statement of the goals and objectives of the institution in order to establish the scope of its functions. The aim, too, is to go beyond high-sounding platitudes and meaningless rhetoric and to arrive at a definitive set of goals. The statement of objectives should set forth as precisely as possible how the team of planners (administration, faculty, trustees, students, and alumni) envisions the institution five or ten years from now.
3. Project environmental assumptions.

4. Design an educational program with plans for implementation and evaluation within a time frame.
5. Work out a budget that will satisfy the financial requirements for implementing the plan.
6. Ensure provisions for an orderly accounting department that reflects the institution's objectives.

The Role of the President

Implicit through this chapter is the assumption of a considerable degree of involvement by the president; there are some fairly clear leadership responsibilities that must be exerted by the president in managing scarce resources. It seems to me that for an institution to achieve meaningful levels of vitality, the chief executive should be someone who has demonstrated the potential for leadership and integrity and has gained the confidence and respect of the board of trustees, the faculty and staff, the students, and, to a degree, the larger community. The president's administrative cabinet should comprise a cadre of competent persons. Any president who is willing to settle for mediocrity in his administrative personnel or faculty deserves what he will receive, mediocrity in performance.

At Saint Augustine's College all unit managers are involved in the budget-making process. All of them have to justify their recommended budgets which must be consistent with the objectives of their units and of the college. All are required to plan a yearly action plan that sets forth (1) continuing objectives; (2) specific objectives; (3) strategies for achieving objectives; and (4) performance standards. All unit managers know which functions they may carry out only with the concurrence of the president; which they may carry out on their own and inform the president after the act; and which they may execute without conferring with the president at all.

In our black colleges, the president must increasingly operate to achieve meaningful levels of vitality through shared authority and responsibility. No longer can a president afford the luxury of trying to operate a college from his hip pocket, if he ever could. To do so will likely bring disaster, both to himself and the institution. As I see it, the president must provide leadership, be an effective manager, be a good fund raiser, and understand the art of bringing the best out of the people on his team to enable them to grow professionally as human beings.

He must be willing and capable of making hard-nosed decisions, based upon the best evidence available to him at a given level. S. M. Nabrit, writing on "Reflections on the Future of the Black Colleges," alludes to this when he states:

> Most institutions are currently experiencing operating deficits or are siphoning off from their endowment in order to balance their budgets. Few are hard-nosed enough to curtail programs and make budgetary cuts in order to live with their income (Nabrit 1971, p. 661).

The president must keep his board advised regularly on the economic status of the institution. He should send out monthly financial statements to the board that establish grid marks representing progress attained over against progress projected in fiscal affairs.

The whole area of student tuition and fees must be monitored carefully even though students attending black colleges, as at other colleges, do not pay nearly what their education actually costs. It is imperative that black colleges observe very carefully the extent to which the costs of education continue to increase tuition and fees. If it fails to take heed of this, an institution might well find itself being priced out of the market because it has placed tuition charges beyond the reach of the overwhelming majority of black students.

In the present crucial period, institutions must be careful about accepting federal funds for initiating innovative programs without having a sustaining base to support the programs once the funds have been terminated. This is especially true during this period of uncertainty when there is an apparent lack of commitment to funding for black colleges on the national level. The Carnegie Commission on Higher Education has stated in this connection:

> They [black colleges] realize the gravity of the problems that face them as they enter into wider competition for students and faculty, and some of them are taking bold actions to meet these problems. American society must respond to their needs with greater commitment and' financial support. (Carnegie Commission 1973, p. 210)

The college president, working with his faculty, must be careful not to get boxed into a situation that calls for a magic formula of twelve or fifteen students to one full-time faculty member. Ruml and Morrison in their *Memo to A College Trustee* state that "a ratio of twenty students to an equivalent of each full-time faculty residence is assumed. Models using this ratio are consistent with good educational practice" (1959, p. 68). The position taken here is that there is per se no magic student-to-teacher ratio. Clearly, class sizes that are substantially beyond

reasonable limits become unmanageable and probably highly un-
productive, depending upon the nature of the class and the type of
teacher. What I am suggesting is that the presidents of black colleges
must take the leadership to provide a balanced student-to-teacher ratio,
one that is sufficiently large to reduce overall costs, but not of such size
as to erode the quality of instruction.

The president of the college must work through his unit managers at
all levels to achieve some of the following specific economy measures,
suggested by the Academy for Educational Development in *319 Ways
Colleges and Universities Are Meeting the Financial Pinch:*

1. Recruit new students more actively.
2. Admit more qualified transfer students.
3. Establish a system for eliminating the cost of utilities through
   unnecessary use.
4. Collect where possible full tuition, room, board, and fees at the
   beginning of the year to reduce billing costs and increase short-
   term investment income.
5. Require larger advance deposits of tuition for entering students.
6. Invest cash balances in short-term securities.
7. Invest cash over the weekend—into the market Friday afternoon,
   out of the market Monday morning.
8. Put new endowment gifts into high-yielding bonds instead of low-
   yielding bonds or the common fund.
9. Utilize where possible the entire plant on a year-round basis in
   order to bring in additional revenue.
10. Rent computer and duplicating facilities.
11. Merge small departments and assign administrators to some
    teaching duties.
12. Restructure the administrative organization toward the view of
    eliminating the number of vice-presidents.
13. Use secretarial or clerical pools instead of providing individual
    secretaries for each department and/or division head. (Academy
    for Educational Development 1974, pp. 15–16)

Cooperation with Other Colleges

Inter-institutional cooperation is a form of husbanding scarce
resources. Clearly, as has been stated, black colleges cannot be all
things to all people. It seems to me that the time has come for these

schools, wherever possible, to think increasingly in terms of entering into cooperative efforts with other institutions within and outside of their own local areas. Among the options that might be considered are the following:

1. "A cluster of small colleges may specialize, emphasizing quality rather than quantity" (Academy for Educational Development 1974, p. 16).
2. Small institutions might enter into cooperative relationships with engineering and technical institutes outside of the state, using the conventional 3–2 plan.
3. A cluster of small institutions might share computer time with a major university or a computer agency within the area. Saint Augustine's has a computer facility located in the Research Triangle—Raleigh, Durham, and Chapel Hill.
4. Small colleges can use the faculty of large neighboring public and private colleges. For example, Saint Augustine's and Shaw University have a cooperative engineering program with North Carolina State University as well as cooperative majors in other specialized high-cost fields.
5. Interlibrary loan systems may be developed between or among colleges in a given area.
6. "Faculty from a distance may serve as visiting teachers on campuses of small colleges such as Brown does at Tougaloo" (Academy for Educational Development 1974, p.16).
7. Professors from small colleges who are research oriented might use the research facilities available at a major university nearby. The faculty of Saint Augustine's College have access to certain research facilities at North Carolina State University.

We have tried to outline some measures that an institution might take through presidential leadership to manage scarce resources. As Nabrit has indicated

> If the Negro private colleges had received one-eighteenth of the 1.8 billion dollars in gifts and grants to higher education from private sources in 1969–70, they would have received 100 million dollars. They, in fact, received approximately 15 million dollars. There was no exception to the rule that where the Negro in America is concerned, it is assumed that he deserves less and receives less. (Nabrit 1971, p. 661)

In my judgment, if black colleges are to survive in the future, they must assign top priority to managing their limited resources; they must vigorously recruit able trustee leadership; they must institute effective and systematic management systems; they must try to secure in their chief administrative ocer—the president—the best qualified person available; if they are related to church bodies, such groups must see in them a valued opportunity to fulfill a prophetic mission. Where possible, black colleges should enter into cooperative relationships with other nearby institutions in an effort to reduce costs. Despite the obstacles confronting the predominantly black colleges today, there will be those that will continue as strong viable institutions, furnishing this nation with a source of leadership and intelligent well-trained manpower that otherwise would not exist. This goal will be attained when the American public awakens to the realization that the black colleges represent a unique national resource.

Chapter 10

The Board of Trustees and the Black College

Charles Merrill

As chairman of the Board of Trustees of Morehouse College for sixteen years, I learned a good deal about what are meant by the terms *board, trustee, chairman,* and *black college.*

Morehouse's previous chairman, an eighty-year-old banker, had wanted to pass the position on to some other representative of the Atlanta business community. Benjamin Mays, the president, and some northern liberals and black alumni on the board, however, wanted a chairman who above all *wasn't* an Atlanta businessman, whose main concern would be to guarantee the college's academic and social predictability. Dr. Mays and I had met a few years before. We rapidly came to like and respect each other. I had some money, was interested in academic matters (at that point I was involved in starting a school of my own in Boston), had a strong commitment to racial equality, and lived 1,000 miles distant. I wouldn't get in the way. In short, I was the machine candidate.

As the machine candidate, I did what Dr. Mays told me to during our annual meetings, a November one in New York, an April one in Atlanta when the dogwood was in bloom. With the opening and closing prayers, the lengthy president's report read from the same document we each held in front of ourselves, the columns of figures, the motions of consolation and commendation related to the lives of the different members, these meetings were largely ceremonial. The membership of the board included the presidents of Atlanta University and Spelman College, a handful of northern bankers and lawyers, a couple of Atlanta

167

businessmen, and half a dozen alumni, most of whom had been chosen
for a lifelong devotion to the college expressed by sustained giving out
of relatively modest incomes, who came to these board meetings much
in the way they would have attended a church service, dozing quietly
unless asked to second or approve one of our motions.

At forty years of age, I was the youngest member of the board; at fifty
that still seemed true. As a young man, I was impatient at the lack of
relevance of whatever we did to either the daily life of the college or to
the strains and changes of southern society. Dr. Mays was sensitive to
both, but he did not see any reason for involving the board in policy
setting or any real action. We gave what money we could afford to the
college, we shared in the corporate ceremonies, we ate tremendous
meals together. Most academic bodies, I feel, run on alcohol, but Dr.
Mays's and Morehouse's Baptist influence meant that, instead, we ate.
My main worry was how to remember my colleagues' names.

I was a chairman of pretty limited ability, but I made three contributions that a more experienced presiding officer might not have. I was
a teacher, even if at the high school level, and saw the world through a
teacher's eyes. I was interested in the courses taught, and I made a
number of good friendships among the faculty. I was also strongly
committed to the value of European education for American Negroes.
To leave the limitations of this country, to expose oneself to totally
different demands and experience in Paris or Vienna or Edinburgh,
experience that world be excitingly free and rich, also disturbing and
lonely, could force a young man or woman to totally reexamine who he
or she was as a black, as an American, as a human being. I financed ten
fellowships a year for students from Morehouse, Spelman, and Atlanta
University, mainly to Europe, the others to Africa. The contacts I made
through that involvement were a rich return for me. Finally, my very
frustration with the ceremonial procedures of the board made me offer
responses that otherwise wouldn't have arisen.

The Morehouse College of twenty years ago was very far away from
the college—any black college—we know today. The formality of it was
special. American society runs on calling the man you met fifteen
minutes ago by his first name, but I still said "Dr. Jones" to the man I
had known for twenty years. I never got used to addressing a sixteen-
year-old freshman as "Mr. Williams." Yet it was not simply a fact of
awarding titles to men (as in Austria, where I had worked as a Fulbright
exchange teacher) because you weren't awarding them much money.
Morehouse was important as an island within the old deep South where

every human being in it, from the dean of faculty to the youngest student and the assistant janitor, was treated with dignity.

Some academic fields were always covered by blacks—chemistry, biology, religion of course, French. But at least one-third of the faculty was always nonblack. For a time physics and math were likely to be staffed by Indians, whose educational system turned out more theoretical scientists than the economy of Bombay or Calcutta could employ. There were refugees from Nazi Germany and Chinese who could not get jobs elsewhere. There were northern whites in fields like sociology or psychology, who saw teaching at Morehouse as a way to fight the American system and who could be both stimulating and destructive as they worked out their personal problems in that role. Some faculty couples were of mixed marriages, accepted on that isolated campus as they would never have been elsewhere, not simply in the South. A few white southerners taught at the college out of a social or Christian conviction, at serious family cost. These were often remarkable individuals.

The students were hard for me to judge. Their style was certainly not mine—so many of them came to the college with few resources and dropped out when these were used up. Some were simply playboys. But a lot of the men I met had a tremendous determination to make an education for themselves, sometimes expressed as a glorious arrogance that no one else was really as good as a genuine Morehouse man.

Sometimes the process of financial control bordered on the grotesque in an institution proud of balancing its budget every year, but doing so on a shoestring. Money assigned for roof repairs might go for office equipment if that bill came in first. When money was obtained for the new typewriters, it might be lent instead to a desperate student who had to hand $300 to the registrar by sundown. The business manager, who kept all these wheels more or less turning and who more or less could find, if he had to, the right papers in the mess on his desk, was an infuriating sort of person. When he was eventually fired, it was hard to find out what the college actually did owe and what were its assets. Nevertheless, to some students who knew him, it was only by such slight of hand that an institution and a community always so short of cash could survive.

By 1960, the civil rights movement began to involve the college and the board of trustees. Morehouse students and some from Spelman went downtown, sat silently at the lunch counter of Rich's department store, were arrested and sent to jail. At one time eighty of our men were in jail, a source of pride to the college and to its president. Because we were a private board of trustees, no matter how sleepy we might be, we supported Dr. Mays in his support of those students, as a public institution (and probably a predominantly white private institution) would not have.

My favorite story out of that earlier liberal period of the Struggle was of a phone call to Dr. Mays from Atlanta's chief of police. "Dr. Mays," it began, "if any of your young ladies and gentlemen are ever going to involve themselves in some sort of demonstration where my police officers will be forced—relectantly—to arrest them, let me know in advance, will you? Most of our officers are real gentlemen, but some are roughnecks, I'm afraid, and I wouldn't want any of your students not treated correctly." This example of southern courtesy did not mean that the heart of the police chief had been touched by Jesus Christ. It meant, as Dr. Mays explained, that the black vote in Atlanta had by then become so important that it was crucial for that police chief to be known as a decent guy.

Even then Martin Luther King, Jr., was Morehouse's most famous graduate, and now, of course, he is the closest this country has to a saint. Nevertheless his relations to his college's board were ambiguous. "To elect King to the board would be a slap in the face of white Atlanta," warned the president of Atlanta University, and it took three years of argument before King could be voted in. He was usually too busy then to attend our long, trivia-choked meetings. At one meeting, the last, I think, before his death, he spoke against the college's acceptance of a Naval ROTC chapter offered by the Department of Defense. It was obviously important to have more black officers in the American armed forces. These ROTC stipends would have been mighty useful to a student body as hard up as ours. But, on the other hand, Morehouse had no business involving itself in the war machinery of a government doing what it was doing in Vietnam. We voted to reject the offer.

Following King's murder, the endless war (to which liberals gave only verbal opposition), and the development of the concepts of black power and black culture, the relationship of Morehouse to the freedom movement changed seriously, as did the relationship of the college administration to its students. The entire thrust of a Morehouse education had been to expose its students, no matter how poor or how poorly prepared, to the whole range of world culture—from Boyle's law to Keynesian economics—to which they had the right of entrance. Dr. Mays gave an almost religious value to the Ph.D., which more Morehouse graduates had earned than the graduates of any other black college in the country. The Ph.D. was the symbol of attainment and authority. We affluent white trustees could speak with pride, back in 1961, of *our* students jailed by *them* in the struggle to gain equal access into American society. *Them* were whites, but they weren't *Us*.

The new militants, however, stated that Boyle and Keynes were whites and that anything they said, as far as blacks were concerned, was simply bullshit. By the fall of 1968 the campus was under siege, not by its traditional white enemies but by these new black warriors. After twenty-six years, Dr. Mays had retired. He had been succeeded by Hugh Gloster, formerly dean of faculty at Hampton Institute, a man of Mays's moral and intellectual integrity, perhaps more pragmatic, with a more current vocabulary. All that year Dr. Gloster worked eighteen-hour days, keeping in touch with student complaints, real or rhetorical, able to respond to each new crisis: A white teacher had been escorted out of (shoved out of?) her classroom because she had made (?) a disparaging remark about a student's black culture; another was answering 2 A.M. phone calls that he'd better quit, Afrika was going to get him.

In our meeting of April 1969 Black Power collided with the board of trustees. The meeting started at 9. By 9:30, ten young blacks in blue-and-white striped robes, led by Brother Abdul (otherwise, Gerald McWhorter, an instructor in sociology at Spelman) carrying a chicken claw as a sign of authority, marched into the board room, and we were ordered to appropriate one million dollars to help establish a Martin Luther King, Jr., University of Black Culture and then to resign. The meeting went on for twenty-nine hours. Boards of trustees in 1969 and 1970 used to boast of how long they had been locked up.

I was chairman of the meeting for most of those twenty-nine hours. Inside the board room were the trustees (unfitted by experience or life style for this challenge), our blue-and-white striped captors, and the Morehouse student government, whom I had invited the day before to join us—a stroke of sheer good fortune. In the hallway outside were the cannon fodder of the takeover, mainly Spelman girls, who carried pressure cans of paint or hair spray in their belts—to attack our eyes, I learned later, in case we called the police. Outside the building was a large, varying number of Morehouse students, essentially loyal to the college and to Dr. Mays and Dr. Gloster, a tribute that many college presidents that year didn't receive.

Despite the threat of violence throughout that meeting, there were some funny details. Trustees are likely to be elderly, and elderly men worry about whether they can get to the toilet. When a New York banker asked to be excused, our captors' "No!" was clearly one more weapon to force our surrender. I suggested we turn a couch on its end in one of the corners, with a doorway to be arranged out of raincoats and, lo, a workable privy. This problem was settled, though the regular bathroom ran out of paper, and I would always advise a college trustee to carry his own supply of toilet paper, toothpaste, soap, dried raisins, and clean socks.

We were locked up, we were afraid of Brother Abdul, a Robespierre excited by images of virtue and terror; we were afraid of the brutality of his henchmen and of the potential hysteria of the students in the corridor. Years later, I feel that our correct position would have been to refuse to negotiate at all, since Brother Abdul represented no body of legitimate concern to Morehouse trustees. Most of his troops came from other colleges of the Atlanta University Center. Moreover our imprisonment denied us any role as legally free agents. Yet we were arguing for the allegiance of the student council members, who were present and judging both sides and would speak to, as well as for, the students outside. Also we were arguing for our own concept of our role as trustees and our own concepts of education and American democracy. Behind the rhetoric of our captors there were some young men and women who for the first time in their lives had forced authority—rich, white authority, usually walled off and distant—to speak directly to them.

Who actually gave the orders at Morehouse? For what purposes? What was the authority of the board of trustees? Whom were we accountable to? We were being asked the questions that were to be repeated to one college board after another and to which few trustees seemed able to give clear and convincing replies. As Brother Abdul interpreted Frantz Fanon, the French-educated black psychiatrist who was the messiah of that time, were not we and Morehouse itself simply representatives of the Colonial Office of the power center in Wall Street, keeping the natives in line? It *was* true that the authority of the college's administration was all too often distant and unresponsive to the needs of black students in an oppressive, unjust society far more brutal—in Vietnam and at home—than the rhetoric of the angriest black militant. My policy, following the image of Kerensky leading and containing his own revolution, was to press for increased student, faculty, and community representation on the board to make it blacker and younger. Furthermore it was necessary to maintain some sort of discipline among my own colleagues, with one faction rigid as Roman senators awaiting the barbarians and another willing to make just about any concession so as to get on a plane for Chicago and order a couple of double martinis.

Fantasy is dangerous, and a fantasy of our captors seemed to be to parlay control of Morehouse's Board of Trustees to those of every other college in the Atlanta Center and under Brother Abdul to convert the combined endowments—maybe $20 million or more—to leadership of the Black Revolution in amerikkka. Or, more tangibly, probably they hoped to provoke us into calling the police and, in the ensuing bloodshed, as the cops fought their way through one locked door after another, tear the college apart and put Brother Abdul on the front page of every newspaper in the country.

How did the confrontation end? Who "won"? It's hard to say. The police were never called. Both sides got tired and finally made some agreement over what seemed the purely symbolic issue of the composition of the board. The added faculty representatives in practice proved to be quite useful. The student representatives, who were supposed to speak for revolutionary change, in later years became preoccupied by questions like parking space for student cars and the right to entertain Spelman girls in their bedrooms. The temper of the times changed, and President Gloster had the tenacity to handle the changes as they came.

The college received some very large grants from the Ford Foundation and from the federal government. Particularly from Ford came increasing pressure for a more organic integration with the other colleges of the Atlanta Center. This seemed like a sensible effort to create a single, federally structured, black educational institution in the South and in the nation instead of six separate fragile ones. It could also mean the suppression of each one of these strongly individual schools into some abstract superbody. In addition, Morehouse set up a two-year premedical program that would help train more black doctors for service in the South.

I resigned from chairmanship of the Morehouse Board in 1973. The college and the budget and the structural changes had become larger than I could deal with. I seemed to have lost touch with the part of the college, the faculty and the students, that was most important to me. By then I felt that I lacked new ideas and no longer cared to run for planes in the Atlanta airport. There was a need for a chairman who could organize the new capital funds campaign, which I couldn't. It was also time for the chairman to be a black man rather than a white.

What are the problems facing the new chairman and his colleagues? First of all, financial strength and survival. The black birthrate did not turn down in 1956 as the white birthrate did, and black colleges are not hurt as much by the demographic slump that is eroding the number of applicants for white colleges. Nevertheless, blacks have been harder hit in this depression than whites, and a lot of black autoworkers in Detroit and black businessmen in Chicago or Atlanta are no longer able to pay tuition for their sons at Morehouse. Grants from foundations and the government are harder to land now, but the administration at Morehouse has the skill still to obtain these funds when other places can't.

Nevertheless, I feel that obtaining money, no matter how crucial it is, has to be a number two priority for both the board and the president. The number one priority is still the intellectual and moral quality of the college: training young men to succeed, to become doctors and lawyers and vice-presidents and still be able to think of someone beside themselves; educating them to speak for the uneducated and unneeded at the bottom of society who have less and less relevance to America. If you are a trustee, what is your personal concept of the good society and the good human being? How does your service on a board of trustees express that? We have to raise money to keep our colleges and schools alive, but, when we do, what do the colleges actually stand for? Why does it make any importance? That's really the main question.

Part III

Teaching and Learning

Overview

Chester M. Hedgepeth, Jr.,
Ronald R. Edmonds,
Ann Craig

Black colleges have traditionally accepted students regardless of their socioeconomic status and their varying high school records, Daniel Thompson informs us. These institutions originated open admissions in the belief that every black youth should have the opportunity to develop his or her talents for service in the community and in the nation. Given the history of denial of access to learning, the early black schools had the difficult responsibility of transforming illiterate former slaves into proud and productive citizens. Then as now, because of the generally low socioeconomic background of black college students and their history of limited exposure to higher education, the faculties of black colleges have dedicated themselves to a highly personalized approach to teaching.

Black colleges, with relatively small student bodies, therefore, tend to be institutions oriented toward teaching, where student-teacher interaction is more common than at larger institutions. In his discussion of faculty and students at black colleges, Thompson indicates that black students regard higher education as an effective economic tool. The successful teacher, he points out, is the one who manages to make a liberal education both personally enriching and economically useful.

The black college teacher is likely to be viewed as a symbol of success and upward mobility by students and citizens in the community. In a much more substantive way, however, the black college teacher possesses the remarkable ability to transform "high-risk" students into community and national leaders. The pedagogic methodologies

177

implicit in such a transformation exist not only in the counseling aspect of the instructional program or in support services but also in the curriculum. Black faculty members have combined traditional and innovative approaches to learning. In the social sciences, Charles U. Smith states that biased and distorted accounts of the attitudes and behavior of blacks disseminated in the media are employed in the classroom for analysis of conscious and unconscious racism. One of the by-products of the student protests that began with black college students in the South has been the heightened interest generally in the social sciences and in particular the image of blacks and black colleges as presented by the media.

Smith states that among "the most persistent and pervasive thrusts of teaching and learning of the social sciences in the predominantly black institution of higher education has been, and is, the utilization of sound scholarship in support of ameliorative strategies for the problems of human welfare—especially those of blacks." The aim of social science teaching as he describes it is to elevate social consciousness and develop its corollary, social action. Insofar as the social science curriculum generally focuses on the importance of increased social awareness and social activism, it is in keeping with the historical mission of black colleges.

Teaching and learning in the humanities have changed considerably in the last ten years, according to Thelma Roundtree. Survey courses in the literature of western European countries have been replaced by interdisciplinary courses that interrelate music, art, literature, philosophy, and history under common themes. Perhaps the major change in courses in the humanities in black colleges has been the inclusion of black and Third World art, literature, and music. The black orientation and the innovative interdisciplinary approach have required retraining many black faculty in the humanities.

The teaching of the humanities is especially important at black colleges because values are derived from the literature that is taught. The spiritual and folk literature of the black American past contain vital historical and ideological content necessary for a full appreciation of the black heritage.

Closely allied to teaching and learning in the humanities is the approach to teaching English language to freshmen in black colleges. John Munro's very basic course in writing is duplicated at a number of other olack colleges across the South. A significant pedagogical consideration is to approach the teaching of writing at the level of student readiness. This usually means beginning a course by expanding vocabulary skills and moving from definition of a word to its use in a sentence. Hence the instructor begins with the most fundamental unit of the English language and progresses to the efficacious use of data to build conclusions in paragraphs. The aim of the course is to write a coherent essay. Munro says, "My own major premise is that it is important and possible for almost all high school graduates . . . to learn to think straight, to deal with reasonably complicated information, and to write out their thoughts in clear, comprehensible standard English phrase." Munro is quick to point out that ideas for student writing derive from the student and not from prescribed textbook readings. Students are enrolled concurrently in courses in black literature and often use ideas from the black experience as themes in their discussions.

What Munro says of students at Miles College is applicable to students at most predominantly black colleges: "The truth is—and all of us on the open-door campuses know this from experience—that a serious percentage of our 'invisible' students are well above average in intellectual ability, either ready right now for the university program or ready after a term or less of preparatory help."

The use of events from daily experience as an important teaching tool mentioned by Smith and Munro is endorsed also by Shirley McBay. Her experience is that students find mathematics less awesome when the student must utilize calculating skills to solve problems of familiar events. Spelman, a women's college, has demonstrated by increased enrollment in mathematics and science courses that special attention to teaching technique in mathematics pays off in increased interest on the part of students.

Chapter 11

Black College Faculty and Students: The Nature of Their Interaction

Daniel C. Thompson

About a century ago James A. Garfield, the twentieth President of the United States, is reported to have said, "The ideal college is Mark Hopkins on one end of a log and a student on the other" (Rudolph 1953, Preface).

It may be persuasively argued that Garfield's definition was little more than a romantic oversimplification of the organization and process of higher education, even at that particular time in history; and that the college of today is far more complex structurally and the academic or teaching-learning process a great deal more involved than it was one hundred years ago. It may be pointed out, for instance, that each of the 2,500 or so colleges in the United States is a very complex entity in its own right, each differing in some important ways from all of the others (see, for instance, Schwebel 1972).

Colleges differ significantly from each other structurally, programmatically, and in regard to sources of control; they also differ markedly insofar as the number, nature, and influence of the public to which they are expected to relate. Fundamentally all well-established colleges must respond to different powerful social pressures exerted on them by individuals, groups, agencies, institutions, and, ultimately, government. These outside forces do, in fact, modify the nature and effectiveness of the teaching-learning process. The black political scientist Tobe Johnson insists that black colleges, more than others, are influenced by such constraints, that they are extremely vulnerable because "for the most part [they are] financed by white philanthropists, controlled by white boards of trustees, initially administered by white presidents, and largely staffed by white faculty" (Tobe Johnson 1971, p. 808).

Nevertheless, despite the complexities characteristic of individual colleges and the almost infinite number of differences that surface when attempts are made to rank, rate, or compare them, when higher education is reduced to its lowest common denominator, Garfield was probably correct in defining the ideal college as essentially the teacher interacting with the student. This may be about the only functional conception of the college that makes universal sense when we attempt to compare the ultimate college products, the *raison d'être* of all colleges—the graduates—with one another.

The Success of Black-College Graduates

In this connection it is important to be reminded that college graduates constitute a distinct social category in the larger society. The fact of having graduated from college, almost any college, sets individuals apart, and society bestows upon them a significant number of rights, privileges, and honors ordinarily withheld from the noncollege population.

Certainly this is not to say that graduates of black colleges or graduates of poor, unheralded, nonaccredited white colleges may reasonably expect to have the same chances in the academic marketplace or enjoy the same level of respect and general acceptance as is characteristically bestowed upon graduates of affluent, prestigious, Ivy League colleges. Overwhelming evidence convincingly shows that they surely will not. The fact is, one of the deeply rooted bases for consistent, flagrant discrimination in American society is the source of one's college education. As a rule, graduates of the more affluent, high-ranking colleges have a distinct advantage over those from lower ranking institutions in the competition for the higher paying, prestigious positions in American society.

Nevertheless American history is replete with exceptions where time, circumstances, and situations have conspired to elevate graduates of low-ranking, nondescript colleges above competing graduates of wealthy, famous colleges with more than their fair share of powerful, successful, nationally celebrated alumni. Some of the colleges that Jencks and Riesman described as constituting an "academic disaster area," an "ill-financed, ill-staffed caricature of white higher education" (Jencks and Riesman 1967, pp. 21–22) have produced graduates who are quite successful and who are making outstanding contributions in practically every major area in American life. Consequently the central question raised in this chapter is, *How can we account for the fact that certain graduates of black colleges, with negative academic reputations, have often managed to compete as equals with graduates of the most prestigious colleges in the nation?*

It is my contention that, while black colleges per se are poor and unable to provide their students with the expensive accoutrements regarded as ordinary and essential in affluent colleges (and which would certainly enhance the teaching-learning process in black colleges), they have been able, by and large, to prepare a relatively large number of highly competent, successful graduates primarily because they have managed, somehow, throughout the decades to produce, attract, and retain a small but devoted core of truly great teachers. *Basically these dedicated, hard-working, diligent teachers, who understand and empathize with the black experience, have made the difference.*

This point was emphasized by a great black teacher, President Emeritus Benjamin E. Mays of Morehouse College, who has himself significantly influenced the lives and careers of many black scholars and leaders in all walks of American life. In accounting for the success Morehouse has had in producing outstanding graduates, he said in part:

> It wasn't affluence . . . It was a few able, dedicated teachers . . . who widened the Negro's horizon and made him believe that he could do big and worthwhile things . . . Salaries were miserably low, but devotion was correspondingly high. (Mays 1971, p. 173)

The work of talented, dedicated, persevering teachers has substantiated the claim of black colleges that they can take certain students who are rejected by most or all of the affluent, high-ranking, prestigious white colleges and produce a relatively large proportion of top-flight college graduates.

With this in mind, let us examine the nature and effectiveness of faculty-student interaction in black colleges.

Black Colleges: The "Log"

At the outset of this discussion it needs to be clearly understood that in actuality there is no such entity as *the* black college. There is, rather, a group of individual colleges that were founded and exist primarily for the education of black youth. These colleges are distinct also because they have maintained very close identity with the struggle of blacks for survival, advancement, and equality in American society.

Black colleges, like all other colleges, differ widely from one another in many important ways. It would be misleading and fruitless to regard them as some sort of academic monolith, as is so often done. There are, however, some basic characteristics they do have in common so that for certain heuristic purposes they may be regarded as a comprehensive entity. One common characteristic is poverty.

As we saw in Chapter 6, throughout their histories private black colleges have been poor, and public black colleges have been grossly undersupported by their respective state governments. In a relative sense, they have never received anywhere near the level of support extended to comparable white colleges in the states or communities where they are located. In an absolute sense, black colleges, whose burden of education is considerably heavier than that of white colleges because their students have, on the whole, greater academic deficiencies, simply have not had the money to build complete, up-to date physical plants and secure badly needed equipment and supplies.

Figuratively, black colleges have received only the crumbs from the tables of this nation's educational funds. This has been true whether funds have been provided by corporations, church bodies, foundations, or government on all levels (Thompson 1973, pp. 245–254). Even during times of prosperity these colleges have had to operate on the proverbial shoestring. There has been no time in their histories when they did not need to be imperatively concerned about their survival. This is so because as a rule the private colleges have had little or no endowment and the public colleges have existed at the will of characteristically hostile, or at best adamant, white legislators.

A systematic study of private black colleges in 1972–1973 (Thompson 1973) revealed something about the extent and consequences of their poverty: Of a representative sample of teachers in these colleges, 60 percent reported that their colleges' physical plants, libraries, classrooms, offices, laboratories, working areas for supportive staffs, and general physical facilities and equipment were barely adequate or definitely inadequate to facilitate the desired level or quality of academic programs and activities needed for the education of their particular students.

First-hand inspection by members of the research team involved in the study revealed that the teachers' evaluation of their colleges' physical facilities was valid: Just about all of the campuses were incomplete in some critical sense. Some lacked long-needed facilities. Often key academic programs and activities were housed in overcrowded, inappropriate, or dilapidated buildings.

Therefore black college campuses differ widely in terms of their physical facilities. As a rule, insofar as the symbolic log of the Mark Hopkins story is concerned, they leave very much to be desired in the task of taking academically disadvantaged students and preparing them for equal competition with other college graduates. The essential challenge of this undertaking is underscored by the fact that

> All attempts to provide a high quality of education for seriously disadvantaged youth . . . have proven that the essential educational cost per disadvantaged student must be considerably higher than the normal cost per average student if comparable achievements are to be attained (Thompson 1973, p. 246).

Consequently hardly any of the black colleges can boast of having an adequate amount of money to afford the very high level of physical facilities and supportive services commensurate with the herculean task of providing the top-quality programs their student's require.

Students in Black Colleges

Today approximately 600,000 black students are enrolled in bonafide senior college programs (U.S. Dept. of Commerce in 1972, p. 63; Table 48, p. 62). About one-third of them are in black colleges.

At every stage in their development, black colleges have made unpredecented efforts to meet the complex, unique needs of their students. During the early years after emancipation, the central urgent mission of these colleges was to take former slaves, or the children of former slaves, and mold them into people with self-respect and dignity and the learning necessary for sheer survival as well as uplift. The primary imperative emphasis had to be preparing blacks for desperately needed professional and business careers and for responsible, challenging leadership roles. This was a formidable task for several reasons:

1. In the first years after emancipation about 90 percent to 95 percent of the black adult population were functionally illiterate. Before these colleges could go about the serious business of higher education, they first had to prepare blacks on the elementary and

secondary levels. Most of the black colleges or universities, therefore, had elementary and high school departments.
2. The white South strongly opposed the education of blacks. Almost
everything was done to discourage the founding of black schools.
State legislatures and local school boards tended to ignore blacks'
efforts to establish schools. The white masses often took drastic steps
to suppress the school movement sponsored by the federal
government, missionary groups, and a few private philanthropists:
teachers were beaten, schools were burned, and black students and
their parents were frequently intimidated (Bullock 1967, pp. 39–44).
3. Some prominent white educators and influential southerners
mounted a well-organized campaign to promulgate the insidious
so-called scientific fact that blacks are mentally inferior and, therefore, ineducable. At the heart of this propaganda was a system of
apologetics designed to explain and justify the South's opposition to
the education of blacks and its refusal to appropriate money for it.
Underlying the apologetics was the perennial belief of white
employers that educated blacks are largely fit for only the dirty,
menial, low-paying jobs traditionally assigned them.

Despite all forms of opposition and the many hardships and
sacrifices it entailed, black youth eagerly sought an education in these
early colleges. They were firmly convinced—as blacks still are today—that education holds the key to equality. They somehow felt that if
they attained a college education they would be prepared for equal
citizenship and that it would then certainly be bestowed upon them.
This belief has motivated black parents to make almost any sacrifice to
send their children to college.

Standards for Admission

These early black colleges set a pattern of admissions that has
persisted in one form or another to this day. They tended to accept
students with little regard to their socioeconomic class or high school
record. Black colleges literally reversed the tradition of social-class and
academic exclusiveness that has always been characteristic of higher
education. *They invented the practice if not the concept of open
enrollment.* Their flexible admissions practices and academic standards
have been without precedent in higher education. This is, no doubt, a
fundamental reason why black colleges have been so widely criticized
by leaders in higher education and why they have been largely ignored
by the most prestigious honor societies.

During the 1970s a few high-ranking white colleges have experimented with various forms of open enrollment. While there are as yet no definitive conclusions about the success of these programs, enough is known to make it apparent that open enrollment can work if it is carefully planned, tightly controlled, and properly financed. Unfortunately black colleges have never had the resources necessary to make a persuasive case for their open enrollment practices. A handful of black colleges have attempted to become increasingly selective in their admissions policies, but recent competition with white colleges for the top black high school graduates has forced even the most prestigious black institutions to retain some modified version of the open enrollment stance.

Black colleges place very little predictive value on national standardized test scores. The Scholastic Aptitude Test (SAT) is widely used by major colleges as a more or less reliable device for selecting students. Minimum scores of 500 on each portion of the test—verbal and quantitative—are regarded as essential for admission to many schools; some colleges that customarily draw from extra-large pools of high school graduates may use a score of 600 or more as a cutoff point and still recruit the number of students desired. However, black colleges do not have such relatively large pools of students from which to select. Consequently the cutoff point for black colleges is quite below the scores of 400 to 500 regarded as minimal by most colleges. Actually very few students in black colleges score into the 500s. Some of these schools ignore SAT scores, and others use them for diagnostic purposes only. Certain leading black educators are seriously advocating that black colleges should cease requiring applicants to take nationally standardized tests, which they claim are biased in favor of the white middle class and have little validity for the selection of black high school graduates.

Insofar as high schools are concerned, black colleges seldom discriminate. Students are usually accepted from any accredited high school regardless of its relative academic reputation. Furthermore, there seems to be a gradient admissions policy adhered to by the predominantly black colleges; students with high grades are admitted first and then the average grade standards are systematically lowered until a desired number has been admitted. It is to be expected, then, that actual admissions standards for a particular college may vary from one year to the next because of the unstable quality of the pool of high school graduates from which it recruits. Also, a given student body may include students whose average high school grades vary from A to C minus.

Socioeconomic Background of Students

In general, students attending black colleges suffer severe financial handicaps. In 1973 two-thirds of the students in black colleges came from homes in which the annual income was less than $5,000; for fully 83 percent the annual family income was less than $10,000. Even today, in the midst of national inflation and the steadily rising cost of higher education, 74 percent of the students in black colleges come from families where the annual income is less than $12,500, or below the national average. The seriousness of this may be better understood if we remember that the annual family income of approximately 71 percent of all college students today is $12,500 and over.

The relative poverty of students in black colleges has important consequences for the quality of education they may expect to receive. For instance, tuition in private black colleges is about 40 percent lower than the national average (United Negro College Fund 1974). (It was $1,395 for colleges in the United Negro College Fund, compared with the national average of $2,240.) This means that income from students contributes far less to the support of black colleges than to other institutions of higher education. Even with such low tuition, some black college officials fear that they may be pricing themselves out of existence. As it stands now, at least 70 percent of the students in private black colleges are receiving federal aid (United Negro Fund 1974, pp. ix–x). Personally, they cannot afford to buy much more than the minimum number of textbooks and to purchase such often-needed supplies as pocket-size calculators, slide rules, notebooks, and other standard learning equipment. Some students find it difficult to purchase even required texts.

Pragmatism of Students

In addition to being academically handicapped as a result of attending substandard, racially segregated public schools, a large proportion of black college students are highly pragmatic as a result of growing up in black ghettos where life is hard. Most of them regard education only as an effective economic tool, an avenue to a good job.

I have no way of knowing whether students in black colleges are more or less pragmatic on the whole than students in white colleges. However, economic pragmatism does seem to be more of a problem in black colleges because it tends to motivate students to prepare for traditional, "safe" careers. Only a few of the many students whom I have known over the years viewed higher education as inherently good and satisfying in itself, as important to the enrichment of life, or as making the individual more useful to his race or to society. Unless these students are led to deal quickly with their crass pragmatism, it too often militates against their academic success because they become bored and frustrated in required courses involving facts and theories with apparently little or no relevance to the occupations they plan to enter. The successful teacher is often the one who somehow manages to make a liberal education both relevant and interesting to the students.

The Faculty at Black Colleges

As we have noted, the central challenging mission of black colleges has always been that of transforming socioeconomically and academically handicapped black youth into productive citizens, competent professionals, businessmen, and leaders. Since black colleges have never had the funds and influence to adequately support this urgent mission, an uncommonly heavy burden has fallen upon the faculty.

Judged by any set of criteria, black colleges, like all other colleges, have had their share of incompetent and mediocre teachers. However, when teachers in these colleges are evaluated according to the relative success of their products or graduates—the final results of their work—it must be agreed that a significant number of them merit the status of great. While none of their students have become president of the United States or billionaires, many have become very successful in all major walks of life. Without great teachers some of these outstanding graduates, who were "high-risk" high school products, would have inherited only the poverty and disesteem suffered by their parents. Almost all experienced teachers in black colleges can cite any number of high-risk students whom they helped prepare for top-level jobs, professional careers, and responsible leadership roles.

Although the overall quality of black-college faculties varies greatly from one institution to the other and from time to time in the history of any individual school, hardly any black college has ever been without a small, stable core of good-to-great teachers. Even the most substandard black college is likely to have some truly successful teachers who have made unique contributions to the art and science of teaching.

There is one important reason why these colleges have been able to recruit and retain outstanding teachers, despite low salaries and often poor working conditions. Until a decade or so ago few white colleges in the nation and none in the South were ready to employ black teachers. Thus, unlike the situation today, black colleges had a virtual monopoly of black faculty members. Consequently some of the most renowned teachers in the nation, such as W.E.B. duBois, Booker T. Washington, Thurgood Marshall, E. Franklin Frazier, George Washington Carver, Benjamin E. Mays, and a host of others, remained on faculties of black colleges.

Some black teachers, who now have attractive opportunities to join white-college faculties, remain in black colleges because they are truly dedicated to black youth, many of whom would have been rejected by white colleges. Teaching is for them a calling in which they find both deep personal and professional satisfaction. Incidentally, many excellent white teachers are in black colleges for this same reason.

Characteristics of Black-College Teachers

Let us turn now to a brief profile of teachers in black colleges (Thompson 1973). About 40 percent of the teachers are female. From 25 percent to 50 percent of the teachers are white; overall about one-third are white. Approximately one-third of all faculty members hold the doctorate; the range is from as low as 25 percent in most colleges to 50 percent or more in a very few of the top colleges. The vast majority of the teachers, 75 percent or more, are experienced, with five years or more in black colleges. Most of the black teachers are themselves graduates of black colleges.

Teaching is not only the primary role but very often the only professional role expected of black college faculties. Few ever take time to do the kinds of research and writing required of teachers in some of the more affluent white colleges and in about all universities. Thus, in a representative sample of teachers, only 5 percent or 6 percent had published in scholarly journals or written books (Thompson 1973).

The reasons why black faculty members are not likely to publish are complex: lack of money to do research; lack of time to do scholarly writing; prejudice on the part of publishers, who fear that there is only a small market for the subjects blacks are usually interested in; and the lack of pressure from black college administrators and colleagues. For whatever reasons, teaching is a great deal more central and more emphasized in a black college than in other colleges. Teachers in higher education in general tend to spend what some believe to be too much time in personal research and writing. Teachers in black colleges, however, are mostly concerned with classroom activities, personal counseling, and sponsoring student organizations. Their interaction with students is many-sided, sustained, and personal.

It is important to note that most of the top faculty members in black colleges teach lower classmen; along with other teachers, they are responsible for introductory courses. Some do so to make up the relatively heavy teaching load expected, but most do so because they want to lay as solid foundation as possible at the start of the students' college career so that their academic development will be sound and continuous.

Faculty-Student Interaction

Teachers in black colleges represent considerable diversity in terms of social backgrounds. Basically, however, their social origins are quite similar to those of their students. Like their students, most of them came from poor families where they were perhaps the first to attend college. Also, about 75 percent to 80 percent of the black teachers were born and grew up in the South and thoroughly understand and empathize with the blacks' struggle for survival and advancement (Thompson 1973, p. 119).

Perhaps the one characteristic that most distinguishes teachers in black colleges from their students is their orientation toward success. Most of them have sacrificed a great deal and striven very diligently to overcome their own social and academic handicaps. They tend to be proud of their accomplishments, and their self-pride is usually reinforced by the high social status bestowed upon them by the black community. There are reasons to believe that black college teachers, on the whole, enjoy a somewhat higher social status among their students than do comparable white teachers. Teachers in a prestigious white college are likely to have students whose parents and relatives are of higher status than their own. This would seldom be the case in a black college; in almost all instances the social status of teachers, even their incomes, will be higher than that of any of their students' parents. Many of the faculty in black colleges are influential local and national leaders. The relatively high status of a teacher affects the nature of his or her interaction with the students. Students from homes and neighborhoods of relatively low status have the best opportunity to learn middle-class ways, manners, and ideas simply by observing the teacher. Some of the good teachers assume this to be one of their primary roles: the preparation of disadvantaged black youth for making it in a white-dominated middle-class environment. Some of the teachers are eminently qualified to do so because they have walked in both worlds.

In this connection it is important to keep in mind that the basic rationale for the small college in American society, especially the private black college, is the belief that it provides maximum opportunities for students to benefit from sustained personal contacts with teachers. The wide differences in social class that usually exist between teachers who are oriented toward the middle classes and the great majority of the students in black colleges can function as a serious barrier to creative teacher-student interaction unless the tensions and conflicts inherent in such situations are skillfully handled. For instance, during the late 1960s and the early 1970s, social-class strains between teachers and students, which in the past had been kept dramatically sub rosa, erupted. On some campuses students and teachers tended to regard one another as antagonists rather than partners in the learning enterprise. Traditional patterns of teacher-student interaction were interrupted and the basic raison d'être of the small black college was threatened.

Patterns of Teacher–Student Interaction

In response to widespread challenging student unrest and rebellion against certain well-established middle-class values advocated by college teachers generally, at least three ideal patterns of teacher–student interaction have emerged on the black campus:

1. A few of the younger teachers have tended to identify with the student subculture, which is very often strongly influenced by "ghetto" or "street" ways. This is frequently reflected in their casual, even esoteric, mode of dress; anti-middle-class life style; characteristically negative attitude toward certain key middle-class values; and a proclivity to compromise academic standards when deemed expedient.

Teacher–student interaction stemming from this stance is seldom successful. Teachers who conduct themselves in that manner are likely to get into serious professional difficulty with their colleagues and administrators, and their credibility and influence with students are generally diminished because of their inability to help students achieve the academic and career goals they have set for themselves.

2. Some teachers in black colleges are more or less completely subject-matter oriented. They have a reputation of being thoroughly familiar with the material they teach. Most seem to be patient with students while still holding them to high academic standards. What sets these teachers apart from their colleagues is the fact that they have little or no interest in their students except the purely academic. If possible, they refrain from functioning in any but a teaching capacity.

On the one hand, students with sound academic backgrounds and strong motivations to succeed usually do very well in the classes of such teachers and go on to successful graduate study or careers, or both. On the other hand, students with relatively weak academic backgrounds, who are uncertain about their academic and professional goals, are likely to make low or failing grades.

3. Increasingly, teachers in black colleges, regardless of their own racial or ethnic identity, are expected to have knowledge of the history and culture of black Americans and be able to interpret relevant aspects of the black experience vis-à-vis their particular academic discipline.

Some respected black educators are beginning to insist that, unless teachers have a functional knowledge of their students' subculture, which is an integral part of the larger American experience, they cannot establish the creative level of interaction desired. This means that basic communication with some students, perhaps most in black colleges, should begin with the students' own experience. In this way, teacher–student interaction can be established upon mutual respect, and differences in social class can be understood and dealt with in such a way that they will function as incentives to self-improvement and self-fulfillment rather than being debilitating strains and conflicts.

This pattern of teacher–student interaction presents the middle-class world, as represented by the teacher, in such a way that it ceases to be threatening and demeaning to certain less affluent students but full of opportunities and challenges for those who are willing to work hard and make necessary sacrifices.

Teaching Methods and Techniques

Since students in black colleges are characteristically recruited from varied social, economic, and academic backgrounds and represent great differences in talents and competencies, the truly successful teachers are those who have mastered a wide repertoire of teaching methods and techniques. They must be able to present a body of information and stimulate learning among both the more gifted and better prepared and the less gifted and poorly prepared. This problem may be met by giving assignments requiring different talents or levels of competency. Thus, while the less gifted or poorly prepared students may be put through what amounts to academic drills, the better students are given special assignments or individual projects. Also the less prepared students may be required to report on routine assignments or respond to basic academic questions while the more gifted, better prepared students are assigned special or independent projects. Also, occasionally the better prepared students may be called upon to lead class discussions or to serve as assistants to teachers.

Varied teaching methods and techniques are regularly employed in such ways that disrupting jealousies and strains among competing students are minimized while at the same time providing ample opportunities for students of very unequal abilities to achieve goals commensurate with their own individual potentials. Therefore the good teacher is not only a master of various methods but is also quite proficient in the *art* of teaching as well.

Counseling

In addition to interaction in the classroom, teachers in black colleges traditionally are expected to give a great deal of time to personal counseling. Most college administrators insist upon this because otherwise far too many of the academically disadvantaged students would be unable to cover the required amount of assigned materials. Most counseling sessions are really tutorial in content. These private sessions provide excellent opportunities for students to better grapple with difficult subject matter and also to acquire added knowledge about how to survive and succeed in white America. Directly or indirectly, teachers in these colleges personally instruct students in middle-class manners and values as well as in formal subjects.

Again, every student organization on campus is expected to have a faculty sponsor or sponsors. Often teachers themselves are members of the fraternities and sororities located on their campuses. As sponsors of student organizations, these teachers have numerous opportunities to teach students from black ghettos how to organize, participate, and lead in our complex, many-faceted urban society.

We may conclude that teachers in black colleges interact with their students in a number of roles. Each role affords its own peculiar dimension of learning. This is the primary reason that, despite other shortcomings, the more ambitious, alert students in these colleges are likely to develop much of the sophistication and poise characteristic of graduates of more affluent colleges. Fundamentally *the faculty makes the difference in the transformation* of an academically handicapped, disesteemed black youth into the urbane, self-confident, competent black college graduate.

Chapter 12

Teaching and Learning the Social Sciences in the Predominantly Black Universities

Charles U. Smith

In this chapter I propose to comment on black institutions of higher education and the education of blacks with special emphasis on teaching and learning the social sciences.

In attempting this, certain cautions must be stated, for although Jencks and Riesman (1967) lump all black colleges together conceptually and analytically (with the exception of nine), more astute scholars recognize the significant differences among the approximately 120 predominantly black institutions currently in existence. Despite the typology implied in the single case depicted in *Uncle Tom's Campus* (Jones 1973), it simply is not accurate to accept this stereotype as typical. The paternalistic and authoritarian president and his chief "hatchet man" described in that supposed exposé (pp. 68–117) are hardly mirrored by many predominantly black institutions, which have constitutions, bylaws, rules, and policies that give faculty meaningful roles in university governance through representative councils and senates.

Diversity among Black Colleges

There is in fact great diversity among the predominantly black institutions in the United States. Important differences exist in community acceptability, indigenous support, and institutional self-concept. The geographic locations of black colleges are associated with

195

variations in ethos and educational philosophy. These schools are dispersed from Florida in the Southeast to Pennsylvania in the Northeast; from Maryland, a South Atlantic state, to Texas in the Southwest; and from Mississippi in the East South Central to Missouri in the North Central regions of the United States. Thus the divergence in sociopolitical position, service requirements, and special functions are manifestly apparent.

Black institutions of higher education differ also in their manner of governance and control. In states like Louisiana and Tennessee, the predominantly black institution is under the supervision of state boards of education (which also govern the elementary and secondary schools) while in Florida and North Carolina *all* public colleges and universities operate under a single governing body.

Likewise, the variations in size, sources of funding, and resources reflect wide variations among these schools. For example, Talladega College in Alabama, with a $1,817,103 annual revenue, 533 students, 59 faculty, and 58,000 volumes in its library can hardly be placed in the same category as Tuskegee Institute in the same state, which has a $15,000,000 annual budget, 2,918 students, 279 faculty, and 185,000 bound volumes in the library (American Council on Education 1973). A look at similar data for two of the larger public land-grant universities is also revealing. Southern University (Louisiana) with approximately 8,000 students has an annual budget of $15,000,000 and a library of 225,000 volumes, while Florida Agricultural and Mechanical University operating with a slightly larger annual budget and library serves nearly 5,000 students (American Council on Education 1973).

Differences of this kind are widespread among the entire population of historically black colleges and universities in the United States. Even when curricula, stated objectives, and course descriptions are virtually identical, the differences of resources and facilities available to the colleges materially affect their ability to deliver similar education.

Similarities among Black Colleges

It now seems appropriate to note certain similarities that most black colleges and universities share. Mack Jones, writing on "The Responsibility of the Black College to the Black Community: Then and Now," has cited the mission of black colleges outlined by DuBois in 1942:

1. Establishing the principle that higher education should be made available to blacks
2. Defending the principle of racial equality by combatting national and international doctrines to the contrary
3. Establishing freedom of Negro colleges to decide what they would teach and to whom it would be taught
4. Promoting democracy and social power for black people by working for enfranchisement and gradual acquisition of political power. (Jones 1971, p. 737)

At a later point in his article, Jones states that this mission, though appropriate for an earlier time, is now obsolete for the modern black college or university. According to Jones, the four phases have been accomplished, and the new mission must be centered around "creating a universally accepted perception of the black predicament and providing a catalyst for serious discussion of goals . . . of black people and the most expeditious means for their realization" (Jones 1971, p. 740). Black students would then

see clearly and understand fully the true position of blacks in American society and the prescriptive implications of that position for normative assessment of international political movements. The incompatibility of their interest—liberation—and that of American capitalism grounded in white supremacy—exploitation—would be obvious. They would be impervious to that legion of pied pipers: black capitalism, soul power, Philadelphia plans, poverty panaceas. (Jones 1971, p. 741)

Henry Allen Bullock apparently agreeing with Jones, believes that the new model of instruction in the black university, especially in the social sciences, should emanate from a central focus on black culture and awareness. Bullock feels that such a method would provide the student with "familiar perceptual windows through which he can view the various disciplines from the vantage point of his own life's situation" (Bullock 1971, p. 597).

One could argue with considerable merit that certain of the goals listed by DuBois are not obsolete and that they have not been adequately realized. It could also be pointed out that what Jones and Bullock propose are extensions or specifications of DuBois's perspective. Without entering into these polemics, we can point out that a fundamental commonality of purpose appears in the ideas of DuBois, Jones, and Bullock and is shared by this writer, namely, *the elevation of social consciousness and the development of its corollary—social action.*

In my observation, one of the most persistent and pervasive thrusts in the teaching and learning of the social sciences in the predominantly black institution of higher education has been, and is, the utilization of sound scholarship in support of ameliorative strategies for the problems of human welfare—especially those of blacks.

Applied Social Science for Social Change

Despite the fact that some trustees, regents, and members of other governing bodies have sought to keep the black colleges and universities structures that will support the dominant value system and the status quo in social, political, and economic matters, the concept of applied social science for social change has persisted. Historically the application of scientific study to human improvement has been a dominant orientation in the social sciences programs of black colleges, especially in sociology.

W. E. B. DuBois, Charles S. Johnson, and E. Franklin Frazier, three of the giants among black sociologists, functioned as applied social scientists throughout much of their professional careers. Undoubtedly they influenced the thinking and approaches of their students and colleagues. DuBois consistently epitomized this approach and produced much survey data, including the classic *Philadelphia Negro*. Although Frazier was associated with the National Urban League early in his career, it is only fair to state that applied orientation was less apparent in his research.

Charles S. Johnson was greatly affected by his association and study with the white sociologist Robert E. Park, who typified a combination of scientific scholarship and a concern with human problems. While Park himself did not do much primary research, he was the moving force behind the outstanding series of studies of social problems produced by his students at the University of Chicago during the 1930s and 1940s. Significantly, Park left Chicago and finished his professional career at Fisk University with Johnson's Department of Social Sciences. Over the years, Johnson left no doubt as to his dedication to the model of sound scholarship and applied sociology—in his writings, the orientation of his staff, the annual race relations institute, the publication of the *Monthly Summary of Events and Trends in Race Relations,* and the development of a community survey service. Many persons have attested to Johnson's ability to marshal objective evidence for the solution of practical problems (Smith 1972). As a former student at Fisk with Johnson, my own perception of sociology and social science research were greatly influenced by him and his staff.

An even earlier influence on my thinking about the nature and uses of sociology and social science research and training was a lesser-known figure, Charles G. Gomillion, who in my judgment was the ideal type of scholar—both social scientist and social activist. It is also worth noting that the five social scientists mentioned above spent most or all of their professional careers at black institutions.

Because of the impact of scholars such as these and the obvious human welfare problems of blacks (and whites) in the South (where most of the predominantly black colleges are located), it is little wonder that many of these institutions developed departments combining social science and social action. While not exclusively the product of black colleges and universities, names like the Department of Sociology and Social Service at North Carolina Agricultural and Technical State University; the Department of Sociology and Social Administration at Tennessee State University; and the Department of Sociology, Anthropology, and Human Services at Florida Agricultural and Mechanical University are common. Furthermore, departments labeled as Sociology or Social Sciences usually include important components of applied action. Thus, when we discuss social science teaching and learning in the black colleges, we must include social work, criminal justice, and corrections in addition to the traditional disciplines.

As Butler Jones (1974, p. 121) points out, the reformist and ameliorative orientation has been typical of sociology, especially in the black colleges. Further documentation of the activist role of black sociologists is offered by Smith and Killian (1974, pp. 191–228), who found that nearly 80 percent of those responding to a survey were "strongly favorable" to social protest and that approximately 75 percent of the black sociologists had been actively involved in protest and civil rights activities.

Black Colleges and White Colleges, South and North

People who work at a predominantly black university, expecially if it also happens to be south of the Mason–Dixon line (as most are), are faced with the necessity of responding to direct or implied questions such as, What kind of school is it? What type of student do you have?

What is your faculty like? These queries are often well-intentioned but are sometimes gratuitously raised by colleagues—most often (but not always) nonblacks—who are smug in the knowledge that they are located at a northern predominantly white mainstream college or university. One rarely if ever hears the question, What kind of school is Harvard? or What kind of school is Oral Roberts?

The assumption seems to be that there is something unique (a euphemism for *weird* or *inferior*) about colleges when they are managed by blacks and located "Down South." Unfortunately cartographers have designed maps so that south is down and north is up. In the symbolism of American society, *up* is good, *down* is bad; *large* is good, *small* is bad; *North* is good, *South* is bad; and *white* is good, *black* is bad. So, when you are associated professionally with a small, black southern university that is "somewhere down there," you and your institution must bear a great burden of stigma. A corollary conclusion is that people who remain in the employ of such a college or university cannot do any better, that no self-respecting major school will have them.

While I have no data specifically relating to students in the social sciences at black colleges and universities, a brief look at the characteristics of their student bodies may be worthwhile and informative. In a recent study, *Black Consciousness, Identity, and Achievement,* Gurin and Epps (1975) report longitudinal data obtained from random samples of students from 10 predominantly black colleges in 1964 and 6 of the same institutions again in 1970. The authors checked the representativeness of their samples for students in black colleges and universities in general. Gurin and Epps present the following summary of data on selected demographic and family characteristics:

> Comparisons with national and southern nonwhite data show that students attending these 10 colleges grew up in families with somewhat atypical socioeconomic characteristics. In terms of occupational distribution, the 1964 data showed that 25 percent of the students' fathers were employed in white collar jobs, as against 15 percent of all nonwhite men and 10 percent of southern nonwhite men. The employed mothers in this student population likewise stood out from other nonwhite employed women: 39 percent of the students' mothers held white collar jobs but only 24 percent of all employed nonwhite women, and 19 percent of all southern nonwhite working women, did so. The fathers and mothers of this student population had also acquired more education: 43 percent of the students' fathers had completed high school compared to 37 percent of nonwhite men and 19 percent of all southern nonwhite men. Similarly 53 percent of the students' mothers held high school diplomas compared to 28 percent of all nonwhite

women and 20 percent of southern nonwhite women. The $5200 median family income reported by the students was also higher than either the $2888 median for southern nonwhite families or the $3724 for nonwhite families in the country at large in 1964. The students' family structures, by contrast, resembled very closely figures for nonwhite families in the south. Three-quarters of the students in our 1964 sample grew up in families in which both parents were present. Census data from 1965 showed that 78 percent of all nonwhite families in the south were two-parent families. (Gurin and Epps 1975, p. 109)

Daniel Patrick Moynihan (1965) wrote that, because of the high incidence of father-absent families among blacks, the home life of young blacks was deteriorating. Such a family structure, according to Moynihan, is dysfunctional and pathogenic for black youth, producing lowered achievement and aspiration levels, distorted values, depressed educational attainment, and dependence on welfare

Moynihan's own data, the Gurin–Epps sample, and the census reports show that three-fourths of all black youth are in two-parent families. Nevertheless, Moynihan placed great emphasis on black families headed by mothers with fathers absent and helped to create a widespread sociological distortion that social science teachers at black colleges and elsewhere are still trying to eliminate from the minds of students and the public. Additional attention will be given later to this type of problem in the social sciences.

The main point about demographic and familial variables among the students at black colleges is that *none* of them produced *any* differences in student performance at any of the ten schools. In coming to this conclusion Gurin and Epps are unequivocal:

How did these socioeconomic and demographic variables relate to student performance? There was no significant correlation between these variables, either separately or combined, and any of our measures of performance. This was true whether performance was measured by entrance test scores, grades in college, or scores on an anagrams task, a test frequently used in achievement motivation research and administered as part of this study. Whether students came from rural or urban settings, from low or high income families where parents had low or high educational attainments, or from two-parent or other kinds of families simply did not relate to how well they performed. This was equally true of men and of women, and it held for every one of the ten colleges. (Gurin and Epps 1975, p. 116)

From this, it may be concluded that, in terms of several typical demographic and family variables, social science and other students at black institutions are not homogeneous; differential performance and achievement by them must be attributed to factors and processes other than those studied by Gurin and Epps.

Poverty among Black Students

Perhaps the most significant characteristic of students at black colleges and universities is that so many of them are *poor*. This alone probably accounts for the fact that many of them choose to attend a black college, where costs are generally lower. Gurin and Epps suggest that there is a direct relationship between the academic rank of the black institutions and the income group of the students' families—the lower the income level, the lower the academic status of the college or university selected by the student.

In 1972, the United States census reported that black families, at a median income of $6,864 per year, had an annual income amounting to only 59 percent of the $11,549 of white families. In 1973, in the South—where most black families and black colleges are and, according to Gurin and Epps, 90 percent of the students at black colleges come from—black families had a median annual income of $6,434 or 56 percent of the $11,508 received by whites. Furthermore, in 1973 over 28 percent of all black families in the United States had annual incomes below the poverty level, and the figure for families headed by black females was 52 percent (U.S. Bureau of the Census 1974, pp. 17;30).

The prevalence of poverty among students at black colleges and universities is illustrated at Florida Agricultural and Mechanical University (popularly called FAMU), where, in 1976, 69 percent of the students had annual parental incomes under $10,000 and 86 percent had annual parental incomes under $15,000.* This compares with national norms of 13 percent and 34 percent, respectively. Of the FAMU students, 73 percent indicated a need for financial assistance of $1,500 to $2,499 per year in order to attend the university (90 percent of all students at FAMU received financial aid from the university). In addition to having anxiety about the uncertainty of financial aid from loans and grants from the university, over 40 percent of the students held part-time jobs, which reduced their energy for study as well as their study time. Since FAMU was one of the universities included in the study by Gurin and Epps, their comment on working students is appropriate:

*This information on the financial status of students at Florida Agricultural and Mechanical University in 1976 was supplied by the university's Office of Financial Aid and the vice-president for student affairs.

... virtually all the students from the low income group, as compared with 40 per cent of the most affluent group, not only worked, but worked an average of twice as many hours. While college jobs can complement academic work and add to character, we need not romanticize their value nor assume they are twice as valuable for the poor as for the more comfortable students. Having to work as many hours as they did and ending college with so much indebtedness clearly put low income students at a disadvantage in financing graduate school. (Gurin and Epps 1975, p. 138)

If all other things were equal between students at black schools and those at predominantly white schools, the sheer fact of the relative poverty of the black students would militate against their ability to attain the academic achievement levels of whites.

Needs of Entering Students

Another handicap shared by many students at black colleges and closely related to the socioeconomic status of their families is that they have been socialized in home and community environments that are at best nonintellectual and at worst anti-intellectual. The pursuit of higher education and excellence in academic achievement are often derided by their peers and are frequently considered unnecessary and too expensive by parents caught in the pressures of day-to-day survival.

Because many black students have lacked out-of-school reinforcement, have developed marginal motivation, and have average-to-poor academic achievement, they enter black colleges with low entrance test scores, poor study habits and skills, an uncertain sense of the future, vague notions of career options, resistance to courses of study without obvious and immediate "practical" utility, and fear of the theoretical and abstract. Such students are particularly challenging (or discouraging) to instructors, expecially those in the social sciences, whose disciplines seem to contain so many of the qualities identified negatively by the students.

In a very real sense, from another standpoint, such high school graduates should be a main focus of attention for all colleges and universities in American society as it seeks to achieve its democratic ideal. The black colleges have long prided themselves on their developmental ability. They take the high school graduate (not yet a college freshman) at his or her achievement level and, after four or five years, produce a college graduate of relatively high competitive ability.

ISSUES IN TEACHING AND LEARNING SOCIAL SCIENCES

A number of other problems and issues are more specifically related to teaching and learning the social sciences in the black university and college. It should be noted that, in general, these observations are based on my personal observations and unsystematic but long-term communication and interaction with colleagues in the social sciences from other black institutions.

Costs

Butler Jones (1974) has written that sociology courses were readily installed in black colleges because of the low cost of teaching them. A similar observation could be made about other social sciences as well. It seems eminently clear, moreover, that black college administrators have been universally dedicated to keeping the costs of the social sciences low by providing only miniscule budgets for them.

By way of illustration, in 1973 the Department of Sociology, Anthropology, and Human Services at FAMU (perhaps the largest social science department among the black universities) had approximately 600 majors in a total student body of about 4,800 (1 out of every 8 students). It had a student service load of 1,300 each quarter and a faculty and staff of 25 full- and part-time persons. During 1973 the University provided only 8 of the full-time faculty, one secretary, and less than $10,000 for expenses and capital outlay. (The sources of the other funds will be referred to later.) Other social science departments at FAMU received even less. Conversations with chairpersons in social sciences at a number of black colleges reveal a similar plight: not only low operating budgets but also limited office and classroom space.

Faculty Recruitment

In some social science fields, there is a surplus of whites who hold the Ph.D. degree. The dilemma of many of the black institutions today is that of recruiting and retaining enough black faculty to balance nonblack personnel, who are in abundant supply.

Although blacks comprise approximately 11 percent of the total population of the United States, the proportion possessing the highest degree in the academic disciplines is far lower than that percentage; a variety of historical, cultural, and economic factors have contributed to this phenomenon, as Butler Jones (1974) noted in his article. Black social scientists who have earned the Ph.D. degree are so scarce that competition for their services borders on the cutthroat, especially in recent years when major white colleges and universities have found it desirable or at least expedient to employ them.

If sociology is illustrative, the situation of the approximately 200 blacks with doctoral degrees in this field dramatizes the problem. Kent Mommsen (1973) published a study that showed that the median nine-to-ten-month salary for black sociologists was over $18,000 plus an average of $2,400 in consultant and other fees. Mommsen found also that an annual salary of over $26,000 would be required to persuade the typical black sociologist to change institutions.

My vision was to establish sociology and the social sciences at FAMU at a level previously held only by Fisk University under the leadership of Charles S. Johnson. Because of the viability and promise of sociology and the social sciences at FAMU as well as the relatively high salary scale (among black universities), it was not difficult in the past to recruit outstanding black scholars for the institution, all of whom received their undergraduate training at black colleges.* Most earned their doctoral degree at major northern white universities, since only two black universities give the Ph.D. (one just beginning); furthermore, until recently southern white universities did not admit blacks. The training that these black faculty had received at undergraduate black colleges was obviously not inferior. While the social science programs at FAMU are in good shape, retention of these eminent scholars would have made them truly outstanding among all universities.

To compensate for such faculty losses, we now recruit teachers from among our own students. We encourage them to pursue graduate study at reputable schools and help them to procure needed financial aid. It is anticipated that their interest in FAMU will cause them to remain on

---

*A few of the social scientists who have taught at FAMU are Dr. Henry Cobb, professor of history and former dean of the Graduate School at Southern University at Baton Rouge; Dr. Edgar Epps, Marshall Field Professor of Sociology at the University of Chicago; Dr. Robert H. Smith, dean of the School of Liberal Studies at Jackson State University; Dr. John Moland, professor of sociology and director of the Center for Social Research at Southern University; Dr. Leonard Spearman, assistant commissioner of education, U.S. Department of Health, Education, and Welfare (psychologist); Dr. Harold Rose, head of the Department of Urban Geography at the University of Wisconsin, Milwaukee; Dr. Emmett Bashful, vice-president of Southern University at New Orleans (political scientist); Dr. Roosevelt Steptoe, professor of economics at Southern University, New Orleans; Dr. Graham Johnson, director of Summer School at Howard University (political scientist); Dr. Ronald Bailey, professor of political science at the University of Florida.

the faculty for significant periods of time. For those who would argue that this is inbreeding, our reply is that it is better to be inbred than unbred.

Careers for Black Social Science Students

Before the 1960s, most students at black institutions of higher education who majored or had concentrations in the social sciences anticipated careers as teachers of social studies in secondary schools. This pattern was primarily a response to the limited professional opportunities for social science graduates with baccalaureate degrees. With few exceptions, up to the middle 1960s, black graduates in the social sciences were systematically excluded from meaningful positions in the human service departments of state and local governments throughout the South.

The civil rights activism of pioneering black students from black colleges in the South (Smith and Killian 1958; Smith 1961) coupled with similar activity by organized civil rights groups contributed greatly to a national climate for social change that had an almost revolutionary impact on career opportunities for black social science students as well as for graduates in other fields in black colleges and universities. Federal legislation during the 60s such as the National Defense Education Act, the Economic Opportunity Act, and the Manpower Development and Training Act were public laws that effectively created new opportunities. However, the Civil Rights Act of 1964 undoubtedly had the most powerful effect in opening up new career options for social science graduates of black institutions. The three titles of this act that were most significant in opening new career doors for graduates of black schools were Title IV, Desegregation of Public Education; Title VI, Non-discrimination in Federally Assisted Programs; and Title VII, Equal Employment Opportunity.

This legislation and the climate for change led the Southern Regional Education Board (SREB) to observe in 1968:

> Job opportunities for educated Negro men and women have multiplied in recent years in this favorable climate, and projections indicate faster expansion in the 1980's. In professional occupations employers are not able to find enough qualified persons of any race to fill the vacancies they have. Many employers are actively promoting equal employment opportunity and seeking Negroes because they need and want them. Others who may be reluctant must, nevertheless, comply with the Civil Rights Act of 1964 and

1968 and meet the inspection of the Equal Employment Opportunity Commission and the Office of Public Contracts Compliance in the U.S. Department of Labor. (Southern Regional Education Board 1968, p. 6–7)

The Commission on Higher Education Opportunity of the SREB further recommended:

> that a summer workshop be held to explore the special needs of Negro students, in terms of both curriculum and services, employing consultants who are trained in all areas related to the problem. This workshop should result in a definitive publication for the use of institutions enrolling significant numbers of Negro students. (Southern Regional Education Board 1968, p.1)

The SREB rationale for deliberate and systematic efforts to evoke curriculum change in black colleges continued:

> Changing conditions have created new opportunities for a substantial segment of our society. In addition, new manpower needs are constantly appearing. It is essential that colleges educate students for these opportunities. Colleges and universities which have traditionally served Negro students have an unprecedented opportunity to contribute to Negro participation in vocations and professions from which their graduates until recently were generally excluded, and to expand and deepen their pre-professional programs leading to post-baccalaureate training. The normal process of curriculum change is slow. The times call for a marked acceleration which is at the same time wisely and carefully executed. (Southern Regional Education Board 1968, p.1)

Subsequently the publication *New Careers and Curriculum Change* was produced by a group of scholars during a ten-day "think–writing retreat" at Warren Wilson College during the summer of 1968. This volume, which contained sections on "Social and Behavioral Sciences" and "Engineering Health and Social Welfare," not only identified new and emerging careers in these fields but also presented specific suggestions for the integration and teaching of the social sciences and related disciplines. Models proposed in this publication were utilized in curriculum planning and development by both black and white colleges and universities.

Grants obtained from the Social and Rehabilitation Service of the U.S. Department of Health, Education, and Welfare (HEW) through state welfare departments and from the Law Enforcement Assistance Administration (to support the Law Enforcement Education Program—LEEP) provided a number of black colleges and universities with substantial support for social welfare and corrections training, respectively. The funds were mostly used for additional faculty positions, student assistantships, student loans and grants, program enrichment, professional travel, and the development of field experience (internships) in the helping professions. These grants have been drastically reduced in amounts and scope in recent years. If they are eliminated entirely (as seems the intent) it will make the continuation of these programs at present levels of development and strength extremely tenuous for some black institutions and totally impossible for others.

The News and Classroom Content

Presentations by the press and other media of the black colleges and universities in comparison with their white counterparts, though often well intentioned, are frequently deleterious to the public image and effective functioning of the black schools. Quite a few of the black

---

Table 12–1
States with Cities Having a Black and a White State-Supported College or University

LOCATION	BLACK INSTITUTION	WHITE INSTITUTION
Montgomery, Ala.	Alabama State University	Auburn University
Tallahassee, Fla.	Florida A & M University	Florida State University
Savannah, Ga.	Savannah State College	Armstrong State College
Baton Rouge, La.	Southern University	Louisiana State University and A & M College
Greensboro, N.C.	North Carolina A & T State University	University of North Carolina at Greensboro
Nashville, Tenn.	Tennessee State University	University of Tennessee
Houston, Tex.	Texas Southern University	University of Houston
Norfolk, Va.	Norfolk State College	Old Dominion University

state-supported colleges and universities are located in the same cities with state-supported white institutions (Table 12–1). However, when the press reports on the feasibility and functioning of black and white institutions in the same city, the stories almost invariably state or imply a threat to the survival and development of the *black* school only.

Newspaper headlines about FAMU (black) in Tallahassee, Florida, with FSU (Florida State University, white) consistently reveal this kind of threat. Here are some examples:

Friday, April 12, 1974   *Tallahassee Democrat*
  AGENCY WEIGHING FAMU STATUS CHANGE
Thursday, May 2, 1974   *Tallahassee Democrat*
  FAMU "MOVING" CONSIDERED
Monday, May 6, 1974   *Tallahassee Democrat*
  REGENTS DECIDE TO HOLD SESSION ON FAMU'S FATE
Friday, May 10, 1974   *Tallahassee Democrat*
  HARRIS ENDORSES MERGING FAMU

Another headline, although not directly germane to the previous point, illustrates that where race relations are concerned, racism is likely to be dominant. It relates to Florida's plan to comply with the mandate of the United States District Court of the District of Columbia for desegregation of the Florida system and reads:

Friday, May 24, 1974   *The Florida Times–Union*
  MAUTZ: DESEGREGATION PLAN WON'T BE POPULAR

This headline is quoting the former chancellor of the State University System of Florida (of which FAMU is presumably a full-fledged and equal member), who "leads" public opinion by suggesting that the citizenry "ought not to like" the desegregation plan. Chancellor Mautz could just as easily and validly have said that the plan would be challenging, or stimulating, or innovative, or would produce great opportunities for interracial and educational growth.

The best example of unconscious bias in well-meant reporting is found in the following lead sentences in an article intended to be favorable to FAMU:

The aroma of collard greens, fried chicken smothered in gravy, and cornbread drifts from the Orange Room across the green lawn of the quadrangle.

A young man with a purple crocheted hat crushing his Afro carries books for the girl whose hand he holds. They, and the students lolling under a sycamore tree on the hillside, wear bright, modish clothing that could double for Sunday best.

Florida A & M University in Tallahassee is different from other universities in Florida. (*The Miami Herald*, March 10, 1974).

It is quite likely that collard greens and fried chicken are eaten with regularity at the University of Florida in Gainesville, and even occasionally by some "southern Scalawags" attending college on the banks of the Charles River at Harvard, but what reporter would ever set out to present the academic value and scholarly position of these schools in such language?

This kind of media coverage makes it more difficult for black colleges to recruit first-rate faculty and students. All was not completely lost in these and other newspaper accounts about FAMU, since I was able to use these stories in the teaching of content analysis to sociology and social science students in a course in methods of social research. The consistency of bias and distortion were identified. Since these reports were close to home and relevant to the students' experiences, motivation was high. It was thus easy to teach this component of social research methods by using these data.

Student Activism and the Curriculum

Of great concern to social scientists at black universities and colleges is the widespread manifestation of bias, omissions, racism, and scholarly irresponsibility in research publications and instructional materials. I have commented on this problem at some length in an article, "Student Activism, Benign Racism and Scholarly Irresponsibility" (Smith 1974), in which I examined seven publications on recent student protests by eminent social scientists.*

Content analysis of these and other publications on student activism revealed that the authors uniformly fail to mention or neglect to indicate the significance of the fact that modern-day student protests began with black colleges and universities in the South, which provided both models and stimuli for students and institutions elsewhere. Although organized student protests started at southern black schools in the midfifties, none of these authors note this fact. They generally leave their readers to believe that all college students were acting beat, having

---

*Articles, books, and journals examined in this regard included Murray Gruber (1973), "Four Types of Black Protest"; *The Annals* (1971), "Students Protest"; Seymour Lipset (1971), *Rebellion in the University;* Gary Marx (1971), *Racial Conflict: Tension and Change in American Society;* Howard Becker (1970). *Campus Power Struggle;* Gary Marx (1967), *Protest and Prejudice; The Annals* (1965), "The Negro Protest."

panty raids, swallowing goldfish, and stuffing telephone booths until 1964 when Mario Savio started the free speech movement among white students at a major white university, the University of California at Berkeley. In fact, by the time that this happened, black students at southern black colleges, utilizing sit-ins, mass arrests, picketing, and protest rallies, had desegregated lunch counters, theaters, and other places of public accommodation.

These activities of students at southern black universities (utilizing indigenous, nonnorthern student leaders) are well documented in research literature but were apparently outside the perception thresholds of the scholars whose work was examined. Consequently, one of the important and time-consuming tasks of the social science professor in the black institution is that of filling omissions, identifying bias, and correcting inaccuracies in much of social science research. While the problem turns up most often in the writing of whites, black scholars are also sometimes guilty of similar racism and irresponsibility.

An incidental by-product of activism on black campuses has been a heightened interest among students in the social sciences and their uses for effecting social change. An additional consequence of activism by southern black college students has been the expansion and diversification of courses and curricula in all colleges on the life and experiences of blacks, courses that had long existed at most black colleges and universities.

Similarly, the differential enforcement of the law, as in the case of John Calley compared with Angela Davis, and such events as the irrational South Boston school desegregation controversy enhance students' interest in the social sciences and provide instructional laboratories for the application of theory to real life.

SOCIAL SCIENCE PROCEDURES AT FAMU

Activities, strategies, and programs that FAMU is carrying on are illustrative of the innovative efforts at teaching and learning the social sciences taking place in many black colleges and universities.

Undergraduate Field Experience (Internships)

With the support of grant funds, FAMU pioneered internships for black sociology majors who were minoring in social welfare and corrections. This program has been used as a model by both white and black, northern and southern colleges and universities. It is in direct accord with views expressed by Alfred McClung Lee, former president of the American Sociological Association, although it had started before he stated them publicly. Lee said that

> our undergraduate departments many times attract curious-minded potential social scientists and then discourage them by showing them that sociology now is something more like applied mathematics, a kind of dehumanized and dehumanizing game or trade. It has often reminded me of the old rhyme
>
> Mother, Mother, may I go out to swim?
> Yes, my darling daughter:
> Hang your clothes on a hickory limb
> But don't go near the water.
>
> How different sociology would be if more sociologists would "go near the water"! The glaring defect of a great deal of undergraduate and graduate training in sociology is a lack of field experiences of an intimate and continuing nature. (Lee 1975, p.20)

In addition to providing training complementary to more didactic on-campus instruction, the field experience program also assists with occupational placement, since many students, upon graduation, are employed by the agency with which they had interned.

Student Volunteering

A program component in the Department of Sociology, Anthropology, and Human Services requires students to give a minimum number of hours of free service to community agencies, institutions, and programs. It is designed to provide assistance, elevate social consciousness, and bring students into contact with real problems of human welfare.

Community Service Center

Grant funds have assisted the Department of Sociology, Anthropology, and Human Services to open and operate a service center in a community near the university. Members of the community are employed in the center and work with student interns and volunteers in an ongoing program of community development, and research.

Off-Campus Certificate Program in Corrections

A continuing grant from LEEP made it possible for the Department of Sociology, Anthropology, and Human Services to provide loans and grants to in-service correctional workers who enrolled in an off-campus certification program in criminology and corrections. Most of the students in this program have been white. Many of them subsequently matriculated in the regular degree program thereby contributing substantially to the racial desegregation at the university. These white students and graduates have proved to be the best recruiters of other nonblack students for the social sciences programs at FAMU.

Faculty Professional Activity and Publications

Because the faculty in sociology, social welfare, and the other social sciences is extremely active in professional associations, public service projects, and scholarly writing, large numbers of students are attracted to these courses of study. A number of these faculty members hold important offices in national, regional, and local organizations and serve on a variety of national, state, and professional boards and commissions. Encountering the published works of local social science faculty in textbooks, research journals, and other instructional materials proves extremely effective in stimulating and motivating students at FAMU, who have perhaps been conditioned to believe that scholarly work came mostly from the Ivy League. Sociology and other social science faculty at FAMU and many other black institutions, while not functioning under the "publish or perish" dictum, nevertheless feel that scholarly research and writing are essential to their personal professional development and also to complement their instructional efforts.

Demographic Training and Research Institute

In 1973 FAMU assisted in the procurement of grants from the Ford Foundation and the Southern Education Foundation. These were supplemented by funds of the Southern Regional Demographic Group of the Oak Ridge Associated University. These resources made it possible to hold at Oak Ridge, Tennessee, a three-week summer training institute in demography for interested faculty members from selected black colleges and universities. The principal thrust of this endeavor was to train faculty who would institute courses in demography in institutions where there were none and to upgrade the understandings and skills of those faculty already teaching such courses.

The following summer, FAMU itself obtained a $20,000 grant from the Cooperative State Research Service in the United States Department of Agriculture and conducted on the FAMU campus a three-week research training institute for sixteen faculty members from the 1890 predominantly black land-grant colleges and universities. The main goal of this institute was to train faculty members in modern demographic research techniques and stimulate ongoing demographic research efforts at the schools involved.

At both of the institutes eminent demographers were used as faculty, and the resulting activity in teaching and research by faculty at the participating institution indicates that these programs were successful.

Grantsmanship

As mentioned earlier, of the twenty-five faculty and staff positions in the Department of Sociology, Anthropology, and Human Services at FAMU in 1973, only eight were supported by regular state-appropriated monies. The remaining positions were funded by outside grants obtained through the efforts of the department chairman and his faculty. In 1973 this FAMU department alone obtained $845,000 in training and research grants in support of its programs and students—no mean accomplishment for a black university with few alumni or powerful friends in the federal granting establishment. Grantsmanship has become vital to the social science programs at many black schools. At FAMU, in addition to continuing faculty efforts, a graduate credit course in proposal writing is offered to social science students in two master's programs.

New Graduate Programs

In response to societal changes, educational needs, human imperatives, and new career opportunities, the social science faculty at FAMU has inaugurated master's degree programs in School and Community Psychology and in Applied Social Science. These programs feature unique internship and research components and are designed to facilitate entry into human service delivery systems by graduates—at a level of responsibility substantially above that of the holder of the baccalaureate.

The master of applied social science program is interdisciplinary and offers a variety of career options while also providing a solid academic base for doctoral study. As far as can be determined, it is not duplicated by any college or university in the United States, although the University of Pittsburgh does offer degree programs in applied sociology.

These programs are staffed by thirty-three faculty members, twenty-seven of whom hold the earned doctorate. FAMU, like most of the black colleges and universities, is fully accredited by the regional accrediting association, and its social welfare program is on the approved list of the Council on Social Work Education.

In discussing the teaching and learning of the social sciences in the predominantly black college and university, this chapter has attempted to outline the diversity of circumstances, problems, processes, and structures that influence such teaching and identify and illustrate the programs, strategies, and innovations employed to enhance and improve social science teaching and learning. Black colleges and universities have pioneered a number of thrusts in the social sciences, and their students with baccalaureates successfully matriculate in graduate programs at major universities throughout the nation.

Chapter 13

Black Students in the Sciences: A Look at Spelman College

Shirley M. McBay

Various studies have been conducted on the number of blacks and other minorities in the sciences. Among these is a report of the National Science Foundation (1975a). This report indicates that in 1972 there were approximately 9,700 black scientists, who comprised less than 2 percent of the total pool of 496,000 scientists. Among the 143,000 scientists holding the doctorate, there were 1,300 blacks, less than 1 percent of the total holders of doctorates in science. There were 4 black scientists per 10,000 total black population, in comparison with 27 white scientists per 10,000 total white population.

Young (1974) indicates that in 1973 an estimated 1,600 black students were enrolled in the sciences at the graduate level. Other sources indicate that among the 17,000 blacks taking the Graduate Record Examination (GRE) in 1974–5, approximately 2,000 took the examination in one of the sciences. If we assume that (a) all 2,000 black students taking the GRE in the sciences in 1974–5 actually enrolled in graduate school, (b) the 1,600 already doing graduate work in the sciences remained in school, and (c) by 1977 all 3,600 successfully completed doctoral programs, with all other factors remaining constant, blacks would still comprise less than 4 percent of the science doctorates.

No specific data were available on the number of black students entering college who chose a science major. The report of the National Science Foundation (1975a) did indicate that in 1973, when blacks accounted for 12 percent of the college-age population, those electing a

216

major in science made up only 8 percent of the total college enrollment. Obviously the causes of serious underrepresentation by blacks in the sciences are numerous. In this chapter, I described barriers to science education for blacks at the college level and some of the strategies employed by black colleges for removing the barriers. In addition, a detailed examination is made of efforts at Spelman College to improve the teaching of the sciences; Spelman is a college for women in Atlanta, Georgia, and the student body is predominantly black. Finally, some general recommendations are made for increasing the representation of blacks in scientific fields.

Why Blacks Do Not Choose Science

When black students enter a predominantly black institution intending to major in one of the sciences or mathematics, they will very likely face a multitude of problems—some that they have brought with them, some ingrained in the institution, and some inherent in the scientific disciplines themselves.*

Among the major impediments to success in the scientific discipline that black students often carry with them to college are the following:

- Lack of experience in the analysis and interpretation of data and in the experimental method of inquiry
- Poor problem-solving skills, poor study habits, and poor standardized test performance, which often cause the belief that the student is a slow learner
- Inability to use scientific or mathematical language
- Inadequate information on traditional and recently emerging scientific careers
- Absence of a firm commitment to major in science, often caused by lack of encouragement or by counseling that directs the student away from science

*A major source of information for the material in this section is a book of published abstracts of projects supported through the National Science Foundation's Minority Institutions Science Improvement Program (MISIP) for the fiscal years 1972-1975 (National Science Foundation 1975b). It should be emphasized that the remarks that follow provide a general picture of black students, faculty, and colleges, rather than variations by specific institutions. Further, the scope of this chapter excludes a discussion of efforts made by predominantly white institutions to increase minority representation in the sciences. Nor is there discussion of efforts by the federal government, business, industry, private foundations, and individuals. It should be recognized, however, that implementation of many of the strategies to be discussed was possible because of financial and other forms of support from these various groups.

- Absence of any prior role models in science
- Lack of adequate financial resources, which make it necessary for the student to work rather than spend time in the laboratory
- Uncertainty about the rewards for long hours spent toward preparing for a career in science in contrast to rewards for long hours spent in pursuit of more certain careers, such as one in athletics
- Uncertainty of job availability in view of national predictions of an oversupply of scientists in the near future.

It should be emphasized that not all black students have these individual handicaps. Those who are so burdened—as well as those who are not—may also enter a predominantly black institution where institutional barriers further contribute to the rejection of a major in science. While this is by no means true of the science program in every black college, many do suffer from deficiencies that turn students away. For instance:

- Lack of well-defined objectives in science at the institution
- A science faculty, some of whose members are inadequately trained in the disciplines that they are teaching and who may have few opportunities for professional development or little time to develop new instructional methods or to update courses
- Excessive teaching loads for science faculty
- Introductory science and mathematics courses offered by instructors whose native tongue is not English
- Inadequate scientific facilities and materials, including laboratory equipment
- Inadequate operating budget
- Inability of the institution to attract and retain promising scholars
- Lack of strong support for the science program by the central administration.

Then there are the barriers discouraging a commitment to science that are inherent in scientific disciplines themselves:

- Mastery of basic and advanced mathematics, which is often required
- Long laboratory hours
- Numerous required major courses and science-support courses
- Little obvious financial or other reward
- The need for expensive equipment and specially designed facilities to make modern instruction and research possible

• Problems of catching up and keeping abreast with advances in traditional science areas as well as the emerging new fields.

Given this overview of deterrents to the selection of a science major by black students, let us examine some strategies employed by predominantly black institutions to overcome the barriers to a career in science by blacks. We will then examine briefly evidence of some successful results.

Strategies for Removing the Barriers

As indicated earlier, support for many of the strategies that have been carried out has come from various sources external to the institutions. It should be emphasized, however, that their development and implementation have come mainly from the science faculties at the predominantly black institutions. Just as all of the barriers identified previously do not exist at each black institution, all the strategies to be described have not been undertaken at all of them. These strategies for overcoming impediments to the selection of a science major by black students may be categorized as student oriented, faculty oriented, and program or facility oriented, with some possible overlap.

1. Student-oriented strategies:

• Special summer programs before the freshman year
• Establishment of a center for developing study skills or learning resources
• Tutorial sessions conducted by students and by teachers
• Seminars and newsletters dealing with career information
• Emphasis on career and personal counseling
• Smaller classes in science and mathematics
• Development of new instructional procedures, including individualized learning modules, team teaching, investigative laboratories, and increased use of audiovisual and audio-tutorial techniques
• The competency-based approach
• Student-exchange program
• Programs for undergraduate research and independent study
• Seminars on techniques for taking tests
• Visiting lectures
• Visits to scientific and medical facilities
• Student involvement in off-campus summer programs.

2. Faculty-oriented strategies:

• Part-time and full-time study leaves

- Summer curriculum-development workshops, departmental seminars, and miniworkshops
- Internships at other colleges
- Faculty participation in special conferences on the educational use of computers and on designing and producing audiovisual materials for instructional improvements
- Provision for research opportunities and facilities for faculty.

3. Strategies that are program or facility oriented:

- Acquisition of modern instructional equipment
- Renovation of existing science facilities or construction of new ones
- Curriculum revisions
- Development of long-range planning, management, and evaluation capability at institutional and departmental levels
- Integrating the use of computers in science and mathematics courses, giving "hands-on" experience to the students
- Increased emphasis on the application of quantitative and statistical techniques in the sciences
- Strengthening the faculty by adding persons with needed expertise
- Improvement of science courses for nonscience majors
- Strengthening training programs for science teachers

Although many of these strategies have been employed to some degree for a number of years, most have gone into effect since 1972 when special programs were established at the national level to support the improvement of science education at minority institutions.

Evidence of Success

It would be unrealistic to attribute to specific strategies any specific increases in science enrollments. However, all evidence of success should be recorded and evaluated for the purpose of eventually identifying a set of minimal conditions that must exist at an institution for its students to be successful in science.

These then are changes at various predominantly black institutions that appear to be associated with increased student interest in science:

- Stabilization or decrease in the level of student attrition in science and mathematics
- Increase in the number of science and mathematics majors and in the number of faculty and students involved in research activities
- Significant increase in job and graduate school success

- Increase in the number of students who apply to medical and graduate schools
- Successful enrollment in graduate schools that require a heavy emphasis on quantitative methods at the undergraduate level
- Statistically significant increase in quantitative test scores on the Graduate Record Examination
- Improvement in faculty morale
- Improvement in student motivation for work and study
- An overall improvement in the academic climate
- Increase in the training level (percentage of doctorates) of the science faculty
- Accreditation of some individual science departments by national groups
- Student interest and enrollment in newly established courses and programs in science.

Again, it must be emphasized that these are collective changes and that all are not operative at an individual institution. Follow-up studies should be done on individual students who graduate in science to see whether they do enter scientific careers. The first freshman class affected by many of these changes graduated in 1976.

From this survey of barriers, strategies, and evidence of success in the removal of barriers to the entry of blacks into science, we move next to a specific improvement plan in effect at Spelman College.

The Spelman College Program

Spelman is a liberal arts college for women and one of six predominantly black institutions comprising the Atlanta University Center.* It is the larger and older of two colleges in the country that have traditionally served black women; the other is Bennett College in Greensboro, North Carolina. In 1972, with the assistance of funds made available under Title III of the Higher Education Act of 1965, Spelman created its first academic division, the division of the natural sciences.† At that time, the young woman entering Spelman who de-

*The six institutions in the Atlanta University Center are Atlanta University, Clark College, the Interdenominational Theological Center, Morehouse College, Morris Brown College, and Spelman College.

†Prior to 1972, Spelman's academic program was organized along departmental lines as opposed to divisional lines. Under the latter structure, related departments were organized into coordinated units; the pilot division took in the natural sciences. As a result of its success, the college moved to establish other divisions, in the fine arts, social sciences, humanities, and education.

sired to major in science faced some discouraging barriers. Among them:

- Inadequate laboratory facilities, equipment, and library materials
- A rigid traditional science curriculum taught by a faculty that was, with few exceptions, unsympathetic to students with a weak background in mathematics and the sciences
- Instruction in a dull and dark science facility that had been constructed in 1925
- A college tradition that emphasized the arts and humanities and a student body of 1,110, of which more than 45 percent were majoring in the social sciences
- Required enrollment in a freshman mathematics course for science and mathematics majors where the passing rate averaged 30 percent.

Faced with the high attrition rates of students in mathematics, the new natural sciences division developed a pilot strategy designed to strengthen the mathematics and reading skills of a small group of entering freshmen during the summer of 1972. A major effort to overcome other weaknesses in the science program was the development in 1973 of a master plan for the improvement of the division. This plan identified goals over a five-year period in staff development, program development, physical facilities, and special student-oriented activities.

In addition, the natural sciences division in cooperation with the college counseling service undertook a number of special activities in connection with the science program. These included:

1. Specialized recruitment of students for science
2. An eight-week summer program for fifty of the top entering freshmen who indicated science or mathematics as a major
3. A counseling program specifically aimed at students seeking careers in health and the sciences
4. An advisory committee for students seeking careers in health and the sciences
5. Tutorials in mathematics, chemistry, and biology, including establishment of a mathematics laboratory
6. Sessions on test-taking techniques and practice under the auspices of the counseling services
7. Establishment of departmental honor societies
8. Opportunities for student research and independent study projects

9. A visiting lecturer series that brought to the college women scientists and Spelman graduates in science.

Table 13–1
Impact of Master Plan on Spelman Students during the Four-Year Period, 1972–1976

TIME	PORTION OF PLAN ADMINISTERED
Recruitment	1. Local high schools 2. Special regional recruitment sessions 3. Brochures 4. Alumnae
Pre-enrollment Summer	1. Instruction in reading, mathematics, introductory biology, scientific instrumentation, and computer science 2. Administration of various standardized tests 3. Provision of stipend
Freshman Year	1. Advanced placement opportunities 2. New teaching techniques 3. Tutorial services (mathematics, biology, chemistry) 4. Counseling services 5. Student-faculty monthly meetings
Sophomore Year	1. Visiting lecturers and recent graduates 2. New teaching techniques 3. Tutorial sessions 4. Counseling, personal and oriented to careers 5. Administration of standardized tests and area tests 6. Science clubs and newsletter 7. Student-faculty meetings, continued
Junior Year	1. Lecture series, continued 2. Testing sessions 3. Intensified career counseling 4. Tutorial sessions (physiology, organic chemistry) 5. Honor societies 6. Student-faculty meetings, continued
Senior Year	1. Lecture series, continued 2. Independent study, undergraduate research 3. Career plans finalized
Postgraduate Period	1. Follow-up

Table 13–2
Number of Students Majoring in the Division of the Natural Sciences at Spelman College, 1972–76

MAJOR AREA	1972–73	1973–74	1974–75	1975–76
Engineering	11	13	47	69
Computer Science	3	7	10	20
Biology, Mathematics, Chemistry, and Physics	128	156	190	230
Totals	142	176	247	319
Total Student Body	1,069	1,135	1,155	1,240

Impact of the Spelman Program

The impact of the master plan on Spelman students over the four-year period from 1972 to 1976 is shown in Table 13-1. The most significant change that resulted from the implementation of the various strategies at Spelman was the increase in the number of majors within the division, which is shown in Table 13-2. Special recruitment efforts in engineering were conducted by means of a program conducted throughout the six institutions of the Atlanta University Center, which accounts for the large number of engineering students.

Table 13–3
Information about Participants at Spelman College Who Completed the Pre-enrollment Summer Program, 1972–1975

YEAR	NUMBER OF PARTICIPANTS	AVERAGE SAT[a] SCORE	READING	MATH ADVANCED PLACEMENT[b]	BIOLOGY ADVANCED PLACEMENT[c]
1972[d]	16	940	All exempted	87%	NC[e]
1973	44	880	All exempted	59%	NC
1974	45	940	All exempted	47%	69%
1975	41	862	39 exempted	61%	83%

[a] Scholastic Aptitude Test
[b] Percentage receiving 1 or 2 semesters advanced placement in mathematics
[c] Percentage receiving 1 semester advanced placement in biology
[d] Four weeks only
[e] Course not offered

The primary factor responsible for more than doubling the number of science majors at Spelman is believed to be the summer program that began in 1972. The program now serves fifty students, who receive eight weeks of instruction in reading, mathematics, and biology with four weeks each of scientific instrumentation and computer science. Advanced placement opportunities exist in mathematics and biology, and exemption from instruction in reading is also possible. Students may receive seven hours of credit in science if they successfully complete the summer program. Participation is at no cost to the student, who also receives a $500 stipend to help compensate for the loss of funds from summer employment.

The original master plan of 1972 calls for the summer program to terminate in 1978; by then it will have provided the institution with a steady stream of science students over a seven-year period and will have helped to strengthen the college's reputation and image in the sciences. Table 13-3 provides information on summer participants who completed the program during 1972–75. Not shown in the table are the results of standardized tests administered to summer students in each discipline at the beginning and the end of the program; significant changes were produced.

Implementation of other phases of the master plan produced a variety of benefits. Faculty and student morale, for example, were greatly improved through complete renovation of the science building and the addition of an annex that provided modern laboratories and research facilities. Curriculum offerings were revised to provide an interdisciplinary and modern thrust with the addition of such courses as biostatistics, biochemistry, science-oriented nutrition, environmental sciences, virology.

In addition to benefiting from activities within the college, Spelman students in science participate in special external summer programs. In 1975, over thirty took part in such programs at medical schools, professional schools, national research centers, and businesses. During 1974–75, thirty-three premedical students participated at a local hospital in a volunteer program in pediatrics, labor and delivery, and in medical and emergency services.

During the period 1970–1975, there were eighty-nine graduates from Spelman College in the sciences. Over 60 percent of them have done some form of advanced study. In 1976, eighteen were enrolled in medical school and four in dental school. Those attending graduate school have enrolled in programs such as operations research, meteorology, biostatistics, engineering, computer science, and master of business administration programs, in addition to the traditional scientific fields. These graduate students are enrolled at major predominantly white universities and medical schools as well as at major black universities and medical schools. Career choices cover medicine and dentistry, research, actuarial science, engineering, statistics, budget analysis, and computer programming. Graduates in science are employed in major white businesses and industries as well as in a black-owned insurance company, a black-owned bank, and predominantly black colleges and public school systems.

With regard to the Spelman science efforts during the period discussed, it must be emphasized that implementation of the plan was possible because of significant external funding, strong support from the college president, general faculty support, various student-support services available at the college, and the total involvement of the entire faculty and students in the sciences.

Increasing Black Representation in the Sciences

What we now know about increasing the representation of blacks in scientific fields points to several lines of activity that should be followed to accelerate the process.

Long-Range Institutional Plans

Many predominantly black colleges, with the assistance of the Office of Education's Advanced Institutional Development Program (established under Title III of the Higher Education Act of 1965), are developing or strengthening their planning, management, and evaluation capabilities. Such an undertaking of necessity involves the complete institution, including, of course, its academic departments or divisions. These programs should enable science faculties to develop realistic and meaningful long-range plans for teaching science.

In developing a comprehensive and cohesive plan for attracting more students to the field of science, it is imperative that the science faculty at each predominantly black institution base its program upon an analysis of existing resources and upon institutional goals in science. Moreover, it must be a program that can be supported by the institution's central administration. In addition to developing staff, program, physical facilities, and special student-oriented activities, support should be sought for endowed chairs and endowed scholarships in science in order to provide financial stability for the program and the institution.

Cooperative Efforts

It is clear that many of the same problems exist at a number of predominantly black institutions. It is clear also that many of these institutions will not have funds to implement the various strategies for increasing black representation in science, or modified versions of them. It seems likely that considerable time, effort, and money could be saved through a program to exchange information on tactics that have been employed, their strengths and weaknesses. The exchange program could take place in two steps:

1. A national conference held for faculty representatives in science that would present curricular and audiovisual materials, instructional modules, new teaching techniques, career counseling information, course syllabi, and other materials that have been successfully employed
2. Establishment of a national data bank containing basic information about these materials that would be available for use by minority institutions

Another project of a cooperative nature could be special training programs for faculty on the integration of computer techniques and statistical and other quantitative methods into science courses. Such programs are necessary if we are to provide students with modern skills that will enable them to be competitive.

In addition, cooperative arrangements should be developed among major universities and groups of minority institutions for funneling graduates of these institutions into the universities. This arrangement could also include additional training for science faculty members of the minority institutions.

Establishing a National Numerical Goal

Securing financial support for institutional improvement in the teaching of science and for cooperative efforts such as those described should provide predominantly black institutions with long-range capabilities in science. This would greatly facilitate access to careers in mathematics and other sciences for black students. However, a concerted effort is necessary to achieve parity.

First, a statistically reliable assessment of black scientists must be made. This should be followed by a similar assessment of potential black scientists at the college and graduate school levels. Using these data and the figure required for parity in the science pool, a national numerical goal can be established to be followed by the establishment of special fellowship programs designed to support minority graduate students and faculty members as a part of an overall effort to achieve this national goal. The period of time required for the development of these programs will be function of the assessment results. Support for the fellowship programs should come from the government, foundations, industry, and business. The primary focus should be on minority institutions, for it is still true that most black students who go on to do graduate work come from the predominantly black colleges.

Summary of Recommendations

1. Development of long-range science plans
2. A national conference featuring successful curriculum materials
3. Establishment of a national data bank
4. Faculty-training conferences on quantitative skills
5. Cooperative arrangements among major universities and minority institutions
6. Establishment of a national goal for parity representation
7. Fellowship programs to aid students

In this chapter I have attempted to identify certain barriers to the selection of scientific careers by black students. Further, I have identified various strategies to remove these barriers and have noted available evidence of success. Implicit in this account is an unstated admiration for the students and teachers involved in these efforts. While others may have managed and organized and still others may have financed these strategies, the credit for achievements belongs to those actually involved in the struggle. They have come up short again and again and yet have managed to endure. Now they are helping to win some small victory for the cause of greater equity in the distribution of our educational resources.

Chapter 14

Teaching in the Humanities

Thelma Roundtree

The fundamental purpose of higher education—its obligation and responsibility—is to transmit purposeful knowledge, facilitate awareness and self-discovery, and develop value priorities. That is why the study of the humanities must occupy a central place in the undergraduate curriculum. It is in these courses that students come to grips with the questions, Who am I? Where am I going? It is in them that they gain personal insights into the diversities among people and societies and the similarities that link them. It is in studying the humanities that students can learn—guided by teachers with the capacity to impart wisdom—to distinguish between the elements of experience that are meaningful and those that are absurd.

There is also a practical side to the matter. As it happens, the humanities provide sound preparation for work at a professional level. Business prefers managerial personnel with an educational background in the humanities, because management involves judgment, analysis, decision making, and the setting of priorities. These functions call for people who operate on the basis of ethics, values, and an understanding of human development, qualities that are fostered by a systematic encounter with the humanities. This is because the humanities are concerned with the study of people as well as things, with rational, spiritual, living beings.

The historian Charles R. Keller is one who has pointed out the connection between study of the humanities and success in the world of affairs. He put it this way:

A study of the Humanities can be most rewarding. While it may not train a person for one particular profession, it can equip that person with a wide general knowledge, judgment, and an understanding of people and events. Study in the Humanities should prepare people for responsibility by teaching them how to go about getting information and finding answers, and how to think clearly, but also to explain themselves clearly and effectively, both in speech and writing. Clarity of thought and of expression, at meetings, in letters and in reports, should be one of the attributes of a well-educated person.

   With this valuable educational background, the Humanities graduate will find open to him a great variety of occupations, indeed a much greater number and variety of occupations than would be open to him if he had confined his studies to a particular profession or trade. (Keller 1967)

The considerations stressed by Keller were, of course, basic to the position of W. E. B. DuBois (1903a) in his historic debate with Booker T. Washington (1901) on the kind of education that blacks should pursue, a controversy with profound implications for the development of black education that is discussed at some length in Chapter 5 of this volume. Washington believed that education should start in a natural and logical order growing out of community needs. He held that success for black students would come from industrial training, which imparted agricultural expertise and the value of occupational skills, industry, and good character. DuBois, to the contrary, argued that industrial education endangered the academic, economic, and social progress of blacks, that high aspirations and occupational success would follow from the study of philosophy, literature, history, languages, and the arts.

What the Humanities Mean at Black Colleges

   The writer has studied humanities programs at sixteen historical black colleges in eight states and the District of Columbia. The study has made clear the unique function of the humanities in the black college. Black education has been enriched and sustained by teaching in the humanities. The past ten years, in particular, have seen changes in the teaching and learning of the humanities at black colleges that have enhanced their value for the black undergraduate. Perhaps the major change has been the inclusion of courses in black and Third World art, literature, and music. In addition, there has been a movement toward interdisciplinary programs that interrelate music, art, literature, philosophy, and history under common themes.

This is not to say that all black colleges define the humanities in the same way. Definitions vary according to the time, place, and the philosophy of education of an institution. Some define the humanities as the classics in world literature, philosophy, and jurisprudence and view them as extending back far enough to include the Greek dramatists. Interestingly, in this conception, works by black Americans are seldom included, with the possible exception of *Souls of Black Folk* by W. E. B. DuBois and *Up from Slavery* by Booker T. Washington.

Other schools conceive of the humanities in terms of the Great Books, including works as historically diverse as Homer's *Iliad* and Dostoevsky's *Crime and Punishment*. The emphasis here is on contents relating to the various forms of joy, happiness, faith, courage, struggle, and aspirations expressed by diverse peoples. In addition aesthetics are used as a touchstone to extend the definition of the humanities to the performing arts, with the arena of performance encompassing the stage, orchestra pit, and art studio.

By and large, the dominant view is one that sees the humanities as a fusion of subject matter from art, music, and literature. The literature may include nontechnical selections from the quantitative disciplines such as mathematics, physics, and chemistry; often history, philosophy, and selections in the behavioral sciences are included. More usually, however, literature is viewed in terms of the conventional genres—poetry, essays, novels, biography, autobiography, and short stories.

Self-discovery and life planning are goals shared by humanities programs in black colleges, whatever their views on content. The emphasis is on confronting the students with questions that create a ferment in their minds. The objectives are very much in line with what Nathan Pusey, the former president of Harvard University, has said about the humanities and their contribution to self-discovery:

> Every human being needs direct personal contact with great stories, myths, and fictions of the human race, and with the history, to begin to know himself and to sense the potentialities—of all sorts, for good and for bad—that lie within his reach and the reach of other men. The reaches of the human soul and the distortions that the human soul is capable of, the meanness that mars our judgments and the great liberations we can achieve, what it is to be a man and what it can be, these things are known through the lives and actions of individuals who speak to us by means of art and the pages of history. (Pusey 1962, pp. 80–81)

Thus you might find a black college student in a humanities course challenged by such statements as:

"Hate destroys all values."—Martin Luther King, Jr.
"The unexamined life is not worth living."—Socrates
"Life is a comedy to the man who thinks; a tragedy to the one who feels."—Horace Walpole

Black Folklore and Music

The outstanding feature of the humanities programs of black colleges today is their emphasis on distinctively black material emerging out of the black culture and experience—particularly in the areas of folklore and music. René Welleck, the literary critic, has pointed out the distinctive importance of folklore as a medium for understanding a people:

> Folklore is an important branch of learning about a group which is only in part occupied with aesthetic facts since it studies the total civilization of a folk, its customs, myths, and tools as well as its arts. Folklore is a common language about a people that expresses an element of reality about its social structure. (Welleck and Warren 1949, p. 106)

Folklore offers values reflecting the past that furnish rich cultural nourishment. Indeed, a cultural heritage can be partly preserved through teaching the folklore of a group. Black folklore contains information about myths and accounts of struggles and oppression. It reveals the economic, social, and educational evolution of black people. These materials have had a unifying effect for blacks and have contributed to the growing understanding of their contributions and diversity. The myths of blacks—like those of other people—are frequently expressed through an oral tradition, in epics, sermons, and musical idioms. One of the most powerful of these forms is the Negro spiritual, a religious song that adapted the narrative style and marked rhythms of the folk ballad to the experiences and life styles of the Negro. The ancestral background of the spirituals and their relationship to the everyday life of blacks is still a matter of some debate. We do know that they were a source of inspiration to the family in everyday life; harmony in the household frequently was expressed through these songs, which were performed to a natural rhythm without instruments. The spirituals were melodies created to express the feelings of the people. Harold Courlander, who has studied various forms of music, finds that African elements survive in the spirituals as well as in other black folk music, particularly in their rhythms (Welleck and Warren 1946, p. 106).

Another powerful form of musical expression for blacks that belongs in the humanities curricula of black colleges is the blues. These songs have a twofold cultural significance: They represent an evolution in musical form, and they communicate the experience of oppression. William C. Handy, father of the blues, said that they expressed the way of life of "honky-tonk piano players, wanderers and other blacks of their impoverished . . . class from Missouri to the Gulf" (Courlander, 1970). The eminent black sociologist E. Franklin Frazier (1939, p. 214) linked the blues to the disruptive experience of black men after the Civil War, when many severed their relationship with their families to look for work in the city, and others, seeking adventure, became solitary wanderers. Often disillusioned and lonely, these men clung to memories of the affection and sympathy they had received from a wife and children left behind. Frazier cites a popular blues song of the period expressing this feeling:

I gotta wife, Buddie
With two little children, Buddie
With two little children, Buddie
Tell 'em I'm comin' home, Buddie
Buddie, I'm comin' home.

Jazz is another black musical idiom that is studied on the black campus, both as a musical form and as part of the humanities. It is, in essence, a response to the changed environment of blacks during the early decades of the twentieth century, an expression of emotions which is not necessarily either sad or happy. Leonard Bernstein has said that "jazz is a vital art with a solid past and exciting future" (Bernstein 1963, p. 48). It is fair to say that jazz is variously the music of the intellect and the emotions, and an aesthetic product.

One of the giants of jazz whose work is being studied on black campuses is Scott Joplin, the nineteenth century black composer of ragtime music. Joplin had an early childhood beset by poverty; in adulthood, he had a large family, which also experienced economic privation. In the face of these hardships, Joplin wrote *Treemonisha*, an opera that expresses his feelings for family cohesiveness. Recent research on Joplin's life and work has revealed the scope of his contribution to the development of ragtime and has increased interest in expanding the understanding and appreciation of this unique black musical idiom.

Innovative Methods

In addition to an increasing emphasis on material derived from the black experience, another conspicuous change in the teaching and learning of the humanities on the black campus is occuring in the area of methods. As has been noted, an interdisciplinary approach is being stressed, with humanities courses related to other subject fields in the curriculum; modular scheduling is frequently utilized. One objective of this thrust is to relate the humanities to the personal problems—emotional and financial—that beset black students.

The study that I conducted revealed that perhaps the most crucial problem confronting the humanities programs at black colleges is psychological, the students' underlying and pervasive feeling of insecurity. Like a third-degree burn, black fears have left an ugly psychological scar since 1619, when slaves were first brought to this country. The schools are attempting to equip their students with the resources for dealing with these fears by connecting the awareness and self-discovery gained in the study of the humanities to other aspects of their academic work and to the totality of their personal experience.

Among the evolving methods of teaching the humanities are the analytical and interpretative rather than the narrative and descriptive. Linguistics, for example, examines the interpretation of symbols; reading is taught as a language art. The inductive method is used in teaching history; this is an approach which analyzes persons, events, periods, and ideas in depth and deemphasizes the chronology of events. Like the black orientation in subject content and the innovative interdisciplinary approach inductive teaching may require the retraining of faculty.

In sum, the teaching of the humanities is of unique importance at black colleges because of the values they transmit and the personal strengths they can foster. At the black colleges, broadening the content of the humanities to encompass the cultural products of the black experience and linking the humanities to other subject fields are uniquely important for accomplishing the basic objectives of a liberal education.

Chapter 15

Teaching and Learning English

John U. Monro

For nine years now it has been my responsibility to conduct and develop the Freshman Studies program at Miles College in Birmingham, Alabama. Miles is a private, church-related, historically black, four-year, accredited coeducational college, established in 1905, and presently enrolling some 1,200 students. This chapter describes some things we think we have learned and what we are trying to do in the English part of the program. I believe it will be useful to start by stating major themes that will be running through my report.

First, my own major premise is that it is possible for almost all high school graduates (call it 90 percent to 95 percent of high school graduates) to learn to think straight, to deal with reasonably complicated imformation, and to write out their thoughts in clear, comprehensible standard English prose.

Second, in any open-door college like Miles College, and there are now hundreds across the country, the freshman class ranges widely in ability, in previous training, in information, and in motivation. All these freshmen come to us hopeful that we can somehow help them on their way. Practically all our freshmen are invisible to the selective colleges; I would include among selective colleges a good many state universities, like the University of Alabama, which screen their entering students with tests. The truth is—and all of us on the open-door campuses know this from experience—that a serious percentage of our "invisible" students are well above average in intellectual ability, either ready right now for the university program or ready after a term or less

235

of preparatory help. Based on what I see at Miles College, I would say that at least 15 percent or 20 percent of the students entering open-door colleges are clearly able to handle demanding college work, given the chance. Our major colleges and universities are losing out on a large number of able students because these colleges do not know how to find them or work with them.

Third, we all wish that the public schools were doing a better job of preparing our students to read and write and think. But since the job is not being done, it is up to colleges to move in and work on the problem. My assumption is that all of us in the colleges, as professional educators, share the general responsibility of the education profession to do the best we can for the nation's youth. I think it is fair to say that most colleges do not yet see this effort as part of their responsibility to the country.

Fourth, a college program designed to deal with underprepared students will require these four elements:

1. A close, professional scrutiny of what each student brings to college in the way of skills, information, and attitudes.
2. A program of teaching and learning that deals directly and efficiently with the needs of students in a firm and supportive way. We cannot afford the wastage of time and of human abilities built into the old introductory courses. We need explicit new objectives and direct and effective new teaching methods that comprehend student interests and differences in learning styles. Students need much individual help and much practice in gaining fundamental skills.
3. A competent, dedicated faculty who are interested in teaching students, rather than just teaching a subject. I will repeat for you here Monro's First Law: Faculty is what matters. If you have a good faculty, they will develop a good program. No matter how good the program, a poor faculty will butcher it.
4. A management that keeps close tabs on what is going on: How teachers and students are doing, what works well and what doesn't, and what new developments in learning theory can help in the work. Needless to say, it is unreal to turn over this kind of management problem to the traditional college academic departments.

As my final major theme: If a college will show such concern and undertake this kind of a program, it will be richly rewarded in human results. Any college *can* do it. The problem is one of awareness, concern, and intent.

The Freshman English Program

Each August we register some 350 new freshmen at Miles. Based on past ACT (American College Testing Program) tests, we can expect that two-thirds will be in the bottom 10 percent in mathematics skills. Half of the entering class will read at ninth-grade level or lower as best we can tell from the Nelson-Denny Reading Test. I start with these tests because they are well known, and this information will begin to set the stage.

Actually these national tests are of little help to us. They are no help at all to us in critical areas of diagnosis. We have known that for a long time. So we have developed our own Inventory Tests in English and Mathematics, which all students take at entrance. These tests tell us quite accurately where our students stand with respect to certain basic skills and information that we know to be important.

The English Inventory Test

The English Inventory Test examines closely the four areas we will be attending to in English 101:

1. *Vocabulary.* Does the student's working vocabulary extend through the 5,000 most frequently used words in standard American English? If not, at what range of frequency does control break down?
2. *Sentence grammar.* Does the student have sufficient control of operational sentence grammar to be able to move information into written, controlled sentences? If not, what particular difficulties is he or she having?
3. *Reading.* Can the student translate a sentence of moderate difficulty into his or her own words? Can he or she take apart an orderly paragraph and state its main idea? Can the student distinguish between general conclusive statements and supporting details? Can he or she discover the writer's program for the paragraph?
4. *Thinking and paragraph writing.* Can the student take a given body of data—say a simple table presenting one or two columns of

statistics—draw a conclusion from the data, state the conclusion, and support it in a five-sentence paragraph?

That is a rough sketch of our English Inventory Test. It takes the student usually about one hour to do the work, though we do not impose a time limit.

This test presents a fairly accurate four-part outline of our curriculum for English 101, the opening course. Thus, it can serve three important functions. (1) *Placement:* If the student does well in the test, he or she obviously does not need English 101; we will therefore move him at once to English 102. (2) *Diagnosis:* The test travels with the student to the teacher of English 101 and conveys, early on, what the teacher needs to know to start working with the student. (3) *Evaluation:* Since the test deals with the substance of the course, we can give Form B at the end of the semester and compare it with Form A given at the start. Thus we find out whether the students have learned anything. Put another way: We can find out how any given teacher is doing the job.

During academic year 1976–77 we began using a second form of the Inventory Test as a required competency exam at the end of English 101. The student must pass all parts of the exam or receive an incomplete grade (the teacher's grade being withheld) until all parts have been passed. A backup tutorial program is now provided to help students with this task.

Neither our Inventory Test nor our curriculum for English 101 was developed overnight. Furthermore, they did not evolve out of any theoretical superstructure. Rather, the course and the tightly related examination grew, bit by bloody bit, out of ten years of daily work in class. It has involved a long, organic process of interaction among teachers and students and materials and methods—paying attention to our students; having in mind what skills and information are involved in thinking, writing, and reading; drawing some conclusions from all that about what we ought to be doing; testing these leads and testing again; and finally getting one more piece identified and in place. Changes are still going on, in some ways more deeply and more rapidly now than ever before.

Before going into the 101 course, it may be useful to report some of the things we find from the English Inventory Test.

About 15 percent of our incoming students do quite well on the exam, are excused from English 101, and go straight into English 102. The record is that 90 percent of this group get A or B grades in English 102; by teachers' reports they are the best students in English 102.

These students, as a rule, have not done especially well on the ACT English test. Thus they have been invisible to the selective colleges. By every indication that we have, however, they are ready for college work or close to it. If you apply these figures across the country, that's many thousands of students whom the major colleges and universities are missing because the testing screens now in use are faulty.

Plainly we need a careful study of where the fault lies in the familiar standardized tests. Based on what we observe in our own college testing, the familiar standardized tests (College Board, ACT) do succeed in identifying certain groups of students who are equipped to do well in college. But these tests fail to identify (and thus serve to exclude) other groups of students who are also equipped to do well in college; our tests identify such students, and the familiar standardized tests do not. Notably, our test calls for the performance of certain tasks common to college work—examining data, repeating the data in the student's own words, and expressing a conclusion or opinion about the data. Standardized tests, built upon the necessities for business-machine scoring, fail to present students with similar opportunities to show their abilities. These observations do not amount to proof, but I believe they are suggestive of the lines our inquiry about standardized tests must follow.

About one-third of the students taking our English Inventory Test will shy away altogether from the exercise on paragraph writing—from the effort of drawing a conclusion from given data and writing a paragraph about it. I do not know why students balk at this unit. I can guess, but I am not sure. I do know that, after three or four weeks of practice in class, they take the data paragraph exercise in stride. They will do better on the reading part of the exam than on the writing, but a good half of them will have trouble with it, expecially with the seemingly simple exercise of sentence translation.

A striking and important fact is that, on the average, our students will have trouble with the vocabulary part of the test. A significant majority, perhaps 70 percent, will show that they need intensive work on the most frequently used 5,000 words, to say nothing of fairly common academic vocabulary beyond the 5,000 mark.

The First Basic Course in English

Now to the English 101 course itself and some of the main things we do in it. As I have pointed out, the course has four specific targets; vocabulary, sentence grammar, reading, and paragraph construction.

Building Vocabulary

I had long been aware of the need to help our students with vocabulary. Indeed, watching them puzzle out passages of prose, working back and forth between the text and the dictionary, I was often reminded of my own efforts to read French or German in recent years. After a long period of not using either language, I found that although I could still understand the grammatical structure, the vocabulary was gone. Also, all those possible meanings offered by the dictionary were no help at all.

In 1971, almost by accident, I happened upon a new paperback dictionary, *The New Horizon Ladder Dictionary of the English Language* (Shaw and Shaw 1970), which presents the 5,000 words most often used in modern English. (Another valuable updating of research into frequency of word usage was done recently for the school edition of *The American Heritage Dictionary*.) Beyond indicating the 5,000 words most often used in modern English, *The New Horizon Dictionary* goes a step further and prints in parentheses beside each word a digit indicating whether it is in the first, the second, third, fourth, or fifth thousand. I had been conscious of Thorndike's scholarly efforts of a previous generation to establish records of word frequency. The new paperback dictionary gave me an idea. Why not set up a fifty-word test, with ten words drawn at random from each of the five ranges of frequency and see how the students made out? We did that. What I discovered was that most of my students had quite good control over vocabulary in the first 3,000 words. After that, control began to break down.

This finding began to give me a handle on the large and complex vocabulary problem. But what to do about it? Malcolm X, as a young man doing time in Massachusetts prisons, set up his own education program by copying one page a day out of the dictionary. Maybe I could have my students buy the new dictionary and somehow make them responsible for learning its contents. A lot of ideas crossed my mind, and a lot of professional advice: for example, Vocabulary can be learned only in context; or You will do best to establish first the ancient Latin roots and suffixes and prefixes. A lot of academic clichés like that.

Eventually we worked out our present system. It involves teaching 35 words a week (7 words a day, 5 days a week) from an assigned list. Across the 15-week term, that comes to about 500 words; across two terms to 1,000 words. The assigned words have been carefully selected from everywhere imaginable: from the third, fourth, and fifth thousands; from a page-by-page reading of two large college dictionaries; from more recent up-to-date studies of word frequencies in various fields, conducted by *The American Heritage Dictionary*. From all this work we arrived at a list of about 3,000 words that must be taught. We then boiled that down to 1,000 super-must words, the number we can hope to teach in thirty weeks.

Learning the words is a cold-turkey business, slugging it out day by day, the way you used to acquire Latin and French vocabulary in school. One difference is that we spend a fair amount of time in class talking about the words, simplifying the definition, arriving at gross recognition equivalents. For instance, after a discussion, my students decided that the *connotation* of a word is really the special *vibes* of a word. Another difference is that the students keep running into these words in their college reading, thus reinforcing their new acquaintances. Otherwise, it is just cold turkey, with testing and retesting, week by week.

I know very well how bad all this is. Indeed, I get admonitions about this from all sides. I will not try to defend what we are doing except to say that it seems to work pretty well. My students groan at first, but then they buckled down and learn the words; they seem to like the specificity of assignments. Every way I know how to observe it, a large precentage of these words, hit thus head-on, is assimilated so that the words become operational. Students in other classes are also interested in the lists.

Learning the Sentence

My students practice writing sentences. To begin with, they write a brief, one-paragraph paper in class almost every day, until the exercise becomes, if not easy, at least familiar. The paper will almost always report on information we have derived that day in class—a numerical table, a bit of reading, a student report, a campus event. I make it a rule to read all these papers, albeit quickly, to give them a grade, to find one thing about the paper I can praise, and to find one way the student can improve it. In addition, once every two weeks (seven or eight times a semester) my students work through a class-long quiz in which they are asked to write at greater length.

Thus the students practice writing sentences or, better, they practice different ways of moving information into sentence form. I have a theory that learning to write is like learning to play the piano. You cannot learn to play the piano until you practice endlessly, programming your mind and fingers to render musical ideas in notes, scales, and chords. Reading a book about the piano or listening to Van Cliburn helps some, but not much. Mainly it comes down to practice. So it is with writing; you must practice, programming your mind and hand to render verbal ideas into sentences. It is my personal conviction, incidentally, that one reason our young ones do not learn to write is that in the main they are taught by teachers who themselves do not know how to write and must therefore try to teach it from a book.

In English 101, we work endlessly at the sentence, coming at it from three directions:

1. From the side of grammar, we learn enough pieces to construct and control phrases and clauses, and we learn to build sentences with phrases and clauses. Ultimately, by my observation, this is what the professional writer does.
2. From the side of data, of raw information to be packaged, we practice writing sentences about a simple action, something seen in class or out, or about the information presented in one line of a statistical table. In class everybody will write a sentence about, for instance, the line in the table. Then we will compare results to see which sentence seems to do the job best. Then everybody will practice writing that sentence form using a new line of data.
3. As we do our reading, we stop to see how Frederick Douglass or Richard Wright or Martin Luther King shaped a given sentence to deal with an idea or a piece of information. We learn from that.

Mainly we study standard sentence forms, we make up sentences of our own, and we practice. Especially we practice working ideas or information into short sentences, ten to fifteen words. If you can program yourself that way, and have it under control, you can write. Indeed, you will write better than most professors.

We read a reasonable amount, ten to twelve pages a day. As I have suggested earlier, one of our central efforts is on what I call sentence translation. I have this notion that if you cannot dig the meaning out of one sentence, then there is not much chance that you will understand a whole bulk of reading, under pressure, in a hurry. The exercise of sentence translation has a good many virtues. A sentence is a workout in problem solving that is the right size for a class. It is small in scope, manageable in details, and is quickly accomplished. Also, this work gives direct feedback into our study of vocabulary and sentence construction and control. It is amazing to see the results you get when you first give a class a sentence to translate.

Constructing Paragraphs

Once we begin to get control of the sentence, especially how you put one together or how you work information or ideas into sentence form, we start work on the paragraph. The paragraph form we start with follows the basic formula: a general topic sentence, stating the writer's general conclusion about the data before him; followed by about three pieces of evidence to back up the conclusion; finishing with another general statement at the end, reminding the reader what it has all been about. I tell students it is a new version of the old preacher's formula for a successful sermon: "First I tell 'em what I'm going to tell 'em. Then I tell 'em. Then I tell 'em what I told 'em."

There are serious difficulties to be overcome in this approach to the paragraph. A good many of my students have never had any experience in class at drawing conclusions of their own from data. I get the impression that many have been in classes where students were positively discouraged from developing original notions of their own. ("We're just not interested in *your* ideas, Johnny! What we want is what's in the book!") So we must work to help our students discover the fun of original thinking and gain the courage to report about it to others.

Another deep-seated problem is that most of my students have a hard time distinguishing the difference between a general statement and the statement of a concrete detail. In the vocabulary of Jean Piaget (1972), most of them are at the stage of "concrete" operational thought. They are not yet at a state of "formal" operations, the free and easy development and use of abstractions. So we must work on that. Further, most of them come to college with surprisingly little information about the world about them. The vocabulary and common facts about geography or contemporary events or politics—the daily news, so to speak—are unknown quantities to them. As a final difficulty, even if the ideas are there, the student is likely to face a simple mechanical difficulty in rendering them in a sentence.

We tackle the problem of paragraph construction from every angle we can think of. A regular staple in our work is the simple table of data. From the table students are asked to draw a conclusion, any conclusion, so long as it is their very own. Then they must state the conclusion and support it with details. We work on this together in class, drawing various conclusions and supporting them, then writing them up. We study paragraphs already in existence to see how the writer did it, in particular to discover the presence of general, conclusive sentences and detailed supporting statements. We watch, too, to see how the writer sets up transitional signposts from general to detail and back again.

Interleaved with our work on simple statistical tables, we do much the same with our reading. In reading Frederick Douglass or Richard Wright, the emphasis is on drawing our own conclusions about the information the writer tells us. What kind of man was Richard Wright's father? How do we know? What were Douglass's feelings about American Christianity? Why did he feel this way?

Our objective is that by the end of English 101, the student will have been given a great amount of encouragement and practice in looking at data and drawing conclusions for himself and in presenting and supporting these conclusions in clear sentences and in a recognizably orderly paragraph form.

The final week or two of English 101 makes the point that the form of the basic *five-paragraph essay* is really just an expansion of the form of the paragraph we have been practicing so hard.

We know very well that this effort in English 101 does not begin to encompass the whole of the art of writing. But at least it tells our students that sentences and paragraphs are made and not just born. It helps them to know the basic forms in both writing and reading. Through practice, it helps them to have the basic forms under some control.

In the next course, English 102, we go on to develop the paper of five to ten paragraphs, to reinforce control over the sentence and paragraph, to expand vocabulary another basic 500 words, and to broaden and accelerate the experience of reading.

How the Material Is Taught

It will be clear from what I have said that, in our teaching at the thirteenth-grade level, I am impressed by the importance of Jean Piaget's work. It is a fact that most of our students are at a level of *concrete* intellectual operations. Our task is to work with them where they are, by reference to details, to specifics, by giving them practice in induction, in discovery, in drawing their own conclusions. Certainly we will do them no good by lecturing to them in traditional, professorial generalities.

I should like to add here, out of simple gratitude, that we at Miles have been helped the most in out understanding of Piaget's ideas by the work of Professor Floyd H. Nordland and his associates in the Biology Department of Purdue University, who have made careful study and application of Piaget's learning theories in biology instruction at Purdue. They have established extensively in the journals (*Science Education, American Biology Teacher, Journal of Research in Science Teaching, Perceptual and Motor Skills*). Furthermore, they have gone out of their way to help Miles College in training a faculty and in helping us to institute a teaching methodology in biology based on their findings and experience. We in freshman English have observed all this closely and learned from it.

Second, we have been helped greatly by the work of a young American psychologist, Arthur Whimbey (1975), whose book, *Intelligence Can Be Taught*, gives us valuable leads to successful experimental work in tutoring and teaching college students who need special help. In particular Whimbey stresses the importance of problem solving as a way of helping students. Also, he has helped me to see that many of the procedures we use in English 101—in translating sentences, figuring out metaphors, analyzing data, or puzzling out the intended form of a paragraph—are really quite important exercises in problem solving.

You will observe that our reading is mostly from black authors. Indeed, at the same time that our students take English 101, they take an opening social sciences course, which is devoted to the history of the black people's experience in the United States. There is a simple rationale behind this: We are a black college; our students and faculty are deeply interested in developing a full and accurate awareness of the American black experience, historically, and its expression in literature. The public school system does not even try to deal with the black experience or contribution. The least we can do is to start by providing our students with the basic information about it, telling the truth, setting the record straight. The country would be much better off if white colleges would do the same. However, the white colleges are not going to do it, or anything like it which is one reason why sensible people prefer to teach in black colleges.

Another pedagogical issue, as we all know, concerns black English as a language with its own vocabulary and grammatical constructions. To what degree should we be teaching black English as opposed to standard English? Indeed, is there a conflict between these two ideas? My own experience and assignment at Miles College have necessarily limited my observations of this matter. I have been dealing all along with students at the thirteenth-grade level; their goals, by and large, are to get a college education as preparation for a professional or business career in society at large. I have had no experience in dealing with grade school youngsters or high school students or school dropouts or more special groups—like prisoners or working adults—whose backgrounds and objectives may be different.

At Miles we have not become involved in the broad political and social controversy surrounding black English. In the area of English language instruction, it has been a general operating premise of the college for many years that our instructional job is to teach standard English—vocabulary, sentence structure, paragraph formation. We know very well that if teachers are thoroughly familiar with black English, they can get closer to the students' use of language and help them more. One excellent example would be the class that undertook to translate scenes from *Oedipus Rex* into black English and to stage the scenes in dialect—a marvelous exercise in translation, and I wish I had thought of it. In my own classes I would be shamming if I tried to make a big deal of black English. But I certainly let my students know that I find the language vigorous and deeply interesting, and I create opportunities for them to instruct me in vocabulary and grammatical forms. It is a reasonable exchange.

Until 1975–76 our freshman program at Miles had not placed much emphasis on any aspect of oral communication—on preparing and delivering brief talks, on helping students (if they wish it) to gain control of standard English speech patterns or on taking notes and writing summaries of material presented orally. We made a beginning in 1975–76 by assigning one-fifth of our English 101 and 102 class time (fifteen hours in the semester) to oral activities conducted by trained speech teachers. The results persuade us that we should intensify our program in all the directions indicated. As many people point out, a significant number of black students deeply resent any instructional efforts to impose standard English speech patterns, especially when the initiative comes from white teachers. Nonetheless, many black students are aware that they may need control of standard English speech for career purposes, and we feel obliged to make this help available in college.

In the end, with us, it comes down to the fact that to succeed in college and later on, our students need careful instruction in standard English. That is what we are there to begin in freshman English; it is what our students expect of us. I try to make it clear, in the opening days, that other teachers on our staff may be far better versed in black English than I am, that those classes will surely be different, and now is the time to transfer. Some students do transfer, as they should.

A final word about pedagogy. A full load for a freshman English teacher at Miles College is three sections, averaging about twenty students per section, meeting five hours a week. Not many faculty members teach a full load of freshman English since we make it a policy to appoint able teachers and to encourage their employment part time in our upper-level courses at the college. Although we now run our freshman English in standard classes—twenty to twenty-five students to a teacher meeting five days a week—we are on the verge of changing that procedure in the direction of self-paced workshops. We are aiming at a modified workshop program in which three or four days a week will be spent in workshop and one or two days a week in full class, for the value of discussion.

For three years now, I have been increasingly impressed by the virtues of the workshop pattern, but our decision to adopt it has been slowed by two basic considerations. First, to develop the lesson units, or modules, and tests, on which a workshop must be based, you need to know specifically what you are trying to do; until now, we have not been sure. Second, I place too high a value on discussion, or group interaction, to go over entirely to the workshop form. Indeed I have found it difficult to decide what should go into the workshop and what to discussion and how to interleave the two. We are now about ready.

Some Results

A final word as to some of our results. Our longitudinal figures tell us that over half of our entering students, somewhere about 55 percent or 60 percent will stick it out for two years and enter the junior year. That is not bad considering that the average reading score at admission is at the ninth-grade level and that two-thirds of our freshmen are in the bottom 10 percent by national norms in English skills. Taking the bottom half of our entering class, with reading scores at the ninth-grade level or below, the longitudinal record shows that over 50 percent of them survive in college, and an interesting percentage eventually get honor records.

Longitudinal records of this kind certainly do not tell the whole story. Nevertheless they tell us something about where we are, and they give us at least one baseline for judging our performance now and in the future.

The Six Basic Elements

Looking back over what I have said here, I can extract six basic elements that are necessary for success in such a program for developing basic English language skills:

1. An awareness of the importance of original thought, of generating one's own ideas, as the basis of any worthwhile writing. Most of our students come to us with no practice in this art, at least not in the classroom setting. We need to develop all our lesson plans to provide constant, daily practice in generating ideas and reporting them.

2. An awareness that our students come to us at different stages of intellectual perception and operations (concrete to formal) and different, individual ways of learning. We will do best if we adapt our teaching styles to these facts.

3. A concentration on reading materials and materials to write about that are alive and interesting to the students.

4. An awareness that we learn to write by writing, by daily practice in writing, not by studying grammar books or reading about writing.

5. The need for teachers who themselves know enough about writing (a) to be able to detect and to praise evidence of good, original thinking even when the piece is badly written; (b) to ignore picky errors of grammar and spelling and help students with the main structural elements of expression; and (c) to move confidently, without apology, to eliminate dependence on the grammar book, and to reduce to essentials what a student needs to know to express his ideas in sound sentences and paragraphs.

6. The need for teachers who care enough about students to see them as individuals and work with them as individuals.

I append a few samples of class materials to afford a somewhat more concrete view of the day-to-day work of our first basic course in English.

Samples of Material

Used in the First Basic Course in English at Miles College, Birmingham, Alabama

Course Outline, Spring 1976

Vocabulary Material
A Preliminary Quiz

Typical Assignment Sheet for One Week

100 "Most Important" Words for Review

Sentence Material
Assignment to Combine Ideas in a Sentence:
Guidance by Teacher

Examples of Sentence Translation:
A Basic Reading Exercise

Paragraph Writing
Assignment to Write a Paragraph Based on Data Table:
Class Response

An Early Assignment in Paragraph Analysis

Assignment to Write a Brief Essay:
Details of Outline and Development

Course Outline

English 101   Course Outline   Spring Term 1976

Books to Own
1. *Dictionary.* Paperback is okay.

2. Chapman, editor, *Black Voices.*
3. F. Douglass, *Narrative of His Life as a Slave.*
4. Richard Wright, *Black Boy.*

Course Outline
The course will place emphasis on five areas, as follows:
1. *Writing.* We will examine how a writer shapes his ideas into sentences and paragraphs and how he manages and shapes ideas in a brief essay, 5 to 7 paragraphs. We will practice writing almost daily. Understanding how ideas are shaped in writing will help a lot in our reading.
2. *Grammar.* We will study particularly the construction of sentences. At the start, this will necessarily involve us in considering the basic parts of speech, the formation of phrases and clauses, and the combination of words, phrases, and clauses into sentences. We will pay particular attention to the various verb forms and to punctuation.
3. *Vocabulary.* Expansion of vocabulary is a major part of the course. We will learn 7 words a day, 35 words a week, pushing toward a vocabulary expansion of 500 words by the end of the spring term. Vocabulary will be tested once each week, as well as at mid-term and final examinations. The learning of vocabulary will require a significant amount of homework each day.
4. *Reading.* (i) In *Black Voices* we will study the expression of ideas in three forms: fiction, nonfiction prose, and poetry.
(ii) In addition, we will read outside of class three other books, as follows:
by February 6, *Narrative* by Douglass
by March 26, *Black Boy* by Richard Wright
by May 30, *Why We Can't Wait* by Dr. Martin L. King, Jr.
These books will be read outside of class. They will be discussed briefly in class. The reading will be tested by essay exams written in class.
5. *Speaking and Listening.* Fifteen or more hours of class time will be assigned in blocks to Dr. Lippke and Miss McQueen, speech teachers, for special work in oral presentation and listening.

A Word about Grading
Like other college courses, this class will follow the A, B, C, D, F grading pattern. But a student receiving a D or F grade at the

end of the course may be allowed to take a grade of *Incomplete* and
develop an individual contract with the teacher to complete the work
of the course and obtain a better grade during the next semester.

J.U. Monro

A Preliminary Quiz to Check Student's Vocabulary Range

Vocabulary Inventory

*Give meanings of these words. In a word or two, come as close
to the meaning as you can. If it will help, use a word in a sentence.*

advice	abandon	blunder	bankrupt	anarchy
bury	competence	defy	demolish	caricature
dignity	envy	elevate	flexible	ferocious
former	glimpse	handicap	hazard	informal
influence	linger	infinite	lust	mediocre
mineral	offend	neutral	obstruct	negligent
pattern	qualify	paralyze	rebuke	pagan
request	resemble	sane	slump	reprimand
trail	thorough	timid	tense	sluggish
widow	vapor	urban	vicious	velocity

A Typical Vocabulary Sheet for One Week's Assignment (Fifth Week)

Vocabulary List

analysis	fiction	mutual	radical	synonym
bibliography	gross	novel	conservative	antonym
casual	homicide	ordeal	remorse	temperature
community	initiative	pattern	sarcasm	tradition
depression	institution	percent	(semi-)	vain
			semiprecious	
domestic	lady	pledge	sociology	visible
encounter	(mal-)	profound	status	withdraw
	malpractice			

Principal Parts of Irregular Verbs

Verbs	Past	Past Participle	Present Participle
break	broke	have broken	breaking
drink	drank	have drunk	drinking
hurt	hurt	have hurt	hurting
steal	stole	have stolen	stealing

Final Selection of 100 "Most Important" Words for Review (15th Week)

Vocabulary Review

I.	controversy	VIII.	folly
detail	integrity	define	epic
general	myth	ghetto	XII.
plagiarism	separatism	moral	bigot
statistics	V.	nation	genocide
fundamental	community	philosophy	metropolis
coherent	fiction	tragedy	pioneer
II.	radical	IX.	tactics
context	conservative	quota	disadvantage
metaphor	synonym	efficient	ethnic
logic	institution	bourgeois	instinct
mortal	pattern	comedy	consensus
propaganda	sociology	urban	XIII.
III.	tradition	technology	theory
anxiety	VI.	X.	corporation
compassion	category	budget	municipal
desegregate	chattel	ego	XIV.
dialect	irony	frontier	standard
integrate	theme	negotiate	style
liberal	token	classic	discriminate
minority	VII.	XI.	anonymous
relevant	capitalism	society	competence
optimist	communism	racism	miscellaneous
recession	socialism	psychology	reproduce

strategy	policy	guarantee	talent
symbol	predominant	economics	compromise
IV.	tolerant	critical	militant
ambiguous	value	virgin	rumor
connotation		intuition	

Assignment to Combine Ideas in a Sentence: Samples of Students' Work and Teacher's Comments on It

The Sentence: How the Writer Combines Two Ideas in One Sentence
    Here we will be concerned with various basic ways that ideas get combined into sentences: Take the following simple sentences:
    John studied hard.
    He passed the exam.

Assignment 1: Combine into one sentence, using two main clauses.

Samples and comments:
    a. John studied hard, *and* he passed the exam.
    Comment: ,and is the most familiar way of combining main clauses. Brings the two ideas into one sentence. One idea is as important as the other.

    b. John studied hard; he passed the exam.
    Comment: ; is a nice, clear, quick way of combining main clauses. One idea still is as important as the other.

    c. John studied hard: he passed the exam.
    Comment: : here conveys the idea of "so" or "therefore." It establishes a closer relationship between the two ideas than the *,and* or the *;*.

Assignment 2: Combine into one sentence, using *one main clause* and *one dependent clause.*

Samples and comments:
    a. *Because* John studied hard, he passed the exam.
    Comment: "Because" makes the first clause a *dependent* clause. The words "after," "if," "when," "since," "whenever" would do the same thing.
    Note: (a) The *main idea* of the sentence is now tagged as the

second clause, the main clause. (b) This kind of sentence *spells out the relationship* between the two clauses: One event causes the other; one event comes after the other; etc.

b. John studied hard *before* he passed the exam.
   Comment: "Before" makes the second clause a *dependent* clause. Other words, such as "when" would do the same thing.
   Note: (a) The *main idea* of the sentence has now shifted to the first clause, the main clause. (b) The subordinating conjunction "before" spells out the relationship between the two ideas.

Assignment 3: Combine into one sentence using *one phrase* and *one main clause.*

Samples and comments:
  a. *Studying hard,* John passed the exam.
     Comment: A participle, "studying," replaces the subject and verb, "John studied." Thus the first clause becomes a *phrase* (lacks subject and verb). The main idea is in the main clause, "John passed."

     Variations to this approach:
       By studying hard, John, passed the exam.
       After studying hard, John passed the exam.
       John passed the exam *by studying hard.*

  b. John studied hard, *passing* the exam.
     Comment: A participle, "passing" replaces the subject and verb, "John passed." Thus the second clause becomes a *phrase.* The main idea is now in the first clause, "John studied hard."

     Variations to this approach:
       John studied hard *to pass the exam.* (Comment: The infinitive "to pass" is used in place of the subject and the verb.)
       John studied hard, *thus passing* the exam.
       To pass the exam, John studied hard.

  c. *By hard study,* John passed the exam.
     Comment: Prepositional phrase "by hard study" replaces clause "John studied hard."

Assignment 4. Other ways of combining some ideas into one sentence.

Samples and comments:
   a. *Hard study* helped John *to pass* the exam.
      Comment: The first clause has now become a noun phrase, "hard study." *The second clause* has become an infinitive phrase, "to pass." We have a new verb, "helped."

   b. John's passing the exam was the result of hard study.
      Comment: Both clauses have become phrases, now joined by the verb "was."

Examples of Sentence Translation, Showing Spread of Student Responses to a Basic Reading Exercise: Sheet Distributed to Class

Sentence Translation: Spread of Student Responses

Sentence (from Frederick Douglass):

   Mr. Gore was just proud enough to demand the most debasing homage from a slave and quite servile enough to crouch himself at the feet of the master.

In your own words, what is Douglass saying?

Student Translations:
   1. He saying Mr. Gore was happy to see slave brought from their homes and throwning to his master feet.
   2. Mr. Gore could demand a slave to do anything he wanted regardless of the extent, but the slave was yet faithful enough to crouch at his master's feet.
   3. He was a cruel man, if he thought a slave said anything he would beat him. He would blame anything on a slave. A slave wasn't allowed to say anything back to Mr. Gore. He made slaves suffer and he would be beaten.
   4. Mr. Douglass is saying that Mr. Gore like to harass the slaves because he knows they will not fight. A slave would crouch; in other words bow down at the feet of the master and do as he say.

The slaves couldn't go or do anything unless they got permission
from the man [master].

5. It means that Mr. Gore was overseer of the slaves and the
big master was over him and the slaves.

6. Mr. Gore was very delight person he didn't mind droping at
his master feet in order to try to get the protion.

7. He is saying Mr. Gore was very cruel to all the slave, when
he command something to be done it had to be done right then. He
had no pity for none of the slaves, yet he pretend to be nice when he
was around Colonel Lloyd.

8. That he treated the slave any kind of way when the master
wasn't there, but when the master came he didn't treat the slave so
bad.

9. He wanted the slaves to be litle and to obey him and Mr.
Gore would do this to the master. He wanted to be the highest
ranked overseer.

10. Mr. Gore would demand low respect from the slave and he
was submissive enough to crouch himself or get down at the feet of
the master.

11. FD is saying that Mr. Gore was proud enough to give the
slaves a harsh and severe treatment, and demand the most lowest
quality from the slaves, but yet and still he was servile enough to
knell or throw himself at the feet of the master after he has done all
of his cruel things to the slaves.

12. This sentence is saying that Mr. Gore was proud enough to
demand the utmost respect from a slave, but humble enough to bow
to the feet of his master. In other words whatever the situation called
for Mr. Gore could adjust to either one.

Assignment to Write a Paragraph Based on Education Data Table: Samples of Students' Paragraphs

Class Response to Education Data Table

Assignment: (a) Draw a conclusion from the table. (b) State
your conclusion in an opening sentence. (c) Support your conclusion
with detailed information from the table (in 3 sentences).

Salaries of Public School Teachers and Percentages of Draftees Failing Army Mental Tests, 1971

	AVERAGE SALARY OF TEACHERS	DRAFTEES FAILING ARMY TESTS
Alabama	$ 5,875	40.0%
California	11,002	5.4%
Michigan	9,832	4.9%
Mississippi	5,772	32.0%
New York	9,800	9.3%
South Carolina	6,883	44.5%

1. The least money you spend on education the higher the percents is for failing the draft test. For example, in 1971 in California, the average salary for public school teachers was $11,002 with a 5.4% failing the draft test. In Alabama the salary for public school teachers was $5,875 with a 40.0% failing the draft test. In South Carolina salary for public school teachers was $6,883, with a 44.5% failing the draft test. The states that spend more money on Education seem to gain more in learning.

2. In an educational data poll taken in 1971, the result appear to that when the teachers earn more money the percentage draftees failing mental tests declines. For instance in the state of Alabama, teachers earned $5,875, and the amount of draftees failing the test was 40%. On the other hand in California where the teachers earn $11,002, the amount of draftees failing was 5.4%. This is a considerable drop from what Alabama had. The same thing with Michigan, New York, with teachers in the states earning $9,800 plus and draftees failing rates being 4.9 and 9.3. Whereas with Mississippi and S. Carolina, teachers earning $5,000 and $6,000, the failing rates was 32% and 44.5. The conclusion I come to is that the teachers that earn more money appear to turn out better mentally prepared students.

3. Alabama, Mississippi, and S. Carolina public school teachers were the low pay teachers in 1971 and have the highest percentage of failing the Army draft tests. For example, Alabama public school teachers salary was $5,875 for 1971. And California school teachers salary $11,002 for 1971. Mississippi percentage of failure of the Army test 32.0 and Michigan 4.9. The salary for school teachers in the south is much lower than the school teachers in the north and the percentage of failure for the Army tests is higher in the south than in the north.

4. The average salary for public school teachers and the percent of Army draftees failing mental tests in 1971 was low. For example, in Michigan, the salary for public school teachers was $9,832 and the percent of Army draftees failing mental tests was 4.9. In New York, the per cent of Army draftees failing tests was 9.3 and the average school teachers salary was $9,800. Also in Mississippi, school teachers salaries were $5,772, whereas there was 32% of Army draftees failing mental tests. From these examples it would seem to be true that for the year 1971 the average salary for public school teachers was low and the percent of Army draftees failing tests was also low.

5. In 1971 the average salary for public school teachers and the percent of draftees failing the mental test was high. In California the average salary was $11,002. In Alabama the failing of the mental test was 40%. In Michigan the salary was $9,832, and in Mississippi the failing of the mental test was 32%. The overall look at the average salary and the Army test was high in 1971.

An Early Assignment in Paragraph Analysis (Third Assignment)

The Paragraph

Read the following paragraph carefully. Then answer the questions about it below.

(1) Greene County, a predominantly Black county in western Alabama, has been a very tough place for Black people to live in. (2) The per capita income in the Black community in Greene County is about $1,000 a year, compared to $3,500 for the whole population of the USA and $2,400 for Alabama. (3) Last year there were 273 Black students in the 7th grade in the Greene County schools and 162 in the 12th grade, showing a 40% dropout from 7th to 12th grades; many of the students get discouraged by the local conditions and "get on the bus" and leave the area. (4) Of 150 Black students graduating from high schools in Greene County last year, about 15 went to college; it happened that the Black high school valedictorian did not go to college. (5) Circumstances are so hard for Black people in Greene County that, if there is not some action to change the situation, soon all the young men and women will leave the area to seek their fortunes elsewhere, and only the old folks will be left.

Questions

1. In 15 words or less, what is the main point of this paragraph?
2. What points of information, or evidence, does the writer produce to support his main point?
3. In terms of "general" sentences and "detail" sentences, what is the pattern of the writer's organization of his material in this paragraph?

Assignment to Write A Brief Essay: Details of Outline and Development

Five-Paragraph Essay

Writing Assignment

1. Write a *five-paragraph paper* (200 words) stating what you think is the major lesson to be learned from Frederick Douglass's *Narrative*, supporting your conclusion by presenting detailed information from the book.
2. Your paper should follow our familiar *pattern* of
   a. general introductory paragraph,
   b. three paragraphs giving supporting details,
   c. general concluding summary paragraph.
3. As a suggestion you may wish to follow this structure:
   Paragraph 1
   "I think one major lesson to be learned from Frederick Douglass is that . . ." (25–30 words in two or three sentences)
   Paragraph 2
   "To support this conclusion, let us look at what Frederick Douglass tells us in reporting the occasion of . . . He notes that . . . He tells us that . . ." (40–50 words in three or four sentences)
   Paragraph 3
   "Further, Frederick Douglass tells us that . . . Of this situation, he said that . . ." (40–50 words in three or four sentences)
   Paragraph 4
   "Finally Frederick Douglass tells us about his experience at . . . He informs us that . . . He concludes that . . ."

(40–50 words in three or four sentences)
Paragraph 5
"Thus the evidence from Frederick Douglass's account is clear that . . ."

4. Please note that paragraphs 2, 3, and 4 are unified within themselves. That is, each of these paragraphs deals with *one idea* or one grouping of similar pieces of information.

5. If you pick up the suggested language of these sentences and flesh them out with information of your own choosing, you will find the paper taking shape quickly and persuasively.

Concluding Statement

Chapter 16

Uniting Method and Purpose in Higher Education

Charles V. Willie

O ur overall conclusion is that black colleges in the United States are a vital national resource. Much that they do is unique. They have pioneered in innovative educational methods, demonstrating that students of varying cultural and educational backgrounds can learn with an effective instructional program. Many of their practices and procedures offer useful models for all institutions of higher education. As far as black students are concerned, they have demonstrated that learning is enhanced when the subject matter relates to ways of coping with social reality—with racism, economic inequality, and institutional arrangements.

More than that, it is in black colleges that the American Dream has been kept alive. If Martin Luther King, Jr., had to graduate from Morehouse rather than Harvard, as Samuel DuBois Cook asserts, it was because his dedication to social justice was bound up with his Morehouse College education. Black colleges have been more concerned with racial advancement than with individual success, and they have also placed greater emphasis on participation in the processes of democracy than most white institutions. Of course, there is no paradox in this; those who are denied the rights of democratic citizenship are likely to·value them more highly than those who can take them for granted.

Their peculiar circumstances and conditions pushed the black colleges into the forefront of developments in higher education that have become major concerns for other institutions only recently. Black

263

colleges, for example, have demonstrated how to desegregate. In years past, they were islands of racial integration in a sea of segregation. They brought black and white teachers together and showed in their own way what can be accomplished when racial groups cooperate. The predominantly black public institutions of higher education have welcomed a considerable number of whites into their student bodies; private black colleges have asked for scholarship help in recruiting whites. On the combined campuses of a score of black colleges discussed in this book, one out of every ten students is white.

Black colleges have operated on the basis of an open admissions policy from the beginning. One reason that black colleges and their students persevere is that education is a form of liberation for them, a sacred possession no oppressor can take away. Black colleges in every generation have been reluctant, therefore, to deny education to the highly motivated who are willing to study and work. Students of varying academic and cultural backgrounds have been brought together on the black-college campus, to teach and be taught by each other as well as by the faculty. The diversity of their campus experience has made black-college students wise in the ways of the world as well as wise in the use of words.

Combining the Pragmatic and the Philosophical

Education in the black college has always been relevant. Education is not an ornament for the black-college student. It is one way of overcoming racial discrimination and a possible avenue out of poverty. Black-college students are looking for an education that provides intellectual substance and also prepares them for a job. Classical and career education has achieved a unity on the black-college campus that is only dimly visible in other institutions. The liberal arts tradition and vocational education complement each other and are not viewed as contradictory or competitive.

It took the student uprisings of the 1960s to give white educators an understanding of the multiple ways in which liberal education can deal with the pragmatic as well as the philosophical. In 1971, Judson Jerome wrote a book describing Antioch's Inner College, with which he was associated at the time (Jerome 1971). A major focus of activity for men and women students in the program, he reports, was baking bread. Young people in college, he notes approvingly, were turning their attention to learning how to survive; they wanted to "rediscover their hands" (Judson 1971, p. 266). The twentieth century was two-thirds spent before some colleges and universities recognized the urgent need for mastering the practical on the part of the young people who came to them for an education.

Black educators were dealing with this need decades earlier, at the beginning of this century. In 1903, Booker T. Washington said that "the very best service which any one can render to what is called the higher education is to teach the present generation to provide a material . . . foundation" (Washington 1970, p. 224). Learning to work with one's hands was what Washington called industrial education. At the same time DuBois was calling for education to develop mind and character, which would "teach life" and not simply work (DuBois 1970, p. 228).

Both DuBois and Washington were influenced by their debate. Washington finally conceded that training the hands without also training the mind was an inadequate educational agenda. DuBois admitted that teaching work was an important function of education; indeed he called it "the paramount necessity." But he added, "Work alone will not do . . . unless inspired by the right ideals and guided by intelligence" (DuBois 1970, pp. 227–228). The essential difference between Booker T. Washington and W. E. B. DuBois was not educational but political, involving strategy and tactics for social change. They wrestled with the problem of education and came to agree that the pragmatic and theoretical go hand in hand.

Their understanding of higher education was ignored. It was not until the second half of this century that an eminent educator like Judson Jerome would write: "If a college is to produce educated people, it should concern itself with both liberal and practical education" (Jerome 1971, p. 264). This affirmation echoes the resolution of the Washington–DuBois debate half a century earlier, which was not acknowledged as the intellectual forebear of a "new" understanding.

Why did it take the leaders of American higher education so long to deal with the issues of the Washington–DuBois debate? The answer I derive is racism. White America ignored Washington and DuBois as two blacks fussing with each other and failed to realize that the issues with which they were wrestling were central to the education of all people. We must not commit the same error again and ignore the initiatives of black educators and black colleges and universities. America has much to learn from them.

Goals and Educational Emphasis

Despite a consensus that higher education is a liberating experience for blacks, the scholars and administrators contributing to this volume express a diversity of views on what the goals of the education should be and what it should stress. Some feel that a college education should enable black students to develop a cosmopolitan middle-class style of life; some, that advanced training should be used primarily to help individuals who are less fortunate. Another position is that college-educated blacks belong in the forefront of community reform movements to achieve a more just society; while still others hold that higher education should provide blacks with the skills to effectively compete with whites in their own institutions. It is fair to say that education is viewed by most of these black educators as an opportunity to contribute to the public good rather than as a resource for private gain.

Directly and indirectly, several of the chapters in this volume stress education as a process in which the capacity for independent thought is cultivated; this probably represents one of the most important functions of higher education from the perspective of administrators and instructors in predominantly black institutions. A few place stronger emphasis on instilling a black perspective on history, the social sciences, and the humanities. Others, more frank in promoting their propaganda, have argued that certain ideologies are more appropriate subject matter of instruction for blacks—for example, collectivism and its many manifestations in economics, politics, and the social order.

While it is true that the educators of blacks have tended to focus more on group advancement than on individual gain, this emphasis has been largely a result of situational determinants—a racially hostile environment that required collective action for effective resistance—rather than a commitment to a particular method of social change. Black education probably is best characterized as pragmatic, as Charles U. Smith and Shirley McBay emphasize. Special methods and particular ideologies have enjoyed a passing popularity in black colleges and universities but have never been able to displace the central function of education: teaching students how to think. Those concerned with the education of blacks have focused, almost as if it were an addiction, upon the development of the mind; the expectation for postgraduate training that Benjamin Mays had for the graduates of Morehouse College has been humorously described as a "Ph.D. mania." The function of education in developing thought is focused upon sometimes to the exclusion of physical and recreational skills and methods and techniques of social and interpersonal relations. Educators in black institutions do not deny the importance of these other functions. In their hierarchy of priorities, however, developing the capacity to think comes first. If there is sufficient time, other mattters may be included in the curriculum. If not, then what time is available should be devoted to cultivating the mind and the capacity to think for oneself.

It is probable that professors in black colleges and universities have focused on this function of education because of the history of blacks and other minorities in America and elsewhere. History has proved that material possessions can be expropriated by superior force but knowledge and wisdom cannot. Thus intellectual development is the only hedge that a vulnerable minority has against the possibility of oppression by the majority. The capacity to think cannot be taken away. Ideologies come and go; skills suffer obsolescence; manners and morals change. But knowledge and wisdom endure. Therefore most persons concerned with the education of blacks have identified the development of the capacity for critical thinking as their number one priority.

Uniting Method and Purpose

Decades ago while still a student at Morehouse College, I had to speak at the daily morning assembly that was held in the chapel. My speech was a response that the president of the junior class customarily made to the charge by the senior class that we should make Morehouse better. As junior class presidents had done before I pledged on behalf of the student body to carry on the honorable traditions. Then, pointing toward the future, I ended my remarks with a rhetorical flourish also customary among chapel speakers of yesteryear. Borrowing phrases from one of Paul's letters to the Corinthians, I said, "And now abideth Yale, Harvard, and Morehouse—these three. But the greatest of these must be Morehouse." My classmates still remember that assembly and have never let me forget that speech. I suspect that they remember because these remarks contained an element of truth that we recognized only dimly then but see more clearly now.

Morehouse was described as the school that must be the greatest in the biblical sense in which the greatest of all is first the servant of all. Morehouse has not, cannot, and will not duplicate Harvard or Yale.

What Morehouse has achieved is the status of *a connecting link* between the great traditions of the predominantly white colleges and universities of this nation and those of the predominantly black colleges and universities.

The predominantly white institutions of higher education tend to emphasize the methods and techniques of education, almost to the exclusion of any focus on goals and purposes. The predominantly black institutions of higher education tend to emphasize the goals and purposes of education, sometimes at the expense of methods and techniques except those that are fundamental. Black schools tend to give more time and attention to the acquisition of knowledge about freedom as the basis of social order, the establishment of systems of justice, and ways of changing the social environment to eliminate racial oppression. If knowledge of freedom, justice, and social change are basic goals of formal education, certainly sophisticated technical skills should increase the probability of achieving them.

Union between goal and method in higher education is needed but has been hampered by the separation between black and white institutions and particularly by lack of knowledge on the part of whites about what goes on in schools that are predominantly black. The possibility of effecting a union has been further hampered by the belief that higher education is a hierarchy of excellence with some predominantly white schools at the top and most predominantly black schools at the bottom. The material presented in this book indicates that black and white schools complement each other; a system of higher education that has a Harvard without a Hampton is incomplete. Further, a hierarchical view of excellence in higher education leads to the inappropriate attempt to reconstruct all schools in the image of an elite ideal type.

We described Morehouse College as performing a unique role of linking within itself the traditions of higher education emphasized by different kinds of schools. Morehouse has emphasized the liberal arts, vocational or career-oriented professional and preprofessional courses of study, health and physical education, and a work-study program for many of its students. On the Morehouse College campus manual effort and mental activity embrace each other, debating and demonstrating are encouraged. It is important to understand the source and consequence of this synthesis and the meaning of both for higher education.

At Morehouse College Benjamin Mays assembled a faculty whose members had doctorates from the major research universities in the nation. He insisted upon high academic performance on the part of the students and qualified his college for a chapter of Phi Beta Kappa. Meanwhile, he gave weekly lectures to the entire student body at its chapel assembly each Tuesday morning. These lectures were on such themes as freedom and truth, love and justice, mercy and forgiveness, aspiration and motivation, perseverance and endurance, reform and resistance. He encouraged the organization of a student government that had power and authority to challenge him. The Morehouse that Mays built focused on the methods and techniques of higher education as well as on its goals and purposes. It is interesting to note that during his career as a professor Mays had respect for the languages of calculation and communication: He taught mathematics and English. As dean of a school of religion, he was at home also with the disciplines concerned with ethics, morality, and human values. His own academic career was a living synthesis of purpose and method.

Morehouse did what neither Harvard nor Hampton had done: It united the unique traditions of the two. As such, it qualified as a marginal institution—one that lives in, between, and beyond the races of humanity (Willie 1975, pp. 24–32). An earlier concept of marginality is that of a unit that falls between two social or cultural groups. However, "the new concept of the marginal person, as I see it, is one who rises above two social or cultural groups, freeing the different groups to work together" (Willie 1975, p. 32). This is precisely what Morehouse College has done for black and white institutions.

One reason Morehouse became a marginal school is that it was led for nearly three decades by a president who was a "marginal" man. In his education, Mays united black and white colleges—spending one year at Virginia Union in the South, a predominantly black school, and the rest of his college years at Bates in the North, a predominantly white school. As a Pullman porter as well as a college teacher, Mays in his adult years performed both blue-collar and white-collar work. As a teacher of mathematics, English, and religion, Mays united science and the humanities. As a college professor and a college president, Mays followed a career of teaching and research as well as of administration. He was a marginal man who brought unity out of diversity, and he led Morehouse College in the way of marginality.

The function of Morehouse as a marginal institution illustrates the inappropriateness of using Harvard, Yale, Berkeley, Oberlin, or any other institution as a model of excellence after which all other institutions, including black colleges and universities, should be patterned.

The future of higher education in America belongs to all institutions. For the benefit of the whole of higher education, then, diversity among colleges is essential until unity of goal and method is found in each institution. Black colleges make an essential contribution by setting forth the goals of higher education. White colleges make a necessary contribution to higher education by identifying the methods of achieving these goals. One emphasis without the other is imcomplete. It would be an academic disaster in the United States to phase out black colleges and their unique contribution to higher education, leaving only those with the unique traditions of whites.

Beyond the necessity for diversity, more black and white colleges are called for today to follow the path of marginaltiy, uniting method and purpose within themselves to provide an education that gives direction to the hand and heart as well as the head. This is the model of higher education that any college or university can follow. It is worthy of emulation by all.

Contributors

Herman R. Branson
President, Lincoln University, Pennsylvania

Jane E. Smith Browning
Assistant to the President, Spelman College, Atlanta, Georgia

Samuel DuBois Cook
President, Dillard University, New Orleans, Lousiana

Ann W. Craig
Office of the Dean of Students, Darthmouth College, Hanover, New Hampshire

Ronald R. Edmonds
Acting Director of the Center for Urban Studies and Codirector of the Black College Project, Harvard Graduate School of Education, Cambridge, Massachusetts

Chester M. Hedgepeth, Jr.
Research Associate, Black College Project, Harvard Graduate School of Education, Cambridge, Massachusetts

Sherman J. Jones
Vice President for Administration, Fisk University, Nashville, Tennessee

Gregory Kannerstein
Haverford College, Haverford, Pennsylvania

Marlene MacLeish
Assistant Professor of Sociology, Northeastern University, Boston Massachusetts

Shirley M. McBay
Professor of Mathematics, Spelman College, Atlanta, Georgia (on leave), and Program Manager, Instructional Improvement Implementation Section, National Science Foundation, Washington, District of Columbia

Benjamin E. Mays
President Emeritus, Morehouse College, Atlanta, Georgia

Charles Merrill
Headmaster, Commonwealth School, Boston, Massachusetts

John U. Monroe
Formerly Professor of English and Coordinator of Freshman Studies, Miles College, Birmingham, Alabama. As of Fall 1978, Professor of Writing, Tougaloo College, Tougaloo, Mississippi

Prezell R. Robinson
President, Saint Augustine's College, Raleigh, North Carolina

Thelma Roundtree
Vice-President for Academic Affairs, Saint Augustine's College, Raleigh, North Carolina

Charles U. Smith
Professor of Sociology and Head of the Division of Social and Behavioral Sciences, Florida Agricultural and Mechanical University, Tallahassee, Florida

Daniel C. Thompson
Vice-President for Academic Affairs and Provost, Dillard University, New Orleans Louisiana

George B. Weathersby
Associate Professor, Harvard Graduate School of Education, Cambridge, Massachusetts; Commissioner of Higher Education for the State of Indiana

John B. Williams
Associate in Education and Research Director at the Center for Urban Studies, Harvard Graduate School of Education, Cambridge, Massachusetts

Charles V. Willie
Professor of Education and Urban Studies and Director of the Black College Project, Harvard Graduate School of Education, Cambridge, Massachusetts

Reference List

Academy for Educational Development, Management Division. 1974. *319 ways colleges and universities are meeting the financial pinch.*

Adams v. *Richardson.* 1973. 356F Supp. 92 (DDC 1973).

American Council on Education. 1973. *American colleges and universities.* Washington, D.C.: American Council on Education.

American Missionary Association.
1848. *Second annual report.*
1861. *Fifteenth annual report.*
1865. Archives. New Orleans, La.: Amidstad Research Center, Dillard University.

American missionary magazine. 1863. 7:271.

The Annals.
1965. The Negro protest. *The annals of the American Academy of Political and Social Science.* January 1965.
1971. Students protest. *The annals of the American Academy of Political and Social Science.* May 1971.

Becker, Howard. 1970. *Campus power struggle.* Chicago: Aldine.

Bennett, Lerone. 1977. Benjamin E. Mays: The last of the great schoolmasters. *Ebony* 33 (December).

Bernstein, Leonard. 1963. *The joy of music.* New York: Simon and Schuster.

Bishop, E. 1971. *The black state colleges and universities.* Cambridge, Mass.: Harvard Law School.

Bogdan, Robert, and Taylor, Steven J. 1975. *Introduction to qualitative research methods.* New York: Wiley.

Bond, Horace Mann. 1960. The origin and development of the Negro church-related college. *Journal of Negro education* 29.

Bowles, F., and DeCosta, F. 1971. *Between two worlds.* New York: McGraw-Hill.

Brown v. *Board of Education.* 1954. 347 US 483.

Browning, J. E. S. 1975. The origins, development, and desegregation of the traditionally black public colleges and universities. Ed.D. dissertation, Harvard University.

Bruner, Jerome. 1960. *The process of education.* Cambridge, Mass.: Harvard University Press.

Buber, Martin. 1955. *Between man and God.* Translated by Ronald Gregor Smith. Boston, Mass.: Beacon Press.

Bullock, Henry Allen.
   1967. *A history of Negro education in the South.* Cambridge, Mass.: Harvard University Press.
   1970. *History of Negro education in South.* New York: Praeger.
   1971. The black college and the new black awareness. *Daedalus* 100:573–602.

Burgess, K. F. 1958. The trustee function in today's communities and colleges. *Bulletin,* October 1958:399–407. Washington, D.C.: Association of American Colleges.

Capon Springs. 1899. *Proceedings of the second Capon Springs conference,* Capon Springs, W.Va.

The Carnegie Commission on Higher Education.
   1971. *From isolation to mainstream.* New York: McGraw-Hill.
   1973. *A digest of reports of the Carnegie Commission on Higher Education.* New York: McGraw-Hill.

Cheit, Earl F.
   1971. *The new depression in higher education.* New York: McGraw-Hill.

Cohen, D. K. 1974. Segregation, desegregation and *Brown. Society* 12:34–40.

Courlander, Harold. 1970. *Negro folk music, U. S. A.* New York: Columbia University Press.

Curry, J. L. M. 1894. *Education of the Negro since 1860, United States statutes at large.* Vol. 25. Washington, D.C.: U.S. Government Printing Office. (New York: Trustees of the John P. Slater Fund.)

DaBrey, C. W. 1936. *Universal education in the South.* Vol. 1. Chapel Hill, N.C.: University of North Carolina Press.

Davis, Harry R., and Good, Robert C., eds. 1960. *Reinhold Niebuhr on politics.* New York: Scribner's.

Dewey, John. 1946. *The problems of men.* New York: Philosophical Library.

Drake, R. 1957. The American Missionary Association and the southern Negro. Ph.D. dissertation, Emory University.

Drake, St. Clair. 1971. The black university in the American social order. *Daedalus* 100:880-90.

DuBois, W. E. B.
1900.   *The college bred Negro.* Atlanta, Ga.: Atlanta University Publications.
1903a. *The Negro problem.* New York: James Platt.
1903b. *Souls of black folk.* Chicago: A. C. Clurg.
1910.   *The college bred Negro American.* Atlanta, Ga.: Atlanta University Publications.
1961.   *Souls of black folk.* Reprint. Greenwich, Conn.: Fawcett.
1970.   The talented tenth. Reprinted in *The Black American: A brief documentary history,* ed. Leslie H. Fishel, Jr., and B. Quarles. Glenview, Ill.: Scott, Foresman. (Originally published 1903)
1973.   *The education of black people: Ten critiques, 1906-1960,* ed. Herbert Aptheker. New York: Free Press.

Edwards, Harry. 1970. *Black students.* New York: Free Press.

Eells, W. C. 1935. The result of Surveys of Negro Colleges and universities. *Journal of Negro education* 4:476-81.

Egerton, J. 1974. *Adams v. Richardson:* Can separate be equal? *Change,* Winter 1974-75:29-36.

Engs, Robert F. 1972. Development of the Negro personality and culture in the emancipation era. Ph.D. dissertation, Yale University.

Enrich, Alvin C. 1970. Plan or perish. *College and university journal,* Summer 1970:55-59.

Federal City College. 1975. *Student affairs annual report, 1974-1975.* Washington, D.C.: Federal City College.

The Florida Times-Union (Jacksonville, Fla.). 24 May 1974. (Daily newspaper.)

Franklin, John Hope, and Starr, Isidore. 1967. *The Negro in 20th century America.* New York: Random House, Vintage.

Frazier, E. Franklin.
    1939. *The Negro family in the United States.* Chicago: University of Chicago Press.
    1957. *The Negro in the United States.* New York: Macmillan.

Gallagher, Buell G. 1966. *American caste and the Negro college.* New York: Gordian Press.

General Education Board.
    1914. *Annual Report.*
    1920. *Annual Report.*

Griffin, John Howard. 1961. *Black like me.* New York: New American Library, Signet.

Gruber, Murray. 1973. Four types of black protest: A study. *Social work* 18:3-18.

Gung Lum v. *Rice.* 1927. 275 US 78.

Gurin, Patricia, and Epps, Edgar. 1975. Black consciousness, identity, and achievement. New York: Wiley.

Hamilton, Charles V. 1967. The place of the black conege in the human rights struggle. *Negro digest,* September 1967.

Harlan, Lewis. 1972. *Booker T. Washington: The making of a black leader, 1856–1901.* New York: Oxford University Press.

Harris, Julian, ed. 1962. *The humanities: An appraisal.* Madison, Wis.: University of Wisconsin Press.

Harris, Patricia Roberts. 1971. The Negro college and its community. *Daedalus* 100.

Haskins, James, ed. 1973. *Black manifesto for education.* New York: William Morrow.

Haven, E. W., and Horch, P. H. 1971. *How college students finance their education.* Princeton, N.J.: College Entrance Examination Board.

Henderson, Vivian W.
1971. Negro colleges face the future. *Daedalus* 100.
1974. Blacks and change in higher education. *Daedalus* 103.

Herzog, Elizabeth. 1966. Is there a "breakdown" of the Negro family? *Social work* 11:3–10.

Hill, John R. 1975. Presidential perceptions: Administrative problems and needs of public black colleges. *Journal of Negro education* 44:53–62.

Holmes, Dwight O. 1934. *The evolution of the Negro college.* New York: Teachers College Press.

Howard, L. C. 1967. *The developing college program: A study of Title III of the Higher Education Act of 1965.* Milwaukee, Wis.: Report of the Institute of Human Relations, University of Wisconsin.

Howe, Harold, II. 1976. Education research: The promise and the problem. Address at annual meeting of the American Educational Research Association, San Francisco.

Jaffe, A. J. 1968. *Negro higher education in the 1960s.* New York: Praeger.

Jellema, William W. 1973. *From red to black: The financial status of private colleges.* San Francisco: Jossey-Bass.

Jencks, Christopher, and Riesman, David. 1967. The American Negro college. *Harvard educational review* 37:3-60.

Jencks, C.; Smith, M.; Acland, H.; Bane, M. J.; Cohen, D.; Gantis, H.; Heyns, B.; and Michelson, S. 1972. *Inequality: A reassessment of the effect of family and schooling in America.* New York: Basic Books.

Jenkins, M. D. 1952. Problems incident to racial integration and some suggested problems—a critical summary. *Journal of Negro education* 21:411-421.

Jerome, Judson, 1971. *Culture out of anarchy.* New York: Herder & Herder.

John, W. C.
    1920. *Agricultural and mechanical colleges, 1917-1918.* Washington, D.C.: U.S. Government Printing Office.
    1923. Hampton Normal and Agricultural Institute. *Bulletin of the Office of Education* 27:89.

Johnson, Charles S.
    1938. *The Negro college graduate.* College Park, Md.: McGrath Publishing Co.
    1954. Some significant social and educational implications of the U.S. Supreme Court's decision. *Journal of Negro education* 23:364-71.

Johnson, Tobe. 1971. The black college system. *Daedalus* 100:798-812.

Jones, Ann. 1973. *Uncle Tom's campus.* New York: Praeger.

Jones, Butler. 1974. The tradition of sociology teaching in black colleges: The unheralded professionals. In *Black sociologists: Historical and contemporary perspectives,* ed. James Blackwell and Morris Janowitz, pp. 121-163. Chicago: University of Chicago Press.

Jones, Mack. 1971. The responsibility of the black college to the black community: Then and now. *Daedalus* 100:732-744.

Jones, Thomas J. 1920. *Negro education: A study of the private and public higher schools for colored people in the United States.* Washington, D.C. U.S. Dept of Interior, Bureau of Education. Reprint. New York: Arno Press, 1969.

Jordan, Vernon E., Jr. 1975. Blacks in higher education—some reflections. *Daedalus,* Winter 1975.

Keller, Charles R.
1965. Statements while directing John Hay Whitney humanities program.
1967. Science and humanities: Two cultures. Unpublished address.

King, Martin Luther, Jr.
1963. *Why we can't wait.* New York: Harper & Row.
1968. *Where do we go from here: Chaos or community?* New York: Bantam Books.

Klein, A. 1969. *Survey of Negro colleges and universities.* New York: Negro Universities Press.

Koch, Adrienne. 1961. *Power, morals, and the founding fathers.* Ithaca, N.Y.: Cornell University Press, Great Seal Books.

Kriegel, Leonard. 1972. *Working through.* New York: Saturday Review Press.

Leavell, Ullin. 1930. *Philanthropy in Negro education.* Nashville, Tenn.: George Peabody College for Teachers.

Lee, Alfred McClung. 1975. Organizing within the ASA. *Invisible socialist newsletter* 2:20.

Leighton, Joseph A. 1930. *The individual and the social order.* New York: D. Appleton and Company.

LeMelle, T., and LeMelle, W. 1969. *The black college: A strategy for relevancy.* New York: Praeger.

Lester, Julius, ed. 1971. *The seventh son.* New York: Random House.

Lipset, Seymour. 1971. *Rebellion in the university.* Boston, Mass.: Little, Brown.

McPherson, J. M.
    1964. *Struggle for equality.* Princeton, N.J.: Princeton University Press.
    1970. White liberals and black power in Negro education. *American historical review* 75:1357–1386.
    1975. *Abolitionist legacy.* Princeton, N.J.: Princeton University Press.

McWharter, G. A. 1968. The nature and needs of the black university. *Negro digest,* March 1968:4–12.

Maritain, Jacques. 1960. *Education at the crossroads.* New Haven, Conn. : Yale University Press, paperback.

Marx, Gary
    1967. *Protest and prejudice.* New York: Harper & Row.
    1971. *Racial conflict: Tension and change in American society.* Boston: Little, Brown.

Mays, Benjamin E.
    1960a. Education—to what end? *The Morehouse College bulletin,* March 1960.
    1960b. The significance of the Negro private and church-related college. *Journal of Negro education* 29:246–247.
    1970. Higher education and the American Negro. In *What black educators are saying,* ed. Nathan Wright, Jr. New York: Hawthorn Books.
    1971. *Born to rebel: An autobiography.* New York: Scribner's.

Meier, August. 1966. *Negro thought in America:* 1880–1915. Ann Arbor, Mich.: University of Michigan Press.

Meier, A., and Rudwick, E. M. 1968. *From plantation to ghetto*. New York: Hill and Wang.

Merton, Robert K.
1949. *Social theory and social structure*. New York: The Free Press.
1972. Insiders and outsiders: A chapter in the sociology of knowledge. *American journal of sociology* 76:9–47.

The Miami Herald (Miami, Fla.). 10 March 1974. (Daily newspaper.)

Miller, J. L., Gurin, G., and Clark, M. J. 1970. *Use and effectiveness of Title III in selected "developing institutions."* Ann Arbor, Mich.: University of Michigan Press.

Mommsen, Kent G. 1973. On recruiting black sociologists. *The American Sociologist* 8:107–116.

Montaigne, Michel. 1958. *Essays*. Stanford, Calif.: Stanford University Press.

Morehouse College bulletin. 1973. Atlanta, Ga.: Morehouse College.

Moynihan, Daniel Patrick. 1965. *The Negro family: The case for national action*. Washington, D.C.: U.S. Government Printing Office.

Myrdal, Gunnar. 1944. *An American dilemma*. New York: Harper & Row. Reissued. New York: Pantheon Books, 1975.

NAACP. 1973. *Dismantling dual systems of public higher education: Criteria for a state plan*. New York: National Association for the Advancement of Colored People Legal Defense and Educational Fund.

Nabrit, S. M. 1971. Reflections on the future of the black colleges. *Daedalus* 100.

National Center for Education Statistics. 1972. *Digest of educational statistics, 1972*. Washington, D.C.: U.S. Office of Education.

National Commission on the Financing of Postsecondary Education.
     1973. *Financing postsecondary education in the United States.*
     Washington, D.C.: U.S. Government Printing Office.

National Science Foundation
     1975a. *Science resources Studies highlights.* September 19,
          1975:F 74–314. Washington, D.C.: National Science
          Foundation.
     1975b. *Instructional improvement project abstracts of the minority
          institutions science improvement program for fiscal years
          1972, 1973, 1974, 1975.* Washington, D.C.: National
          Science Foundation, Division of Higher Education in
          Science.

Niebuhr, Reinhold
     1956. *An interpretation of Christian ethics.* New York: New
          American Library, Meridian.
     1960. The problem of a protestant political ethic. *The Christian
          century,* September 21, 1966.

O'Brien, Gael M. 1976. Colleges' concern grows over ethical values.
     The chronicle of higher education 11:5.

Padover, Saul K., ed. 1946. *Thomas Jeffe·son on democracy.* New York:
     New American Library, Mentor.

Peck, Elizabeth S. 1955. *Berea's first century.* Lexington, Ky.:
     University of Kentucky Press.

Phelps–Stokes Fund. 1932. *The twenty-year report of the Phelps–Stokes
     Fund, 1911–1931.* New York: The Phelps–Stokes Foundation.

Piaget, Jean. 1972. Intellectual evolution from adolescence to adult-
     hood. *Human development* 15.

Pifer, Alan. 1972. The higher education of blacks. Address delivered
     under the auspices of the South African Institute on Race
     Relations, Johannesburg, South Africa, August 1, 1972.

Plessy v. *Ferguson.* 1896. 163 US 1138.

Pressley, Samuel W. 1976. Educator backs black universities, *Evening Bulletin* (Philadelphia). 26 April. (Daily newspaper.)

Pugh, W. C. 1974. The inflated controversy: DuBois vs. Washington *Crisis* 81:132-133.

Pusey, Nathan. 1962. The centrality of humanistic study. In *The humanities: An appraisal*, ed. Julian Harris. Madison, Wis.: University of Wisconsin Press.

Redding, Saunders. 1964. *On being Negro in America.* New York: Bantam Books. Original publication. New York; Bobbs—Merrill, 1951.

Reed, Addison. 1962. The life and works of Scott Joplin. Ph.D. dissertation, University of North Carolina.

Reuter, Edward. 1927. *The American race problem.* New York: Thomas Y. Crowell.

Riesman, David, and Jencks, Christopher. 1968. *The academic revolution.* New York: Doubleday.

Robinson, Prezell R. 1973. The predominantly black colleges and universities. *Proceedings of the fifty-third annual meeting of the North Carolina Association of Colleges and Universities,* November 1973:12-23.

Rose, W. L. 1967. *Rehearsal for reconstruction.* New York: Random House, Vintage.

Rudolph, Frederick. 1956. *Mark Hopkins and the log.* New Haven, Conn.: Yale University Press.

Ruml, Beardsley, and Morrison, Donald H. 1959. *Memo to a college trustee.* New York: McGraw-Hill.

Shaw, John Robert, and Shaw, Janet, eds. 1970. *The new horizon ladder dictionary of the English language.* New York: New American Library, Signet.

Schuck, P. H. 1972. Black land-grant colleges: Discrimination as public policy. *Saturday Review,* June 1972:46–48.

Schwebel, Milton, 1972. Pluralism and diversity in American higher education. *The annals of the Academy of Political and Social Science* 404:88–100.

Smith, Charles U.
 1961. The sit-ins and the new Negro student. *Journal of intergroup relations* 2:223–29.
 1968. Problems and possibilities of the predominantly Negro college. *Journal of social and behavioral sciences* 13:3–8.
 1972. Contribution of Charles S. Johnson to the field of sociology. *Journal of social and behavioral sciences* 18:26–31.
 1974. Student activism, benign racism and scholarly irresponsibility. *Florida A & M University Research Bulletin* 20:65–76.

Smith, Charles U., and Killian, Lewis.
 1958. *The Tallahassee bus protest.* New York: Anti-Defamation League of B'nai B'rith.
 1974. Black sociologists and social protest. In *Black sociologists: Historical and contemporary perspectives,* ed. James Blackwell and Morris Janowitz, pp. 192–250. Chicago: University of Chicago Press.

Southern Education Foundation.
 1972. *Small change: A report on federal support of black colleges.* Atlanta, Ga.: Southern Education Foundation.
 1974. *Ending discrimination in higher education.* Atlanta, Ga.; Southern Education Foundation.

Southern Regional Education Board. 1968. *New careers and curriculum change.* Atlanta, Ga.: Southern Regional Education Board.

The Tallahassee Democrat (Tallahassee, Fla.). 12 April 1974; 2 May 1974; 6 May 1974; 10 May 1974. (Daily newspaper.)

Tappan, Lewis.
    1855. *History of the American Missionary Association.* New
      York: no publisher.
    1869. *American missionary magazine* 13:83.
    1873. *American missionary magazine* 17:183.

Thomas, T. 1973. Student movement at Southern University.
    Freedomways 12:14–27.

Thompson, Daniel C. 1973. *Private black colleges at the crossroads.*
    Westport, Conn.: Greenwood Press.

Tyack, D.B. 1975. *The one best system.* Cambridge, Mass.: Harvard
    University Press.

United Negro College Fund.
    1974. *Annual statistical report, 1973–74.* New York: United
      Negro College Fund.
    1976. *Annual statistical report, 1975–76.* New York: United
      Negro College Fund.

U.S. Bureau of the Census.
    1974. *The social and economic status of the black population in the
      United States, 1973.* Special studies. P-23, No. 48. Wash-
      ington, D.C.: U.S. Government Printing Office.
    1976. *Statistical abstract.* Washington, D.C.: U.S. Government
      Printing Office.

U.S. Department of Commerce. 1972. *The social and economic status of
    the black population in the United States, 1972.* Washington, D.C.:
    U.S. Government Printing Office.

U.S. Department of the Interior, Bureau of Education.
    1872. *Report of the Commission, 1871.* Vol. 2. Washington, D.C.:
      U.S. Government Printing Office.
    1896. *Report of the Commission, 1895.* Vol. 2. Washington, D.C.:
      U.S. Government Printing Office.

U.S. Office of Education. 1942. *National survey of the higher education of Negroes.* Vols. 1–6. Washington, D.C.: U.S. Government Printing Office.

Walden, Daniel, ed. 1972. *W. E. B. DuBois: The crisis writings.* New York: Fawcett.

Washington, Booker T.
    1901. *Up from slavery.* New York: Doubleday & Co.
    1970. Industrial education for the Negro. Reprinted in *The black American: A brief documentary history,* ed. Leslie H. Fishel, Jr., and B. Quarles. Glenview, Ill.: Scott, Foresman. (Originally published 1903.)
    1974. *Up from slavery.* Reprint. New York: Dell.

Welleck, René, and Warren, Austin. 1949 *Theory of literature.* New York: Harcourt Brace Jovanovich.

West, Earle H. 1972. *The black American and education.* Columbus, Ohio: Charles E. Merrill.

Whimbey, Arthur. 1975. *Intelligence can be taught.* New York: E. P. Dutton.

Whitehead, Alfred North. 1947. *The aims of education.* New York: New American Library, Mentor.

Williams, John B. 1976. The American Missionary Association and the founding of Berea College. Special qualifying paper, Harvard University.

Williams, John A. 1970. *The King God didn't save.* New York: Coward, McCann & Geoghegan.

Willie, Charles V.
    1966. Into the second century: Problems of higher education of particular concern to Morehouse College. *Morehouse College bulletin* 35:9.

1970. (ed.) *The family life of black people.* Columbus, Ohio: Charles E. Merrill.

1973a. A theoretical approach to cultural and biological differences. In *Assessment in a pluralistic society* (Proceedings of the 1972 Invitational Conference on Testing Problems.) Princeton, N.J.: Educational Testing Service.

1973b. Perspectives on black education and the education of blacks. In *Does college matter?* ed. Lewis C. Solomon and Paul Taubman, pp. 231–238. New York: Academic Press.

1975. *Oreo: A perspective on race and marginal men and women.* Wakefield, Mass.: Parameter Press.

Wilson, T. L. 1972. Notes toward a process of Afro-American education. *Harvard educational review* 42:374–89.

Winkler, K. J. 1974. Desegregation: In accepting eight plans HEW comes closer than ever to setting integration guidelines for public higher education. *The chronicle of higher education,* July 8, 1974:4.

Winston, Michael R. 1971. Through the back door: Academic racism and the Negro scholar in historical perspective. *Daedalus* 100.

Woodward, C. Vann. 1951. Reunion and reaction. Boston, Mass.: Little, Brown.

Work, John W., 1940. *American Negro songs and spirituals.* New York: Crown, Bonanza.

Wright, Nathan, ed. 1970. *What black educators are saying.* New York: Hawthorn Books.

Wright, Stephen J.; Mays, Benjamin E.; Gloster, Hugh; and Dent, Albert W. 1967. The American Negro college: Four responses and a reply *Harvard educational review* 37:451–467.

Young, H. A. 1974. Survey of black scientists in the United States. *Journal of chemical education* 51:781–782.

Zinn, Howard.
    1965. *SNCC; The new abolitionists.* Boston, Mass.: Beacon Press.
    1966. A new direction for Negro colleges. *Harper's Magazine,* May 1966.